LETTERS TO HAZEL

THE HISTORICAL SERIES OF THE REFORMED CHURCH IN AMERICA, NO. 46

LETTERS TO HAZEL

Ministry within the Woman's Board of Foreign Missions of the Reformed Church in America

MARY L. KANSFIELD

WILLIAM B. EERDMANS PUBLISHING COMPANY
Grand Rapids, MI / Cambridge, U. K.

Wm. B. Eerdmans Publishing Co.
255 Jefferson Avenue, S.E., Grand Rapids, Michigan 49503 /
P.O. Box 163, Cambridge CB3 9PU U.K.

Printed in the United States of America

Library of Congress Cataloging-in-publication Data

Kansfield, Mary L.
      Letters to Hazel, Ministry within the Woman's Board of Foreign Missions of the
Reformed Church in America / Mary L. Kansfield
         p.   cm. — (Historical Series of the Reformed Church in America, no. 46)
     ISBN 0-8028-2870-1
         1. Reformed Church in America — Mission History. 2. Reformed Church in America
— Woman's Board of Foreign Missions. 3. Biography — Hazel B.Gnade.

The Historical Series of the Reformed Church in America

The series was inaugurated in 1968 by the General Synod of the Reformed Church in America acting through the Commission on History to communicate the church's heritage and collective memory and to reflect on our identity and mission, encouraging historical scholarship which informs both church and academy.

General Editor,
  The Rev. Donald J. Bruggink, Ph.D, D.D.
  Western Theological Seminary

Commission on History
  James Hart Brumm, M.Div., Blooming Grove, New York
  Lynn Japinga, Ph.D., Hope College, Holland, Michigan
  Scott M. Manetsch, Ph.D., Trinity Seminary, Deerfield, Illinois
  Melody Meeter, M.Div., Brooklyn, New York
  Jesus Serrano, B.A., Norwalk, California
  Robert Terwilliger, M.Div., Kalamazoo, Michigan

To Norm

Contents

Illustrations

Acknowledgments

I wish to acknowledge with gratitude those who contributed to the writing of this book—perhaps unknowingly. The women students at New Brunswick Theological Seminary, who struggle to respond to God's call to ministry, deserve recognition. Their support for one another and for my research and writing is a testament to the long history of Reformed Church women supporting one another.

Reformed Church women seminary graduates who feel strongly the call of God to pastoral ministry and are unable to find appropriate positions within the church struggle to fulfill God's calling. This issue speaks to the whole church and begs for greater understanding and acceptance. God calls, and these women are prepared to answer that call.

Retired Reformed Church in America staff members, ministers, spouses, and surviving spouses gather at New Brunswick Theological Seminary for a holiday party each December. Their stories and witness in the life of the church—especially the contributions of women—need to be acknowledged and remembered. I thank them for their inspiration and encouragement.

The discontinuation of Reformed Church Women's Ministries in 2001 has moved Reformed Church women to a new place in their history. At times like this, a glance backward often helps bring clarity. I hope the glance backward this book offers will contribute to the identity and shape of the witness of RCA women in the future.

Without the Gnades, Jerry and Ruth Ann and Ken and Mari, this story would not have been written. To Dr. Jerry Gnade I am indebted for sensing the importance to others of remembering his mother's ministry and for finding time in his busy schedule to meet with me. I also appreciate his support for my work in telling not only Hazel Gnade's story, but also the history of the Woman's Board of Foreign Missions. To Ken Gnade I am grateful for generously taking time to help put together the details of his family's history, and to Mari Gnade I am grateful for serving patiently as the Gnade family genealogist.

The Travelers' Club of New Brunswick is a women's literary club begun in 1890, and annually each member presents a paper on a given theme. Thank you to my wonderful Travelers' Club friends for allowing me to write on Hazel Gnade's life for our program, "Uncommon American Women." To each member and dear friend go my thanks for support and encouragement. You are each and all Uncommon American Women.

Although writing itself is a solitary exercise, the work of research and scholarship relies both directly and indirectly on the help of others.

I am indebted to Russ Gasero, Reformed Church archivist; to Geoffrey Reynolds and Lori Trethewey at the Joint Archives of Holland, Michigan; and to Rita Hollenga, archivist, and the staff of the Collegiate Corporation Archives, as to the many church secretaries and pastors who scoured their membership books for women's first names and who made available congregational archives for my research.

I am grateful to Marsha Blake and Reneé House, librarians, and the other members of the staff at the Gardner A. Sage Library at New Brunswick Theological Seminary for their patience and continuous help in the process of research for this book.

For technical assistance, I am grateful to Sandra Sheppard, who amazes me with her delight and capacity to meet computer and technical challenges, and who has always found time to help me. To Steven De See goes my appreciation for graciously helping me keep my computer operational throughout this writing project.

I wish to thank my dear friend Lois Speckman for editing this manuscript. With sensitivity to both the author and the text, the task of criticism was accomplished quickly and with great affection.

My deep appreciation is extended to Elaine Strauss, E. J. Emerson, and Philip Greven, who read the manuscript and offered insightful suggestions. For their scholarship and their friendship I am grateful.

I deeply appreciate the encouragement and support for this writing project given by the many family members and friends whose individual names are not recorded here.

I do wish to note, however, the names of three individuals who contributed to making this book possible by relieving me of customary duties and responsibilities. To Dee Geist for helping keep the President's House in a clean and welcoming state, to Norna Fairbanks, who manages Promise Catering Service and feeds the New Brunswick Seminary community each night of classes, and to Edmond Nicholson, who makes airport drives any time of day or night, I am thankful.

I wish to thank my sister-in-law Carole Kansfield Verkaik for recognizing the importance of and arranging for my initial contact with Jerry Gnade. The written story of Hazel Gnade's ministry began with this connection.

To my sister Susan Klein Torp, who never doubted my skills or my judgment to write RCA women's history, and who was always there to encourage me, I am grateful.

I am grateful to our children, Ann and John Kansfield, for helping me see clearly why the stories of their foremothers in the RCA and the foremothers of all Christian children need to be remembered, inasmuch as the stories of church women and men not only make history come alive, but also testify to the value we place on their lives. For your own fascinating lives and the myriad ways you have helped "to pull on the rope together" in support of my research and writing, I am grateful.

I wish to thank my husband, Norman, with whom I have shared a passion for history for thirty-nine years, and with whom I have shared an understanding that the common tasks of living and of raising children rest less on gender than on who is available at the time. Our shared love for our work, our children and family, and our friends has made life an interesting adventure for which I give abundant thanks.

Letters to Hazel: Ministry within the Woman's Board of Foreign Missions of the Reformed Church in America was copyedited and proofread by Laurie Baron. Page composition was designed by Russell Gasero, who also prepared the indexes. The cover was designed by Willem Mineur of William B. Eerdmans Publishing Co.

Introduction

We are making history every day.
To a great extent we must live our life in the light of the past.

> The Reverend William J. R. Taylor
> Chair of the General Synod's Committee on Publications
> *Christian Intelligencer*, XXVI.2 (July 12, 1855), 1

It may not be totally valid to say that the Reformed Church in America (RCA) does its "theology by genealogy." Yet there is a ring of truth to the description. Within our comparatively small denomination, family connections, childhood relationships drawn from growing up in Dutch ethnic areas, and college friendships, particularly those established at RCA colleges and seminaries, have long formed a network of connections which serve to keep us in touch with one another.

By means of one such connection Dr. Gerard R. Gnade Jr.,[1] a physician at Ingalls Memorial Hospital in Harvey, Illinois, spoke one day with my sister-in-law Carole Verkaik, who is a nurse at the same hospital. Jerry asked Carole if I continued to be interested in Reformed Church women's history. If so, he had a book of letters he wanted to show me. This he did in the summer of 2000. The bound volume contained sixty-six letters, some of which were illustrated, some in poetic form, and one in the

---

1. This branch of the family pronounces the family name Gc-nä´-dee or Guh-nä´-dee. Gnade is the Dutch word for "grace."

1

form of a story. The book had been presented to Jerry's mother, Hazel Gnade, in 1955 at a dinner party honoring her ministry of hospitality to RCA missionaries and denominational guests, which began officially in 1946 and continued officially through 1959. It was at this dinner party that the master of ceremonies, the Reverend Barnerd Luben, program secretary for the Board of Foreign Missions, publically referred to Hazel Gnade as "Tugboat Annie."[2] That reference appears in the letters and was originally considered as a title for this volume.

When I asked Jerry Gnade how he hoped the letters would be used, he responded by saying his only hope was that his mother, Hazel Gnade, and her ministry to missionaries and guests of the denomination would be remembered. After reading several examples of the letters, I recognized that the letters revealed the substance of Hazel Gnade's life as described by sixty-six different people. Hazel Gnade was obviously a very special person to many people; she was also the kind of person one would wish one's children would emulate. The letters also furnished a unique insight into the lives of our foreign missionaries. Thus began my interest in and commitment to a writing project that finds completion in these pages.

The story of Hazel Gnade's ministry, as viewed through the lens of these sixty-six letters, cannot be understood fully apart from the larger context of RCA involvement in the foreign mission movement, and especially the role of women in that involvement. When I agreed to edit the letters to Hazel Gnade, I realized that some kind of historical background was needed against which Hazel Gnade's life and the letters could be understood. However, at the outset, I never intended to research and write that context, to tell the story of RCA women collectively, or to tell the story of the Woman's Board of Foreign Missions (WBFM) and its role in the mission movement.

It didn't take long to discover that very little history on Reformed Church women had been written. In 2000 Firth Haring Fabend wrote *Zion on the Hudson: Dutch New York and New Jersey in the Age of Revivals*,[3] which is a scholarly history of Dutch church women prior to 1876. However, other than Russell Gasero's essay, "The Rise of the Woman's Board of Foreign Missions," which was published in 1999 in *Patterns and Portraits: Women in the History of the Reformed Church in America*,[4] and short biographical references to individual women identified in Una Ratmeyer's *Hands, Hearts, and Voices: Women Who Followed God's Call*, published in 1995,[5] there simply was no evaluative history of RCA women from 1875 to the present or any scholarly history of the WBFM (1875-1946) beyond the history written in 1925 by Mary Chamberlain[6] to

---

2. Although use of the name was foreshadowed by the popular TV character of the 1950s, the name as used here stemmed from Hazel Gnade's familiar presence at the docks. This was not a totally unknown nickname for Hazel Gnade, especially among the children of missionaries. She was also referred to affectionately as "Waterfront Hazel."

3. (New Brunswick, New Jersey: Rutgers Univ. Press), 2000.

4. Reneé S. House and John W. Coakley eds., The Historical Series of the Reformed Church in America, no. 31 (Grand Rapids: Eerdmans, 1999).

5. (New York: Reformed Church Press).

6. Chamberlain, *Fifty Years in Foreign Fields China, Japan, India, Arabia: A History of Five Decades of the Woman's Board of Foreign Missions Reformed Church in America* (New York: Abbott Press, 1925).

mark the fiftieth anniversary of the Woman's Foreign Board. Following Mary Chamberlain's history, the following anniversary histories were added: The *Sixth Decade of the Woman's Board of Foreign Missions Reformed Church in America 1926-1935* by Sarella Te Winkel;[7] *The Story of the Seventh Decade 1935-1945*, a collection of essays published by the WBFM;[8] and, in 1975, an eight-page history by Dorothy Burt, *I Call to Remembrance My Song*.[9] Out of necessity then, I have had to write a history of the Woman's Foreign Mission Board in order to provide a historical background for viewing Hazel Gnade's ministry of hospitality to missionaries and denominational guests.

This history is divided into nine chapters. Chapter 1 traces the General Synod's prolonged struggle to finance the RCA's growing commitment to world missions and the shape it gave to WBFM formation. Chapter 2 outlines the origins and formation of the WBFM as a group, that is, its external organization. Chapter 3 serves as a case study. It seeks to prove that RCA women unintentionally and unknowingly became feminists[10] and joined other church women in the mission movement to become the primary force in what historians refer to as the first wave of feminism.[11] Chapter 4 begins an examination of the internal organization of the WBFM. The organization's foundational documents—that is, the constitution, the by-laws, and the other documents drawn up when the WBFM was established—serve as the structure for examining how the board managed itself. Chapter 5 continues this examination and focuses on how the board organized its work both on the home front and in the foreign field. Because the original documents could not reflect how the organization would develop over time, chapter 6 examines those areas beyond coverage in the foundational documents that contributed directly to the shape of the WBFM.

In Chapter 7 an examination is made of the 1946-1960 post WBFM years.[12] In order to provide the necessary historical context for Hazel Gnade's ministry of hospitality, which extended officially from 1946 to 1960, the history of the

---

7. (New York: Woman's Board of Foreign Missions, 1935).

8. (New York: Woman's Board of Foreign Missions Reformed Church in America, 1945).

9. (New York: Reformed Church Women, 1970). Dorothy Burt retired in 1970, after working for thirty-three years for the Board of World Missions and the office of Promotion and Communications, RCA.

10. Throughout my research, I understand and employ the term "feminism" to describe any effort among women to assert and obtain equal standing with men. I will use this term to describe those efforts within the church as well as within the broader North American culture.

11. Within my research, I use the term "first wave of feminism," in reference to the first major drive among women to achieve legal rights equal to those of men.

12. Due to cultural differences associated with living in "separate spheres," women during the earlier days of the Woman's Board of Foreign Missions were known by their husbands' names. Unmarried women were recognized or spoken of as "Miss." Among themselves, however, women sometimes spoke and signed their letters and reports using their own first names. In signing Articles of Incorporation, women had legally to identify themselves using their own legal names. Throughout this text, women's first names will be used whenever those names are known; and in the first use of a woman's name, her husband's name and title will be noted in parentheses.

organization of RCA women needed to be extended to the end of her ministry, hence this additional chapter.

The details of Hazel Gnade's life also provide context for understanding the letters. For this reason a biography of Hazel Gnade has been pieced together from information provided by her family and friends. This biography forms chapter 8.

The sixty-six letters themselves form chapter 9. To retain the character and original flavor of the letters, no corrections or emendations of the letters have been made. For ease of reference, the letters are arranged in alphabetical order by the writer's last name.

Chapter 1

WBFM Formation in the Wake of General Synod Debt

Oh for more Hannahs to consecrate their sons from their birth to the service of the sanctuary! And why may we not expect recruits from the ranks of our young men of spirit, intelligence, piety, and wealth, who shall feel that the noblest calling on earth is that of the Christian ministry.

State of Religion Report
Minutes of General Synod, 1874, 64

In 1864, a year before the end of the Civil War, both the General Synod and the Board of Foreign Missions (BFM) began to experience lean financial times, which accelerated in unforeseen and devastating ways. As a result of its separate legal incorporation in the State of New York, which occurred in 1860, the BFM maintained its own financial account with the General Synod, kept its own separate financial records, and reported its audited finances to the synod independent of the General Synod treasurer and the Board of Direction.[1] Because of this, the General Synod debt and the debt of the BFM accumulated independently and grew in parallel with each other. These financial travails relate directly to the formation of the WBFM; therefore, a review of the story of this debt provides the necessary context for understanding the founding of the WBFM.

---

1. The Board of Direction functioned as a corporate board with legal responsibility for the corporation.

In 1864, much of the attention of the General Synod focused on financial problems arising from its direct administrative oversight of its seminary in New Brunswick, New Jersey. At the same time the synod undertook to support the Holland Academy, a new educational institution "in the West,"[2] which would in 1866 develop into Hope College and Western Seminary. For these, and for the synod's own operations, there were sufficient permanent endowment funds to cover the core, continuing functions. What the synod lacked was any ready source of income to fund the growing cost of doing business, that is, to cover expenses which today are known as administrative costs.

To combat the denomination's growing debt, the General Synod in 1864 took two actions. It voted a major change in the financial system that was used to transact the business of the General Synod. (This change would quickly result in disastrous financial consequences.) It also "directed an assessment of $20,000 to be laid on the Classes."[3] General Synod had hoped that if only the classes would pay the assessment of $20,000,[4] the debt problem would be solved. This did not happen. The classes did not pay.

As the General Synod's debt began to mount, an individual contributor stepped forward and donated a $40,000[5] bond. The donor was the Reverend Nicholas E. Smith D.D.[6] The bond, backed by investments in oil, was given to the General Synod

---

2. This designation was frequently used within the RCA at that time. Although the frontier had moved to California by that time, the location of Dutch immigrants in the Michigan, Wisconsin, and Illinois area in the 1840s gave rise within the denomination to viewing that area as "the West," and it is from this understanding that Western Seminary in Holland, Michigan, or the seminary "in the West," received its name.

3. Reformed Church in America, *Minutes of the General Synod* (hereafter *MGS*), 1864, 653. The governmental structure of the Reformed Church in America is composed of four assemblies. The smallest and most local assembly is called a consistory. A consistory is the governing council of each congregation. It is made up of the pastor (or pastors), plus elders and deacons. Elders are responsible for the spiritual care and direction of the congregation. The work of the deacons includes meeting the physical needs of the congregation and overseeing the congregation's charitable ministry. Elders and deacons are elected by the congregation. A pastor (or pastors) is "called" by a congregation with the permission of the classis.

A classis (plural: classes) is a group of congregations within a geographic area. There are, at present, forty-six classes in the United States and Canada, ranging in size from six to forty-one congregations.

Each classis is a member of a regional synod (formerly called a "particular synod"), an annual regional assembly. At the present time there are seven regional synods in the United States and one in Canada.

Each classis is also a member of the General Synod, the annual binational assembly. The General Synod is based on representation from the classes and serves as the highest assembly and judicatory of the denomination.

4. Throughout this text, figures will be calculated for inflation through 2002, and these calculations are based on the work of Robert C. Sahr, Political Science Dept. Oregon State University, Corvallis, OR 97331, found at infcf17002002.xls. Figured for inflation, $20,000 in 1864 would equate to $227,273 in 2002.

5. Figured for inflation, $40,000 in 1865 would equate to $439,560 in 2002.

6. The Reverend Nicholas Everitt Smith was born in Jamaica, Long Island, New York, August 11, 1820. He received AB and AM degrees from Rutgers College in 1841 and 1844 respectively. In 1845 he

to help underwrite the remaining half or $20,000 cost of endowing a third professorate at the seminary in New Brunswick.[7] The bond was also intended to help cover those expenses for which no endowment existed. This generous gift brought great relief to the General Synod, and based on the projected income from the bond, the General Synod pressed ahead by hiring a fourth professor for New Brunswick Seminary and undertaking construction of the first of three new faculty residences in New Brunswick.

The excitement of General Synod was short-lived, however. In 1867, the bond's donor lost his entire fortune and was unable either to redeem the bond or to pay the interest, making the bond worthless. As a result, the synod suddenly found itself in the midst of a still more complex financial crisis. The crisis was underscored by the lack of income derived from the synod's $20,000 assessment on the classes in 1864.[8]

Having estimated that of approximately fifty thousand church members, none had yet contributed anything to alleviate the financial difficulty, the General Synod of 1869 passed another assessment. The Board of Direction was authorized:

> to apply to each of the churches either directly or through the classes for a subscription from each, equal in amount to one dollar per capita for their respective memberships, to meet the present wants of the Synod, and replace deficiency occasioned by past demands upon the Fund.[9]

The response went unmet and was reported in 1873:

> A *pittance* only was requested–the Master's cause was represented in the appeal, and in His name was the appeal made—*yet*, apart from two or three churches which contributed very small amounts, *not one response was made throughout the entire Church. In no one instance was there a compliance with the appeal.*[10]

This response, coupled with the failed response to the $20,000 assessment, brought home to the General Synod a new and clear understanding that nonbinding assessments would not solve the problem. Although generous individuals contributed to the expansion of buildings at New Brunswick Seminary,[11] the annual operating

---

graduated from New Brunswick Theological Seminary and was licensed and ordained by the Classis of New York. In 1861 he was honored by Rutgers College with a D.D. degree. At the time of his gift, Smith was serving as pastor of the Middle Reformed Church in Brooklyn, New York, which at that time was the largest member RCA church in the South Classis of Long Island. In the *Biographical Notices of Graduates of Rutgers College*, June, 1891, 20, it says of Smith, "Dr. Smith was an intimate friend of the late Henry Ward Beecher, whom he resembled considerably in appearance. A widow and four daughters survive him." No information is provided that gives insight into his financial interests.

7. The gift came with the condition that another $40,000 be raised for yet another—the fourth—professorship. By 1865, $30,012 of this amount had been raised.

8. For a listing of the classes in arrears of this assessment as of May 1, 1866, see *MGS*, 1866, 15.

9. *MGS*, 1870, 48.

10. *MGS*, 1873, 658. Italics are original.

11. Both Suydam Hall, which was built in 1871-1873, and Sage Library, which was built 1873-1875, were donated by individual generous seminary supporters.

expenses of an expanded campus continued to contribute to rising General Synod debt.

With denominational debt spiraling out of control, a committee of the Board of Direction was appointed to prepare for the 1873 General Synod a major statement detailing the history of the debt, as well as a plan for extinguishing the debt.

It was a scathing review:

> That the difficulties under which the Board of Direction is laboring, and the causes which have produced the burden upon the Treasury may be understood, the following statement has been prepared, and will show that either ignorance of the actual condition of the Funds and the revenues therefrom, and the demands upon them, or thoughtlessness on the part of recent Synods, have brought an evil upon the Church which may be calculated to raise the question of faithfulness to its engagements.[12]

There was no going back to reverse the fateful decision of the General Synod of 1864 to change a financial system which had worked well up to that time. In its statement of June, 1873,[13] the Board of Direction projected that it would need an income of $80,000[14] to meet the General Synod's expenses for the coming year. Numerous resolutions were passed, including authorizing the Board of Direction to employ an agent or agents to aid in securing the funds as deemed necessary.[15] The synod also created a representative committee from the Particular Synods of Albany, New York, and New Brunswick, whose task it was to "awaken a due sense of the importance of the work, – maturing plans, soliciting contributions, and if an agent be appointed by the Board of Direction, facilitating his labors."[16] This was where the matter rested at the end of General Synod in June, 1873. At least it was a plan.

Underlying this entire history is the stated conviction, found in the BFM's founding documents, that God's call to evangelize the world was God's act, and every man, woman, and child was called to the task of world mission. To this end, who could say no? It was therefore believed by synod's board, and indeed by the synod itself, that the funds for the task of mission were there, within the resources of church members.

> ...And, having put our hand to the plow, our Church dare not, and we are sure would not wish to look back. Nor can we go on, allowing our debt to accumulate. In that way lies utter and shameful ruin. Nor is there any need for us to stop, nor to go back, nor to plunge deeper in debt. *The Church has the money, and it is not hers, but her Lord's.* He asks it *now*, and who will take the responsibility of withholding it?[17]

---

12. *MGS*, 1873, 650-51.
13. See *MGS*, 1863, 650-65.
14. Figured for inflation, $80,000 in 1873 would equate to $1,194,030 in 2002.
15. *MGS*, 1873, 666.
16. Ibid.
17. Italics are original. *MGS*, 1868, 489.

For the years 1864-1871, the closing years of the Civil War and the beginning years of postwar reconstruction, the General Synod tried to move ahead in its effort to evangelize the world. To accomplish this task, the synod had to find a way to bring its recurring debt under control. This meant inspiring denominational interest in missions and establishing a system whereby local churches would provide regular and consistent annual giving in support of the denomination's mission program.

During these years, the General Synod was inspired by reports from missionaries in the field, who pleaded for reinforcements. The synod was embarrassed in 1864, when a recent New Brunswick Seminary graduate wanted to serve on the mission field and there were no funds to send him. Fortunately, the young graduate obtained his own funding, which enabled the BFM to sponsor his tenure on the foreign field.[18] Fervent prayers for missionary recruits led the recruits to come, and, in 1868, the General Synod sent out two new missionaries and three unmarried women—without knowing how they were going to be funded. It was the conviction of the General Synod that this was God's answer to their prayers for new laborers in the mission field and that God intended for the synod to send out the new missionaries.

To resolve the recurring problem of debt during the years 1864-1871, the General Synod solicited and placed great hope on the recurring kindness of individual donors. Such efforts failed to meet the larger problem of establishing an organizational base to provide consistent annual income. However, it often did meet the emergency financial needs of the moment. One such instance occurred in 1866. The BFM report reads:

> In order to make the members of the Churches in New York city [sic] and its immediate vicinity more accurately acquainted with our necessities and their cause, and that they might know the legitimate claims of the work, it was concluded to invite a number of gentlemen to meet at the house of Jonathan Sturges, Esq., on the evening of Nov. 12th. At the appointed time there was a large attendance of ministers and laymen. A statement was presented of the history and then present condition of our Missions. A warm appeal was made by the Rev. H. D. Ganse. As he sat down, the Rev. Talbot W. Chambers, D.D, arose, and announced that on the morning of that day, Warren Ackerman, Esq., of the Collegiate Church, had set apart $31,000[19] to remove the debt of the Board, $15,500 to discharge its expenses from Oct. 1st, 1866, to Jan. 1st, 1867, and

---

18. The student was J. Howard Van Doren, who graduated from New Brunswick Seminary and was licensed and ordained by the Classis of New Brunswick in 1864. "Notwithstanding the pressure upon the Treasury, the Board could not withstand the plea of Rev. J. Howard Van Doren to be sent to China, inasmuch as he accompanied the plea with the offer of money to pay his outfit and passage, as well as meet his salary for a time" *MGS*, 1865, 6. To this end, "$1,855 was paid to the Board of Foreign Missions for his outfit, passage to China, and expenses in the field." *MGS*, 1865, 5. Van Doren continued to work at the Amoy mission until 1873, when he returned to the United States "as his constitution proves to be not adapted to the climate." *MGS*, 1873, 7. He continued to serve as an RCA parish pastor until his death on June 6, 1898.

19. Figured for inflation, $31,000 in 1866 would equate to $348,315 in 2002.

$10,000 to be invested for the support of the work in the future, in all $56,500. The effect of this announcement upon the meeting cannot be described. The gladness of those present was expressed in a prayer of thanksgiving offered by Rev. Peter Stryker, D.D.[20]

By 1871, the General Synod faced a $22,000[21] debt, and for the first time the synod requested pastors to organize the women in their churches into missionary societies auxiliary to the BFM.

> *Resolved*: That each pastor endeavor to comply as soon as practicable, with the request to organize the Christian women of the Church under his care, as a Missionary Society, auxiliary to the Board.[22]

The General Synod's Committee on Foreign Missions[23] evaluated the situation this way:

> It is certain that heathen women are now becoming accessible as they never have been before, to Christian instruction. It is certain also that our Churches at home deprive themselves of a great element of usefulness and source of power, by not taking advantage more specifically of the influence of Christian women in carrying on the missionary work. The union of these two objects, it is proposed to accomplish by such organizations. Your Committee coincide in the decision of the Board, that the end may be better secured by the method proposed, than by organizing, as has been done in other denominations, a distinct "Woman's Board of Foreign Missions." In the opinion of your Committee, this is neither advisable or necessary. The organization in each Church should be auxiliary to our present Board; and female teachers who may offer themselves for this work among the heathen, should be commissioned by, and come under the regulations of the Board.[24]

Still, the 1872 BFM report to General Synod noted sadly:

> But at this time the burden of debt was so heavy, the payments to be made in a few weeks or months so large, that a reduction in the appropriations could not be avoided....The Church has been liberal. The outlay of our income has been economical. But our work has constantly increased, and we have endeavored to assume and sustain the enlargement. We have simply undertaken to maintain a larger work than our income has enabled us to pay for. We have struggled

---

20. *MGS*, 1867, 4-5.

21. Figured for inflation, $22,000 in 1871 would equate to $323,529 in 2002.

22. *MGS*, 1871, 327-28.

23. The Committee on Foreign Missions was the General Synod's own internal committee and spoke on the synod's behalf. Advisory committees today serve in a similar capacity.

24. Ibid.

earnestly, as the Church has directed us to do, to continue our operations without diminution, and have at last been compelled to relinquish for the present a part of our work in India.[25]

Much of the General Synod of 1873 was taken up with discussing the synod's debt. BFM debt "of $33,500 and more than $3,000 in interest"[26] was paid from the year's contributions, although a new debt of $9,000 would appear in the coming year. Meanwhile, the synod lamented "that the Arcot Mission will soon be reduced to two efficient working men, and the Amoy Mission has now but two men in the field."[27]

In the fall of 1873, what became known as the Panic of 1873 overtook the nation, and everyone felt the impact of this major economic recession. Railroad speculation, falling stock prices, overexpansion in industry, agriculture, and commerce–all contributed to growing inflation and unemployment. It was an uneasy time in the nation, and, like everyone else, church members felt the impact of the economic recession. This uneasiness was compounded by the death and destruction brought about by the Chicago fire just two years earlier.[28] For many people, God's anger could be felt clearly in these unsettling times.

All this contributed to form the context within which the General Synod of 1874 met in Poughkeepsie, New York. The synod's Committee on Foreign Missions took note that for the BFM "it has been impossible, successfully, to maintain operations upon the scale of former years."[29] The committee made only two recommendations, both of which were passed by the synod. The first recommendation:

> That General Synod recall the attention of the Churches to the value of monthly Missionary Concerts as demonstrated through the entire history of the work, and as insuring a direct obedience to the command of our Savior, – Pray ye the Lord of the harvest to send forth laborers into His harvest," –and also as keeping before the minds of our people the condition and progress of our Missions, so encouraging to Christian faith and liberality.[30]

25. *MGS*, 1872, 5.

26. *MGS*, 1873, 741.

27. *MGS*, 1873, 742. It is not possible positively to identify the "two efficient working men at the Arcot Mission" (and their wives!) to which the *MGS* refer. However, the two men at the Amoy Mission included the Reverend Leonard W. Kip (missionary to China 1861-1898) and his wife, Helen A. Culbertson Kip, and the Reverend Daniel Rapalje (missionary to China 1858-1899) and his wife, Alice Ostrom Rapalje.

28. The late autumn of 1871 was exceptionally dry. During the second week of October, fires destroyed large portions of Chicago, Illinois; at least three communities in Wisconsin; and most of Holland, Michigan.

29. *MGS*, 1874, 141.

30. *MGS*, 1874, 142.

The second recommendation was recorded this way:

> Your Committee also call the consideration of the Synod to the establishment of a Woman's Missionary Society, substantially upon the form of those now existing in other denominations, auxiliary to our Foreign Board. The organization of associations of ladies in the other benevolent enterprizes of the Church, has been most effective. By branches of these auxiliaries, in different cities, neighborhoods or churches, we shall be enabled far more fully to district congregations, and generalize the support of our missionary work, and, instead of devolving its burdens upon the few, reaching many who have not heretofore contributed to this Board, thus securing regular annual membership subscriptions. It is proposed also, to give these organizations an auxiliary character, by requesting, through them, the selection and recommendation of such ladies as we may send into the foreign field to teach in the girls' schools, and to gain access to others of their own sex. In reference to the above, your Committee suggest the following action:
>
> ...*Resolved,* That General Synod recommends the organization of a "Woman's Missionary Society," having in view the objects heretofore named, with auxiliary associations in all those Churches where it is practicable, in the work of which our Board shall fully sympathize and co-operate, accepting nominations by this Society for that branch of the service especially committed to it.[31]

It was this invitation from the General Synod of their denomination that caused women to gather in New York City that stormy January day in 1875. Their understanding of the purpose for their meeting was absolutely clear. They were beginning the work committed to them by the General Synod.

The meeting was also the answer to many of their prayers. On the one hand, not in their personal memories had church women been allowed, much less invited, to leave their sphere of household duties and childcare responsibilities to move and breathe the rarefied air of the public sphere of men, and of Reformed Church men in particular. On the other hand, the General Synod's request for the women to organize meant that Reformed women were needed. It was just that simple. Women of the Reformed Church in America were needed to be God's voice and to be God's special messengers to heathen women and children, just like Sarah, the wife of Abraham; Miriam, the sister of Moses; Deborah the judge; and Priscilla, whose teaching Paul admired; Lois and Eunice, who became models for the training of young children; Mary the Mother of Jesus; and all the other women recorded in the scriptures who had been called by God to do their special jobs.[32]

Were not the women who met on January 7, 1875, and those who followed called by God to a sacred task? Was not the impact of the gospel reflected in their willingness

---

31. Ibid.

32. The names of these biblical women were chosen by the author. Historian Patricia R. Hill makes an interesting observation: "The signs of the times, as interpreted by the leaders of the woman's foreign mission movement, indicated that use of Sarah as a model ought to be discarded in light of a reexamination of the 'relation of woman to the New Testament church.'" Professor Hill then uses an

to brave the brutal weather of that day, as well as in all of the successes that followed? In the true Calvinist tradition of believing in God's sovereignty and God's gift of grace freely extended to all, these women arrived convinced of God's passionate love for all humankind in this broken and sinful world. On that day in January, 1875, did not these women passionately believe that they and all their sisters in Christ were being called by God to a new leading of the Holy Spirit? Was not God's call to them absolutely real, and did they not trust the God of Abraham, Isaac, and Jacob and their heavenly Father who sacrificed his only Son our Lord Jesus Christ on a cross for the redemption of all humanity? These women fully believed that they were on a mission for the Master and his church, and above all else, they wanted to be faithful to the Master.

Over the course of seventy years, thousands of Reformed Church women sought to be faithful servants by participating in the work of the WBFM. For most women, involvement with other women to advance the cause of foreign missions brought affirmation and value to their individual lives and roles within the church, no matter how large or how small the roles were. Through the work of the WBFM, women found a place at the table of the Lord. Women's understanding of God's world was broadened, and women were changed because of it.

---

interesting quote from a woman identified only by her initials, S. W., in "Woman As a Christian Factor," *Woman's Work for Woman* 11 (December, 1881): 417-18. It reads:

> Our grandfathers dwelt lightly upon that exceeding honor which Christ in assuming human form had cast upon woman....Strangely too was it forgotten that Anna, the prophetess, spake of the Babe of Bethlehem to all them that dwelt in Jerusalem, that Mary Magdalene and Joanna and Susanna and many other women, abandoning their homes, followed the weary steps of our Master...and that to the women who labored with Paul in the gospel many of the tenderest of his messages...were addressed. More strangely still was it forgotten that almost the only acts of great self-sacrifice narrated by the evangelists were performed by women; that no man cast all his living into the temple treasury, but a woman and she a widow; only a woman anointed the Saviour with precious ointment, while men disapproved this expression of grateful love; only a woman washed His feet with tears; women were the last at the cross and earliest at the sepulchre.

Patricia R. Hill, *The World Their Household: The American Woman's Foreign Mission Movement and Cultural Transformation, 1870-1920*, (Ann Arbor: Univ. of Michigan, 1985), 74.

For RCA women, Ruth the gleaner appears to be the model. In her article, "Women Raising Women: The Urgent Work of the *Mission Gleaner*, 1883-1917," Reneé House notes:

> ...Even before the *Gleaner* was published, the women identified themselves with Ruth, the gleaner....When the *Gleaner* began as an autonomous publication of the woman's board in 1883, the women reiterated in their annual board report their intent to be "a gleaner, not a reaper in the field of the churches which belong by inheritance to Synod's Board. But on the pages of the *Gleaner* itself, this publication by and for women only, there is never any further explanation of this title. It appears to me that the woman's board identified themselves with Ruth, at least in part, as a means of signaling to the men their intent to stay in their proper place in relation to the men's board. The women do not claim to own the field, or to have planted the seeds, or to be the primary laborers in the harvest. Like Ruth, the women signal their intent to remain in their rightful place.

In Reneé House and John Coakley, eds., *Patterns and Portraits, Women in the History of the Reformed Church in America*, The Historical Series of the Reformed Church in America, no. 31, (Grand Rapids: Eerdmans, 1999), 106.

Chapter 2

Origin and Group Formation

How often we forget that the Church of Christ ought to be concerned more for people outside its doors than those within. *Our* church, *our* building, *our* program. . .these become the focus of our attention and our concern until the institution has become an end in itself. This is an entirely human tendency, but it is not biblical.

Carol Hageman
November, 1967, Guild Program
"What in the World is Social Ministry?"

The origin of the Woman's Board of Foreign Missions[1] dates from 1875, but long before this time women and men in congregations of the Reformed Protestant Dutch Church in North America supported the work of missionaries.[2] The General Synod,

---

1. Note should be taken that according to its Certificate of Incorporation dated January 30, 1892, the name of this Foreign Mission Society is the *Woman's* Foreign Mission Society. In the Constitution of January 1, 1883, the Woman's Executive Committee of Domestic Missions of the RCA is identified specifically as the *Woman's* Executive Committee of Domestic Missions of the RCA; and according to the Certificate of Incorporation, which appears in the 1910 *Annual Report of the Women's Board of Domestic Missions*, this name officially becomes the *Women's* Board of Domestic Missions.

2. For an overview of RCA historiography and a bibliography of RCA history, see John Coakley's essay, "Women in the History of the Reformed Church in America," in Renée House and John Coakley, eds., *Patterns and Portraits, Women in the History of the Reformed Church in America*, The Historical Series of the Reformed Church in America, no. 31 (Grand Rapids: Eerdmans, 1999), 1-15.

John Henry Livingston

in 1786, made "the Extension of the Church" a regular agenda item at its annual meeting. In 1796, Reformed, Presbyterian, and Baptist churches in New York City joined to form the New York Missionary Society, and among the officers of this society were the Reverend Dr. John Henry Livingston and the Reverend John N. Abeel, both ministers of the Reformed Protestant Dutch Church in North America.[3]

During gatherings of the New York Missionary Society, John Henry Livingston (1746-1825), the first professor of theology in the Reformed Protestant Dutch Church, preached two powerful sermons in support of the call to world mission within the Reformed Protestant Dutch Church. The first sermon, "The Glory of the Redeemer," was preached April 23, 1799. It was based on Colossians 3:11.[4] "The Everlasting Gospel," the title of the second sermon, was preached April 3, 1804, and was based on Revelation 14:6-7.[5] The sermons were quickly published and widely distributed. Both sermons called urgently to Christ's followers to answer the call to mission and spoke of the necessity of sharing the gospel with all cultures prior to Christ's second coming, which Livingston believed would occur no later than the year 2000. Thus Livingston's sermons carried with them a sense of timeliness and

---

3. Arie R. Brouwer, *Reformed Church Roots: Thirty-five Formative Events* (New York: Reformed Church Press, 1977), 94.

4. Colossians 3:11 reads, "In that renewal there is no longer Greek and Jew, circumcised and uncircumcised, barbarian, Scythian, slave and free; but Christ is all, and in all!"

5. Revelation 14.6, 7 reads: "Then I saw another angel flying in midheaven, with an eternal gospel to proclaim to those who live on the earth—to every nation and tribe and language and people. He said in a loud voice, "Fear God and give him glory, for the hour of his judgment has come; and worship him who made heaven and earth, the sea and the springs of water.""

urgency. In response to Livingston's call, and further encouraged by the enthusiasm for foreign missions that was sweeping across England, the General Synod in 1806 created a Standing Committee on Missions, which was later designated a Board of Managers, to implement the task of missionary work.

In 1810, the Reformed Protestant Dutch Church joined the Congregational and Presbyterian churches to form the American Board of Commissioners for Foreign Missions (ABCFM).[6] With the support of the ABCFM, the first missionaries from the Reformed Church, John Scudder, M.D., and his wife, Harriet Waterbury Scudder, sailed in 1819 for Ceylon, and, in 1829, the Reverend David Abeel sailed for China. When in 1832 the Reformed Protestant Dutch Church formed its own Board of Foreign Missions, it did so as a means of supporting world mission through the ABCFM, and this relationship continued until 1857.[7]

In 1857, however, when the Reformed Protestant Dutch Church in North America incorporated its own Board of Foreign Missions, it undertook world mission on its own. It did so in the belief that such a change would result in greater financial support and care, "greater efficiency and a more faithful conformity to the Divine requirement."[8] In making this change, the denomination was following the example of others, which had earlier taken similar steps. Nevertheless, the Reformed Protestant Dutch Church remained committed to cooperative ecumenical mission strategies.

Since the beginning of the nineteenth century, church women had banded together to form "cent societies."[9] Membership in cent societies required each woman to commit one penny a week from her household funds. This money would be used to support indigent students at the Reformed Protestant Dutch Seminary, which in 1810 was relocated from New York City to New Brunswick, New Jersey.[10]

During these early nineteenth-century years, and later during Victorian times, the place in society occupied by all women in general was given clear definition. Men were in positions of authority over women as understood in the literalists' interpretation of certain biblical passages such as Genesis 3:16, Ephesians 5:22-24,

---

6. Eugene P. Heideman, *From Mission to Church: The Reformed Church in America Mission to India*, Historical Series of the Reformed Church in America, no. 38 (Grand Rapids: Eerdmans, 2001), 10.

7. Edward Tanjore Corwin, *A Digest of Constitutional and Synodical Legislation of the Reformed Church in America* (New York: The Board of Publication of the Reformed Church in America, 1906), 297. According to an annotated chronology prepared for the 125th anniversary of the BFM, and appearing in the 1957 *Annual Report of the Board of Foreign Missions*, "The Hon. Theodore Frelinghuysen was president of the American Board for ten years" (*MGS*, 1957), 3.

8. *MGS*, 1857, 263.

9. Corwin, *Digest*, 120. See also *MGS*, 1818, p. 18; 1820, p. 46. For a history of the earliest "cent societies," see Ellen C. Parsons, "History of Woman's Organized Missionary Work as Promoted by American Women, An Address presented at the Congress of Missions, Columbian Exposition in Chicago, 1893" (Chicago: American Tract Society 1894), 84-85.

10. It was one year later, in 1811, that students at New Brunswick Seminary established the Berean Society. The Berean Society focused on discussions relating to foreign mission work and became a great influence within the student body. In 1820 the Berean Society changed its name to the Society of Inquiry Concerning Missions, which continues to function today as the student government within New Brunswick Theological Seminary.

and 1 Corinthians 14:34-35.[11] Men were intended to assume responsibility for public and political matters, and as heads of households they were expected to provide for the needs of their wives and children. Women were entrusted with the oversight of the home and care of the family. It was believed that the virtues of piety, purity, submissiveness, and domesticity belonged especially to women and formed the guidelines for women in their aspirations for "true womanhood." Morality especially was believed to reside with women.[12]

Women and men lived in "separate spheres." Here, clear lines of authority marked the boundaries between the sexes and delineated the behavioral expectations of both women and men.[13] Living in separate spheres was also reflected in church life and architecture. In many Reformed congregations, women and men were seated separately. Since church sanctuaries often had no central aisle, women and children were seated in a large central section of pews, and men were seated in smaller sections on either side of the nave.[14]

---

11. Genesis 3:16 reads, "To the woman he said, 'I will greatly increase your pangs in childbearing; in pain you shall bring forth children, yet your desire shall be for your husband, and he shall rule over you.'" Ephesians 5:22-24 reads, "Wives, be subject to your husbands as you are to the Lord. For the husband is the head of the wife just as Christ is the head of the church, the body of which he is the Savior. Just as the church is subject to Christ, so also wives ought to be, in everything, to their husbands." 1 Corinthians 14:33b-35 reads, "As in all the churches of the saints, women should be silent in the churches. For they are not permitted to speak, but should be subordinate, as the law also says. If there is anything they desire to know, let them ask their husbands at home. For it is shameful for a woman to speak in church."

12. As noted by Dr. John W. Beardslee III, professor of church history at New Brunswick Theological Seminary 1964-1984, "With all its faults, the Christian church and western society demanded moral responsibility of women." John W. Beardslee III, "The Dutch Women in Two Cultures: Looking for the Questions?" in House and Coakley, *Patterns and Portraits*, 65.

See Barbara Welter, "The Cult of True Womanhood: 1820-60," *American Quarterly*, XVIII (summer 1966), 151-74, which defines and describes the nineteenth-century attitudes. See also: Linda K. Kerber and Jane De Hart Mathews eds., *Women's America: Refocusing the Past* (New York: Oxford Univ. Press, 1982), 14-19; Steven Mintz and Susan Kellogg, *Domestic Revolutions: A Social History of American Family Life* (New York: The Free Press 1988), 52-57; and Renée S. House, "Women Raising Women: The Urgent Work of the *Mission Gleaner*, 1883-1917," in House and Coakley, *Patterns and Portraits*, 109.

13. For an interesting review of women's ideology, see the introduction to Kerber and Mathews, *Women's America*, 14-17.

14. Examples of this include the First Reformed Church in South Holland, Illinois, whose *Centennial Book, First Reformed Church of South Holland, Illinois: 1848-1948* shows on page 32 a plan of the second church building (1863-1890). It has the pews marked "men" on both side sections and "women" on the center section.

In the centenary anniversary history for the First Reformed Church in Cedar Grove, Wisconsin, it is noted, "During the pastorate of the Reverend Herman Borgers, 1875 [1874-1881] the families were requested 'to sit together in the service.'" This meant that no longer were the men to sit on one side of the high partition between the seats and the women and children on the opposite side." *First Reformed Church Centenary 1854-1954 Cedar Grove, Wisconsin*, (Port Washington, Wisconsin: Pilot Print, 1954), 5.

See also Robert P. Swierenga, *Dutch Chicago: A History of the Hollenders in the Windy City* (Grand Rapids: Eerdmans, 2002), 110-11.

During the early decades of the nineteenth century, American culture did not allow women to speak in public—either in a public role or in a public setting.[15] Women spoke primarily among themselves and in the privacy of their homes. It is generally agreed among historians that the nine-month tour that Sarah and Angelina Grimké undertook in 1837, during which they spoke in public against slavery, marks a major change for all women.[16] This was true for church women as well.

Women of the Reformed Protestant Dutch Church and their sisters in Christ in other denominations listened to and became inspired by the stories they heard about the work that missionaries were doing. Hearing these stories and learning about the needs of the missionaries moved church women increasingly to want to play a role in assisting missionaries in their work both at home and overseas.

Within the New York City area, a group of interested church women began meeting to discuss the exciting work that missionaries were doing. Sarah Doremus was one of those women, and often she would open her home for such gatherings.[17] In 1829, David Abeel, recently graduated from New Brunswick Seminary and ordained by the Classis of Rensselaer, sailed for the Far East under the supervision of the ABCFM. At the time of his departure, Sarah Doremus was among those women who were present at the docks to say farewell to David Abeel. When he returned about six years later, Sarah Doremus and her friends were again waiting for him at the docks.[18] This practice of women saying farewell to and welcoming home missionaries at the docks in New York City has a long and distinguished history. This is the ministry that Hazel Gnade would one day carry out with distinction—a tradition begun with Sarah Doremus. The women waiting on the docks for David Abeel's return could hardly wait to hear about his mission work and to learn what he had discovered in the Far East, especially in China.[19]

It is not surprising, then, that shortly after his return in 1835, Abeel met with a group of church women at the Doremus home and pleaded for American church

---

15. Gerda Lerner, *The Grimké Sisters from South Carolina: Pioneers for Woman's Rights and Abolition* (New York: Houghton Mifflin, 1967), 5.

16. See Lerner, *The Grimké Sisters*. See also Eleanor Flexner, *Century of Struggle: The Woman's Rights Movement in the United States* (New York: Atheneum, 1974), 43-44; and Sandra Opdycke, *The Routledge Historical Atlas of Women in America* (New York and London: Routledge, 2000) 46-47.

17. In March, 1877, the *Missionary Link* dedicated its entire issue in tribute to Sarah Doremus. It contained a broad review of her life. *The Missionary Link for the Woman's Union Missionary Society of America for Heathen Lands*, 9, no. 2 (March, 1877) 2-29. For an interesting description of Sarah Doremus and her work, see Helen Barrett Montgomery, *Western Women in Eastern Lands* (New York: Macmillan, 1910), 161-66. See also James I. Good, *Women of the Reformed Church* (n.p., 1901), 287-95, and Una Ratmeyer, *Hands, Hearts, and Voices, Women Who Followed God's Call* (New York: Reformed Church Press, 1995), 2-3.

18. According to Edward Tanjore Corwin, in *A Digest of the Constitutional Legislation of the Reformed Church in America* (New York: Board of Publication of the RCA, 1906), 833, "It had been her [Mrs. Doremus's] custom to look after the comfort of almost all outgoing and incoming missionaries from the time of the departure of David Abeel in 1829, until her death in 1877."

19. For further reading about David Abeel and the RCA mission to China, see Gerald F. De Jong, *The Reformed Church in China 1842-1951*, The Historical Series of the Reformed Church in America, no. 22 (Grand Rapids: Eerdmans, 1992).

women to organize. He told stories of women and children in China and their suffering from the torturous practice of foot binding, their lack of medical care and education, and most importantly their ignorance of the gospel message. Helen Barrett Montgomery (1861-1934), noted Greek scholar, reformer, and dynamic pioneer leader on behalf of American Baptist women, describes David Abeel's request for aid this way in her history, *Western Women in Eastern Lands*:

> The helplessness and misery of the women of the Orient had profoundly touched [Abeel], and he had seen also the hopelessness of attempting to dislodge heathenism while its main citadel, "the home," was unreached, and unreachable by the agencies then employed. Thinking long and deeply over the problem, he had come to hold the then revolutionary doctrine that it was absolutely necessary to bring into the field unmarried women to reach and teach the women and children. Men were shut out from ministry by the iron bars of custom that imprisoned women in zenanas, secluding them from all contact with the world. The missionary wife at best could give only a fragment of her strength and time to the work; then why not send out women to minister to the uncounted millions of women in non-Christian lands? [20]

At this point David Abeel's anguish on behalf of women makes clear how directed toward men the mission efforts had been. It was a concern for the souls and lives of men that preoccupied missionaries up to this time—not the souls and lives of women.

David Abeel's appeal, "especially for unmarried women to consecrate themselves to this work,"[21] had prompted women in England to establish the Society for Promoting Female Education in China and the Far East. This society became the very first Protestant woman's foreign missionary society to support independent missionary work in foreign lands.[22]

In 1836 a group of church women led by Sarah Doremus approached the ABCFM and asked to be allowed to organize a women's board of foreign missions. In response

---

20. Helen Barrett Montgomery, *Western Women in Eastern Lands: An Outline Study of Fifty Years of Woman's Work in Foreign Missions*, (New York: Macmillan, 1910), 21.

21. Corwin, *Digest*, 833.

22. See E. Jane Whateley, "The Society for Promoting Female Education in the East," in E. M. Wherry, comp., *Woman in Missions: Papers and Addresses Presented at The Woman's Congress of Missions October, 2-4, 1893, in the Hall of Columbus, Chicago* (New York: American Tract Society, 1894), 73-82. In her presentation at the Columbian Exposition, Miss E. Jane Whateley, "one of the vice presidents" of the Society for Promoting Female Education in the East, described David Abeel's meeting with English women in 1834 this way:

> Mr. Abeel had come from the scene of his labors with a heart full of sorrow for the misery and degradations of the women of the country. He felt that his efforts and those of his fellow-workers could not reach their case. The gospel, even when preached in their country, was virtually shut out from them.

> When the Christian Church first awoke from its long sleep of indifference to the call to "teach all nations," the work of missionaries was, naturally enough at first, purely general. In some countries this might make no practical difference; but in India, China, and the East generally, domestic and social habits completely excluded women from the preaching and teaching of men.

David Abeel

to their request, the Reverend Rufus Anderson, secretary of the ABCFM, asked the women "to defer indefinitely" the organization of a women's board. To this response, David Abeel is remembered, "with tears rolling down his face," to have asked, "What is to become of the souls of those who are ignorant of the offers of mercy and of the Bible?"[23] For those women desiring a women's board, waiting was not easy. They were not pleased. In one memorable response to the ABCFM's recommendation, Joanna Bethune declared, "What! Is the American Board afraid the ladies will get ahead of them?"[24]

By 1861, Sarah Doremus and her friends could wait no longer. As Dana L. Robert asks in her 1997 study titled, *American Women: A Social History of Their Thought and Practice*:

The existing schools were usually only for boys. The missionary had no means of addressing the wives and mothers of his hearers. This was painfully impressed on Mr. Abeel's mind. He pictured to his English friends the state of this vast mass of Eastern women, oppressed, trampled on, secluded, and utterly ignorant: unable to be a power for good, and yet capable of being a mighty power for evil; for the despised heathen mother had her own means of influencing her sons, and could often effectually prevent them from listening to the gospel message. What was to be done for this poor, down-trodden, benighted multitude? Only their own sex could reach them. Would not some of the Christian women of England stretch out a helping hand? This was the substance of Mr. Abeel's appeal.

23. Mary Chamberlain, *Fifty Years in Foreign Fields, China, Japan, India, Arabia: A History of Five Decades of the Woman's Board of Foreign Mission, Reformed Church in America* (New York: Abbott Press, 1925), 5-7.

24. Chamberlain, *Fifty Years*, 7. Joanna Bethune was the mother of the Reverend George Washington Bethune. For information on Joanna Bethune, see Edward Tanjore Corwin, *A Manual of the Reformed Church in America (Formerly Ref. Prot. Dutch Church)* (New York: Board of Publication of the Reformed Church in America, 1902), 321.

What caused Mrs. Doremus and the other women to change their minds and to defy Rufus Anderson, the most powerful mission administrator in America? For one thing, public opinion as to the role of women was advancing along with the wider availability of women's education. Social trends favored the increase of wider public roles for women as the nineteenth century wore on....But more specifically, two reasons for the decision to reject Anderson and the counsel of most missionary men in 1861 was the continued reluctance of the Protestant mission boards to send out unmarried women, and the limitations of Anderson's three-self theory for the particular missionary contribution of women.[25]

A child of wealth, Sarah Platt Doremus was married to Thomas C. Doremus, a well-to-do New York doctor who firmly supported his wife in her charitable undertakings, of which there were many.[26] Even as the mother of their nine children, Sarah Doremus continued to lead a privileged life. She and her family were members of the South Reformed Church, located at 5th Avenue and 21st Street in New York City, where Thomas Doremus served as elder.[27] Such wealth and privilege were disciplined by years of concern for the salvation of a lost world and concern for the welfare of women in particular. With energy, insight, and social grace, Sarah Doremus

---

25. Dana L. Robert, *American Women in Mission: A Social History of Their Thought and Practice* (Macon, Georgia: Mercer Univ. Press, 1977), 115. Dana L. Robert further explains:

> The mission executive who presided over the great expansion of girls' schools and their transformation into female seminaries was Rufus Anderson, Secretary of the American Board from 1822 to 1866. Anderson was the preeminent American mission theorist of the nineteenth century. His "three-self" mission theory was evangelistic in focus, arguing that the conversion of the world could best be effected by founding self-supporting, self-governing, and self-propagating churches. An "evangelizer" rather than "civilizer," Anderson evaluated all mission policies through the lens of whether the work promoted world evangelization (89).

26. See R. Pierce Beaver, *American Protestant Women in World Mission: History of the First Feminist Movement in North America*, (Grand Rapids: Eerdmans, 1968), 90-91, for an insightful list of Mrs. Doremus's charitable involvement.

27. South Reformed Church was no longer part of the Collegiate Church at this time. Pastors at South Reformed include James M. Mathews, 1811-1840; associate pastor Mancius S. Hutton, 1834-1837; John M. Macauley, 1838-1861; Ebenezer P. Rogers, 1862-1881; Roderick Terry, 1881-1904; and T. R. Bridges, 1906-1914. The congregation was disbanded in 1914.

Sarah Doremus's husband, Thomas C. Doremus, was an elder and also keenly interested in foreign missions. According to a *Historical Sketch of the South Church (Reformed) of New York City*, compiled by Mr. Frederic C. White and Rev. Roderick Terry, for the 75th Anniversary of the Separation of the Church from the other Collegiate Churches (New York: Gilliss Brothers and Turnure, 1887), page 35, Thomas Doremus played a pivotal role in establishing the RCA mission in Japan. According to the account, one stormy evening in 1854 following a prayer meeting, Thomas Doremus read a letter from a friend that spoke of the ratification of the Treaty with Japan, which opened two ports for American commerce. The pastor then recounted,

> When he finished I remarked that the Dutch had once carried the Gospel into Japan and I did not see why they should not do so again. With characteristic promptitude he [Thomas Doremus] asked: "What would it require to do it?" I answered, A Mission of at least three warm-hearted Christian men; if possible, a Minister, a medical Missionary and a master of the useful arts of Western civilization. To his inquiry as to the expense, I replied, Five hundred a year for each of the

Sarah Doremus

organized the Women's Union Missionary Society of America for Heathen Lands. This union of churches was interdenominational, and Sarah Doremus served as president of the society from its inception in 1861 until her death in 1877.[28]

Following the turbulent years of the Civil War, various denominational women's boards came into existence. These were separate from the Women's Union Missionary Board, although the Women's Union Missionary Board remained "the mother and inspiration of all those denominational societies and can claim a share in their

---

three men; and I thought there was no use in attempting it unless the money could be pledged for at least three years. After a moment's thought he [Thomas Doremus] said, I will be one to subscribe five hundred a year for three years. I said, I think I can tell you who will be another if you go now and ask him, and I named Mr. D. Jackson Steward. Mr. Doremus went immediately through the storm, called on Mr. Steward, and received his generous subscription of $1,500. The third $1,500 was soon subscribed by others of the congregation. This provided for the three Missionaries. Subsequent arrangements provided for the support of their wives...Our Mission to Japan has been a most successful one. To God be the praise!

28. According to Edward T. Corwin,

Mrs. Doremus's Union Society proposed to send out only unmarried ladies. It at once secured 100 collectors, each of whom would be responsible for $20 per year, for five years. "The Missionary Link" was issued as its organ of information. In the first 25 years, 1861-1886, this Society raised about one million dollars. Its annual receipts before 1886 reached about $70,000, and there were then about 70 lady missionaries under its care. Zenana work has been the strong feature in the labors of these missionaries. Many Reformed churches organized Women's Societies in connection with this Union Society, before the R.C.A. formed a Woman's Board of its own in 1875 (*Digest*, 833-34).

At the time of her death, a marble tablet was placed on the wall of the South Reformed Church which read, "In Memory of Sarah Platt, Wife of Thomas C. Doremus—who peacefully fell 'asleep in Jesus,' January 29, 1877. Aged 74 years. She united with this church September 11, 1823. 'Well reported

achievements."[29] Women in the Congregational Church were the first to form their own board in 1868, and they were followed in rapid succession by their sisters in the Methodist Church (1869), the Presbyterian Church (1870), and the Baptist Church (1871). Women in the Reformed Protestant Dutch Church, (renamed the Reformed Church in America in 1867 and hereinafter RCA) were organized in 1875, the last of the five major women's foreign boards to organize on a denominational basis. In her fifty-year anniversary history of the WBFM, Mary Chamberlain comments:

> It is an interesting, if not a puzzling question why the women of the Reformed Church, with both Dr. Abeel and Mrs. Doremus of their own Church to lead the way, should have been the very last to organize. We are told that "the mills of the gods grind slowly" and we are not unaccustomed, perhaps, to the idea that the mills of the Dutch gods grind slowest of all. It may be so. Yet in seeking for some solution to this perplexing problem a fairer and more flattering explanation has been found. There are many proofs, as we have seen, that Mrs. Doremus exerted a wide influence among women outside of her own denomination. There are many more indications that she enjoyed great popularity among the women of her own Church. It was very natural that those women, accustomed to look upon her as their leader, should have felt a peculiar devotion to the society of which she was the head and that they should have been slow to organize in her own Church another woman's board of foreign missions.[30]

---

of [sic] for good works, she hath brought up children, she hath lodged strangers, she hath washed the saints' feet, she hath relieved the afflicted, she hath diligently followed every good work'—1 Timothy, 5-20. This tablet is erected as a tribute of affection by the ladies of the South Reformed Church."

In delicate contrast to this, the sermon preached at her memorial service by the Reverend Talbot Chambers, is recorded in the South Church 75th Anniversary book this way:

This Church has the credit of having produced what I take to be the most distinguished ornament to Christianity, of the female sex, which this country has seen or is likely to see. And it has often been a matter of great wonder to me that there was not adequate printed memorial of the life and character of Mrs. Doremus, of whom it is enough to say, that while being on the one hand a wife and mother in whom nothing was lacking from beginning to end, she superadded to the performance of domestic duties an amount of service to the cause of Christ, at home and abroad, which is almost incredible. Every good enterprise, no matter of what name or under whose auspices, found in her a wise adviser and an efficient helper. She was like "the beloved Persis which labored much in the Lord," and yet never overstepped the limits of her sex or gave occasion to unfriendly criticism. It is an honor—a bright and distinguished honor—to the Church, to have had such a woman reared here and live here for so many years, unto the last without a spot, without anything that required explanation—her own presence anywhere a blessing and a delight.

Sketch of the South Church (Reformed) of New York City, 40-41. For the most complete description of the life of Mrs. Doremus, see the *Missionary Link for the Woman's Union Missionary Society of America for Heathen Lands,* March, 1877, vol. 9, no. 2., 2-29. See also Mary S. Benson, "Sarah Platt Haines Doremus," *Notable American Women 1607-1950: A Biographical Dictionary,* Edward T. James ed., vol. 1 (Cambridge: Belknap Press, 1971), 500-501; Ratmeyer, *Hands, Hearts, and Voices,* 2-3.

29. Beaver, *American Protestant Women,* 92.

30. Chamberlain, *Fifty Years,* 8-9.

Within the Reformed Protestant Dutch Church, early women's missionary societies contributed to the mission work among women and children in foreign lands by sending their donations to the Women's Union Missionary Board, which was under the leadership of Sarah Doremus, or to the General Synod's Board.[31] With the formation of denominational women's boards, however, the financial resources of church women increasingly became directed toward the support of the separate denominational women's boards.[32]

Having become incorporated in 1857, the Board of Foreign Missions of the Reformed Protestant Dutch Church observed by this time the kind of financial support their own church women were giving to the Women's Union Board. Within twenty years of this shift to an independent denominational mission board, the women of the church were asked by the General Synod to form their own Woman's Board of Foreign Missions.[33] This Woman's Board of Foreign Missions was not to be a totally independent board, but it was to serve as an auxiliary board "to aid the Board of Foreign Missions of the Reformed Church in America."[34]

The beginning of the story of the Woman's Board of Foreign Missions is recorded this way:

> The meeting for organization was called at the Chapel of the Reformed Church, corner Fifth Avenue and 29th Street, New York City,[35] January 7th, 1875. The morning could scarcely have been more inauspicious. One of the severest storms of the winter was raging at the time when the trains, which were to bring the ladies to the chapel from various suburban towns, left there for the city. The pavements were sheeted with ice, while the rain and sleet fell steadily all the forenoon. Yet, at the appointed hour there were present in the lecture-room twelve or thirteen ladies, representatives from as many churches, six of these being from the towns referred to, viz.: Brooklyn, L.I.; Yonkers, Millbrook, and Saugerties, N.Y.; Belleville and Hackensack, N.J. Rev. Dr. [John Mason] Ferris, Secretary of the Board of Foreign Missions, to whose suggestion the Church is largely indebted for the formation of the Woman's Board, was present, and contributed, at that and at subsequent meetings, his counsel and assistance in the organization. A constitution and by-laws were prepared and adopted, permanent officers and a Board of Managers chosen, and an appeal issued to the ladies of the Reformed Church in America, appended to which was a form of constitution, to be adopted by auxiliary associations.[36]

Who were these determined ladies in their long skirts and winter muffs, who somewhat foolishly left the safety of their homes and traveled on public

---

31. Corwin, *Digest*, 833.

32. Beaver, *American Protestant Women*, 92.

33. *Annual Report of the Woman's Board of Foreign Mission* (hereafter *ARWBFM*), 1875, 3.

34. A good review of the formative years of the WBFM can be found in Heideman, *From Mission to Church*, 159-71.

35. That is, Marble Collegiate Church.

36. *ARWBFM* 1875, 4.

transportation into New York City on a day like this? What could be so important to them that they would risk leaving the safety of their homes in this inclement weather to attend a church meeting?

These were no ordinary women, and this was no ordinary church meeting. The lives of these women, and the ministries of Reformed Church women who followed them, including Hazel Gnade, tell a story that speaks of a powerful and aching passion for the gospel that led to an equally powerful commitment to share the gospel with and to care for all women and children throughout the world.[37] It was an auspicious moment. As Mary Chamberlain noted in her fifty-year history of the WBFM, "It was a movement destined to set free the unsuspected energies of multitudes of women in behalf of other multitudes less fortunate than themselves."[38] It is a story rich in excitement and hope. It also remains a largely untold story of American women and how the women's mission movement loosened the shackles of the cultural confines of "separate spheres" that marked the place of American women from Victorian times to the 1960s. Reformed Church women eventually came to a monumental empathy for the suffering of all women and children throughout the world—a world about which the women in 1875 knew little if anything.

When the General Synod convened in June 1874 in Poughkeepsie, New York, and voted to establish a Woman's Board of Foreign Missions, the synod's action revealed clearly that it needed women to do a job that the Board of Foreign Missions could not itself accomplish on behalf of the General Synod.[39] Although the BFM had been

---

37. In 1874 the Woman's Christian Temperance Union was founded, and it quickly grew to become a major organizational force for women. As with other denominations, Reformed Church women were encouraged to join in support of this organization. In her presentation delivered at the Woman's Congress of Missions in 1893 in Chicago titled, "History of Woman's Organized Missionary Work as Promoted by American Women," Ellen C. Parsons analyzed the temperance and mission movements this way:

> What was it that shook the Church, roused the women to united, systematic, concentrated action, that moved on and on, a compelling force, until we now have in this country the spectacle of hundreds of thousands of women, representing every branch of the Christian Church, banded together in chartered societies and disbursing from one to one-and-a-half millions of dollars every year? Only one other movement, that of the Temperance Union, compares with it in numbers and moral power. Whence came that powerful voice which evoked so much energy and action? It was not patriotism warning of the menace in an incoming tide of immigrants; that came later. It was not national remorse demanding reparation for the exiled Indian. It was not even the last command of Jesus, "Disciple all nations," like a clarion call to the conscience. It was a *human cry* appealing expressly to woman's tenderness, and it pierced her heart.

"History of Woman's Organized Missionary Work as Promoted by American Women," in Wherry, *Woman in Missions*, 89-90.

Within the RCA, the denomination's weekly newspaper, the *Christian Intelligencer*, noted in its December 17, 1874, issue that the WCTU had met "at Cleveland, Ohio, a few weeks ago." The article reviewed what transpired at the Cleveland meeting including all the strategies to be used by the WCTU in its war on liquor. RCA women were strongly encouraged to participate in the WCTU cause. "Women and Temperance," *Christian Intelligencer*, December 17, 1874, 9.

38. Chamberlain, *Fifty Years in Foreign Fields*, 4.

39. Sometimes referred to by the women as "Synod's Board" or "the Men's Board." See House and Coakley, *Patterns and Portraits*, 106.

operating for forty-two years and had sent both married and unmarried women into foreign mission fields, their missionary call to women had remained largely unmet. It had taken time finally to reach the point of recognizing that only women had access to other women. As the *First Annual Report of the Woman's Board of Foreign Missions* notes:

> The conventional laws that exclude instructors of the other sex from the family apartments of the jealous master, do not shut out the gentle sisterhood who are nurses, housewives, teachers of needlework, and sympathizing companions, as well as preachers of righteousness.[40]

---

40. *ARWBFM,* 1875, 6.

Chapter 3

A Case for RCA Women as Feminists[1]

> In the last war a "substitute" was sent by those who could not themselves go against the invader. Through the collections we ask you for your substitute in this war against ignorance and sin. As this has been a year of pecuniary trouble, do not take more from the income of your family, do not, dear sister, ask it of husband or father, but deny yourself, and lay upon the Lord's alter the sum that you have saved from your own wants.
>
> Gertrude Lefferts Vanderbilt
> Foreign Corresponding Secretary
> *ARWBFM*, 1909, 11

The General Synod's request for assistance from women was a long time in coming, and the request was specific. The synod asked that a Woman's Board of Foreign Missions be established "to aid the Board of Foreign Missions of the RCA by promoting its work among the women and children of heathen lands."[2] By working through their own foreign mission board as a means of aiding the denominational Board of Foreign Missions, the new Woman's Board functioned as an appendage or "auxiliary to" the BFM. Not totally independent, the new WBFM worked with the BFM in a supportive way. By the time the Woman's Board was organized in 1875, women were speaking in public, although they were expected to take their cues from what men said and respond appropriately in any situation. Clearly women were expected to stand behind the men—not to stand next to them.

---

1. Please be reminded of my definition of feminism in footnote 10 of the introduction.

2. Edward Tanjore Corwin, *A Manual of the Reformed Church in America (Formerly Ref. Prot. Dutch Church)* (New York: Board of Publication of the Reformed Church in America, 1902), 321.

Against the American cultural backdrop of women and men living in separate spheres, scholarship concerning women and the mission movement owes much to the research, analysis, and writing of R. Pierce Beaver.[3] In 1968, Pierce Beaver wrote a text titled, *All Loves Excelling, American Protestant Women in World Mission,*[4] which spoke of the grand passion for foreign missions felt and acted upon by Protestant women in the nineteenth and twentieth centuries. This book continued to be so helpful that in 1980 it was revised and republished. In the revised edition, the title of the text was changed to *American Protestant Women in World Mission: A History of the First Feminist Movement in North America.*[5] This title suggests that women's role in the combined foreign and domestic mission movements formed the beginning of the first feminist movement. This is significant, because many scholars have assumed that the Women's Rights Convention, which took place at Seneca Falls, New York, in 1848, represented the primary expression of women's drive for equality with men.

In her ground-breaking essay, "The Role of Women in the India Mission, 1819-1880," Barbara Fassler states:

> The girls' schools had a far different purpose. They were to change the role of women in Indian society, but only in the ways in which that role differed from American ideas of the proper role of women. The missionaries were appalled by the practices of child-marriage, compulsory widowhood for girl children whose intended husbands died, immolation of widows on the funeral pyre of their husbands, female infanticide, and temple prostitution. These practices were opposed by the missionaries and by the British government, and were eventually outlawed. Beyond these most shocking practices, missionaries were concerned about those kinds of oppression which it is more difficult to outlaw: woman's isolation in the home, callous and brutal treatment by their husbands who beat them or laid on them the most irksome manual labor, their total lack of education, and what the missionaries called their "superstition."
>
> Missionaries, through their schools, tried to encourage a different role for women—a role like that of women in American society. The missionaries were convinced that the role they envisioned was a much better role.[6]

Building on Fassler's scholarship, Eugene Heideman readily acknowledged that for American women:

> their vision for women's place in India was the same as it was for their own place in America. They believed that a woman, whether in India or America, should be

---

3. For a beautiful tribute to the legacy of R. Pierce Beaver and a measure of the seriousness with which Beaver's scholarship continues to be regarded, see F. Dean Lucking, "The Legacy of R. Pierce Beaver," *International Bulletin of Missionary Research*, vol. 14, no. 1, January 1990, 2-5.

4. Grand Rapids: Eerdmans, 1968.

5. Grand Rapids: Eerdmans, 1980.

6. Barbara Fassler recognizes that RCA women acknowledged and were repelled by *all* forms of oppression experienced by *all* Indian women. They hoped to claim for *all* Indian women, not just a few select women, the place American women held in American culture. In James W. Van Hoeven, ed., *Piety and Patriotism: Bicentennial Studies of the Reformed Church in America, 1776-1976* (Grand Rapids: Eerdmans, 1976), 157. Subsequent publications by Barbara Fassler appear as Barbara E. Walvoord.

educated, respected in the home, free to participate in making her contribution to the welfare of the whole society, and have access to good health care. She should be free to remarry after the death of her husband and essentially to be a person in her own right. In other words, women's advocacy for foreign missions can rightly be understood to be an extension of the nineteenth-century movement for women's rights in America.[7]

For Heideman, the foreign mission involvement of American women represented an extension of the women's rights movement. Both Pierce Beaver and Eugene Heideman make a strong case for understanding the role of women in the foreign mission movement as intimately related to the struggle for the advancement of women's rights in America.

At this point Mary Chamberlain's assessment of the impact of the Civil War years is helpful:

> The Woman's Union Missionary Society was founded during the strife of the Civil War....The war, however, had made it inevitable that some kind of "woman movement" should ensue. The ideals and ideas of women had changed since the beginning of the nineteenth century. Old things were passing away and if all things had not, as yet, become new, they were fast taking on a new aspect. The abolition movement, woman's suffrage, woman's rights, woman's sphere, were burning questions of the hour, in the discussion of which the voices of women rose high above the din of masculine strife. Men and women everywhere were revising their ideas of the relation of woman to the universe. The ministry of women to soldiers in the war had proved that they possessed great executive ability and an amount of energy which, once set free, could not be and ought not to be suppressed. The vision of national need which they had so clearly seen in the struggle of the war, developed at its close into a wider comprehension of world demands and they were ready at the end of that decade to begin the most strategic and far-reaching enterprise in which they had ever yet engaged—the work of carrying their vision to the women and children of far Eastern lands.[8]

Perhaps the most accurate assessment is that the women's rights movement and the women's missionary movement grew in parallel, and that both of them existed and advocated on behalf of other women.[9] Women in both movements were not

---

7. Eugene P. Heideman, *From Mission to Church: The Reformed Church in America Mission to India*, Historical Series of the Reformed Church in America, no. 38 (Grand Rapids: Eerdmans, 2001), 166.

8. Chamberlain, *Fifty Years in Foreign Fields*, 8. Or, as historian Barbara Welter notes, "The war had also dislocated the living patterns of American women, whether North or South, and drawn them into the Hallelujah Chorus of the missionary drama." Barbara Welter, "She Hath Done What She Could: Protestant Women's Missionary Careers in Nineteenth-Century America," in Janet Wilson James, ed., *Women in American Religious History* (Philadelphia: Univ. of Pennsylvania Press, 1980), 119.

9. During the nineteenth century, many women's reform societies came into existence, including the WCTU, in 1874, and its forerunner organization, the American Temperance Society, organized in 1828. Out of the gatherings of women in Hillsboro, Ohio, in December, 1873, the WCTU was born. In

concerned only for their own "rights" but for the "rights" and needs of others. The women's rights movement, however, faced opposition from other women, many of whom believed that living in separate spheres with men as heads of households reflected the biblical imperative for their lives. Participation in the women's world mission movement, however, produced no such opposition from other women within the church. As historian Barbara Welter points out in her essay, "The Feminization of American Religion: 1800-1860":

> Religion carried with it the need for self-awareness, if only for the examination of conscience. Organizational experience could be obtained in many reform groups, but only religion brought with it the heightened sense of who you were and where you were going. Women in religion were encouraged to be introspective. What they found out would be useful in their drive towards independence. The constant identification of woman with virtue and with religion reinforced her own belief in her power to overcome obstacles, since she had her own superior nature and God's own church, whichever it might be, behind her. Religion in its emphasis on the brotherhood of man developed in women a conscious sense of sisterhood, a quality absolutely essential for any kind of meaningful woman's movement. The equality of man before God expressed so effectively in the Declaration of Independence had little impact on women's lives. However the equality of religious experience was something they could personally experience, and no man could deny it to them.[10]

Reformed Church women were not consciously feminist. There is no evidence to suggest that they ever intended to change the culture of the times—only to extend American culture and their own privileged position to women and children less fortunate than they.[11] As historian Patricia R. Hill notes:

---

its December 17, 1874 issue, the *Christian Intelligencer* provided its readers with a thorough review of a recently held WCTU meeting in Cleveland, Ohio, at which WCTU strategies and plans were identified. Reformed Church women were strongly encouraged to take part in the work of the WCTU, although thus far no data exists for knowing exactly how many RCA women were directly involved in the organization. The first action noted in the *MGS* regarding temperance is the creation of a permanent committee on temperance in 1914.

In my research, I refer to the women's rights movement as the drive among women to win the right to vote. The question of the involvement of RCA women in the women's rights movement cannot be commented upon at this point, since no data on this subject has been collected. It can only be presumed that there were some RCA women who participated in any or all of these women's movements.

10. In Mary S. Hartman and Lois Banner, eds., *Clio's Consciousness Raised: New Perspectives on the History of Women* (New York: Harper Torchbooks, 1974), 151-52.

11. In 1900, Mary Loring Cushing, the home corresponding secretary, closed her annual report with these words:

> It is not possible to give any record of our work without a new desire to share our Christian blessings with the women whose lives form so striking a contrast with our own. They need exactly what we have, to make them what we are. This Board stands pledged to help the women and

...Women who took up the cause of foreign missions after the Civil War were explicit in their rejection of egalitarianism and felt compelled to dissociate themselves and their movement from the woman's rights crusade. An editorial in the first issue of *Woman's Work for Woman*, the journal of the Woman's Foreign Missionary Society of the Presbyterian Church (North), offers an extended comparison of the "two very different movements going on at this time among the women of our country." What the writer gives as a descriptive account of the woman's rights crusade uses language that reveals her negative attitude toward that movement.[12]

The editor of *Woman's Work for Woman* wrote that the women's rights movement:

> insists upon what its promoters call the equality of woman with man. It seeks to give to her whatever advantage in the battle of life is supposed to belong to man, to afford her the opportunity (and more than this to lay it upon her as a duty) to push her way into public life, to the polls and the rostrum....They insist upon *rights*, they talk of the downtrodden position of women in this free and happy land.

Missionary women, however, seek to take an active part:

> in extending the blessings which they enjoy to their less favored sisters in heathen lands. These women feel that to the Gospel they owe the place of honor and of dignity which is theirs in this Christian land...so they...reach forth to the other side of the world to bring love and hope to those who are wasting their lives in idle ignorance of the capabilities of true womanhood...the blessings of wifehood...the holy responsibility of motherhood.[13]

There is another significant difference that waits for scholars to explore. While it is true that the Civil War years represent pivotal years for change in the higher education of women, not all women were able to participate immediately in these changes. Between the beginning of the Civil War in 1861, and 1875 when the WBFM was established, many women's colleges came into existence. Several pioneer colleges founded in the middle states as coeducational institutions flourished, and other colleges and state universities increasingly came into existence. Within the Reformed tradition, and RCA history in particular, education had always played an especially important and formative role. A high value had been placed on reading the Bible for

---

children in heathen lands. Woman's Work for Woman. It must be through the influence of Christian women, entering into the home life and reaching the mothers where superstition reigns supreme before the world can be won for Christ.

ARWBFM, 1900, 16.

12. Patricia R. Hill, *The World Their Household: The American Woman's Foreign Mission Movement and Cultural Transformation, 1870-1920*, (Ann Arbor: Univ. of Michigan, 1985), 74.

13. Hill, *The World Their Household*, 35.

oneself and studying and memorizing the Heidelberg Catechism as the primary tool for learning. There had been insistence upon an educated clergy.[14] All of these do attest to the importance the Reformed Church has traditionally placed on education. But, for thousands of RCA women, it was the world mission movement that became their education—their entry into an exciting and unknown world beyond themselves. This new form of education became elevating; it was invigorating; and at the same time, it was a means by which to be faithful to God and to Jesus Christ.

There is an old proverb that asserts, "A little knowledge is a dangerous thing."[15] There is no sequel to this proverb. What happens when a mountain of knowledge is acquired? The quest "to aid the BFM of the RCA by promoting its work among the women and children of heathen lands" began with little or no knowledge of the lives of women and children in foreign lands. However, acquiring knowledge about the lives of these women and children quickly became an obsession.[16] They knew from the start that in order to help other women in foreign lands, they had to know who these women were, how they lived and what their lives were like. Learning about the lives of women and children in foreign lands and the work of missionaries, women and men alike, opened unforeseen doors and windows into the world. It removed Reformed Church women from their limited and self-contained lives and opened before them a vastly new and exciting world. And they acquired new knowledge in abundance. They did not intend to be feminists. It was in their commitment to follow Jesus that church women were changed. The call to mission was clear. The vision of a new age and a new task was made manifest, and Reformed Church women recognized it in the Great Commission found in Matthew 28:19:

> Go therefore and make disciples of all nations, baptizing them in the name of the Father and of the Son and of the Holy Spirit, and teaching them to obey everything that I have commanded you. And remember, I am with you always, to the end of the age.

They believed that commission pertained not only to the disciples, but to all who embraced the gospel message, which included women and men together. That which limited the early mission work overseen by men became the pivotal point of RCA women's feminism. The limitation for men, and the denomination's BFM, was that

---

14. For a history of the value which the RCA has placed on education, see "The Hereditary Interest of the Reformed (Dutch) Church in Education, Common and Collegiate," by Ransom Bethune Welch in *Centennial Discourses: A Series of Sermons Delivered in the Year 1876, By Order of the General Synod of the Reformed (Dutch) Church in America*, 2nd ed., (New York: Board of Publication of the Reformed Church in America, 1877), 203-24. See also "Its System of Catechetical Instruction," by W. H. Campbell, ibid., 283-91.

15. The proverb, "A little knowledge is a dangerous thing," was recorded to be in use in the United States and first cited in 1881 in Huxley, *Science and Culture*, according to Wolfgang Mieder, Stewart A. Kingsbury, and Kelsie B. Harder, eds., *A Dictionary of American Proverbs* (New York: Oxford Univ. Press, 1992), 353.

16. Such an obsession is evidenced, for example, by women who would walk eight or twelve miles to attend the first Classical Union meeting April 10, 1883, in Utica, New York. See *ARWBFM*, 1883, 18.

male missionaries did not have access to and could not share the gospel with women in foreign lands. David Abeel was expressing concern for women when he cried out, "What is to become of the souls of those who are ignorant of the offers of mercy and of the Bible?" With the creation of the WBFM in 1875, the male-controlled BFM and the all-male General Synod had reached the point of needing to ask women to join them in a task men alone could not do.[17] Out of this call for church women to come to the aid of other women and children came a church women's organization so large and so effective that it changed decisively the position of women in the church and in society. That first wave of feminism was born of the conviction that women were needed to help other women and children, and it was nourished by the compassion of Christian women for the *shalom*[18] of other women and children. This is the tradition out of which RCA women today have come, and it is a tradition within which Hazel Gnade and thousands of other church women found their ministries.

17. *ARWBFM*, 1875, 7.

18. *Shalom* is the Hebrew word for peace. However, peace does not mean simply the absence of war, but carries the meaning of total well-being. John Calvin is said to have translated the word *shalom* as "virtuous prosperity."

Chapter 4

Foundational Documents and Organization

There are open doors and beckoning hands and pleading voices from which we cannot turn aside. God has called us to this service and we must press forward.

> Mary A. Loring Cushing
> Home Corresponding Secretary
> *ARWBFM*, 1902, 17

Little old ladies they were not. They were charged up and ready to go—and no winter storm was going to stand in their way.

In her fifty-year anniversary history of the WBFM, Mary Chamberlain wrote:

We are told that thirteen women of the Dutch Reformed church assembled in the lecture room of the Marble Collegiate church at the corner of Fifth Avenue and Twenty-ninth Street, New York City, on January 7, 1875.... Every available record has been searched for the names of these heroic ladies. Yet it does not seem to require the gift of second sight to imagine who some of them were."[1]

---

1. Mary Chamberlain, *Fifty Years in Foreign Fields, China, Japan, India, Arabia: A History of Five Decades of the Woman's Board of Foreign Mission, Reformed Church in America* (New York: Abbott Press, 1925), 10. Given the hindsight of this study, it seems reasonable to imagine that at least Mary Myers and Margaret E. Sangster were present also. This is based on their intense involvement in the organization starting with its formation in 1875.

Mary Chamberlain surmised that the following ladies were present:

Clarissa Cochran Ormiston	(Rev. William)	Marble Collegiate[2]
Louise Frelinghuysen Chambers	(Rev. Talbot Wilson)	Middle Collegiate
Elizabeth M. Cumming	(Mr. James P.)	Yonkers, N.Y.
Abigail D. Wyckoff Cole	(Rev. David)	Yonkers, N.Y.
Matilda Van Zandt Cobb	(Rev. Henry Nitchie)	Millbrook, N.Y.
Mary A. Cushing	(Mr. A. Loring)	Bellville, N.J.
Amelia A. Letson Romeyn	(Rev. Theodore Bayard)	Hackensack, N.J.
Charlotte Fountain Westervelt	(Mr. Erskine)	Hackensack, N.J.
Jeanie G. Inglis	(Rev. David)	Brooklyn, NYC
Anna F. Enos	(Dr. DeWitt C.)	Brooklyn, NYC
Amelia Lent Van Cleef	(Rev. Paul D.)	Jersey City, N.J.

All of the women were married. Of the eleven women whom Mary Chamberlain listed, eight were ministers' wives. Two of the husbands served Collegiate churches; the others served churches in Brooklyn, Yonkers, and Millbrook, New York; and in Hackensack and Jersey City, New Jersey.[3]

The Reverend John Mason Ferris, secretary of the Board of Foreign Missions, was present to conduct the meeting and to serve as secretary. On behalf of the General Synod he restated the purpose of the meeting, and "gave in detail the present appropriations of the Board for work among the heathen women of India, China and Japan, amounting in all to $7,442 annually."[4] According to the minutes of the meeting, which were reported in the *Christian Intelligencer*, January 14, 1875, Ferris then read a letter from Mrs. W. E. Schenck, president of the Woman's Foreign Mission Society of the Presbyterian Church. Her letter read:

> Ever since the meeting of the Synod of your Church in June last, I have looked for such a notice as I find in the *Christian Intelligencer* of December 31st, regarding the formation of a Woman's Foreign Missionary Society, to aid your Board of Foreign Missions.
>
> That this is a movement in the right direction none can doubt who have watched the success of denominational societies, such as you propose. God has blessed them in developing the resources of prayer, sympathy, and means in the church

---

2. In 1875 there were three congregations in the Collegiate Church of New York City: (1) Middle Collegiate, the Rev. Talbot W. Chambers, pastor, located at Lafayette Place at 4th Street; (2) Marble Collegiate, the Rev. William Ormiston, pastor, located at Fifth Avenue at 29th Street; and (3) St. Nicholas Collegiate, the Rev. James M. Ludlow, pastor, located at Fifth Avenue at 48th Street. From 1729 to 1871 the Collegiate pastors preached in rotation. By 1875 the rotation had ceased. In addition, the Collegiate Church included four chapels, each overseen by a "pastor in charge." The four chapels included De Witt Chapel, located at 160 West 29th Street; Knox Memorial Chapel, located at Ninth Avenue, above 38th Street; Seventh Avenue Chapel at Seventh Avenue and 54th Street; and North Church Chapel, located at the corner of William Street and Fulton. It was in the North Church Chapel that the Fulton Street Prayer Meetings were held.

3. Nothing is known to the author about the husbands of the remaining women.

4. *Christian Intelligencer*, January 14, 1875, 3.

at home, while to workers in foreign lands they have opened up sources of strength, blessing and material support of inestimable value. May God prosper and bless the organization of the sisters of the Reformed Church abundantly.

We send you a copy of the Fourth Annual Report of this Society, also the last number of the magazine published by it, assured you will find in both great encouragement to go forward in the new work before you. If, from our experience we can render you or your co-workers any assistance we will rejoice to do so.[5]

According to the *First Annual Report of the WBFM:*

> ...A constitution and by-laws were prepared and adopted, permanent officers and a Board of Managers chosen, and an appeal issued to the ladies of the Reformed Church in America, appended to which was a form of constitution, to be adopted by auxiliary associations.[6]

How to explain the immense amount of business transacted at this first meeting is a difficult question to answer. Did the women who arrived at Marble Collegiate Church on January 7, 1875, already have an organizational structure in mind? Did they arrive with a tactical strategy for an organization already identified? Furthermore, how did they know the names of the women who would agree to serve as officers of the new organization? Didn't these women need first to be asked? This would be especially true for the new president, Mary Sturges, whose life had been altered radically by the death of her husband as recently as November 28, 1874.

To be sure, the women who met that January had enjoyed six months of time to plan since the June 1874 meeting of the General Synod. They would have had an opportunity to contemplate, to discuss among themselves, and to design the kind of organization they envisioned. It would also have given them the opportunity to acquaint themselves with how other women's foreign missionary societies were organized, such as the Presbyterian Woman's Foreign Missionary Society represented in Mrs. Schenck's letter. One thing was eminently clear. These women didn't want to make mistakes. This was carefully noted in the first *Annual Report*:

> So far as human foresight can determine the prospect, none of the conditions of success are wanting to our undertaking, if the women of the Reformed Church in America will but interest themselves actively in behalf of it. The work is not an experiment. The only excuse that can be offered for our seeming inaction in days past, is that we have watched the movements of other societies bearing the same banner as that we now raise—"Woman's Work for Woman"—and learned from their mistakes, as from their achievements, lessons that may serve us in the stead of dearly-bought experience. Thanks to the pioneers in the field, we enter it with a full comprehension of its nature and facilities, of the stumbling blocks to be avoided, the advantages we should seize. Our way is marked out for us by the

---

5. Ibid.
6. *ARWBFM*, 1875, 4.

footprints of those who have toiled and fought, as we need not do if we are wise observers and willing pupils.[7]

"Wise observers and willing pupils" aptly described those women. They were thoughtful and they were cautious. They prepared a constitution and by-laws, even though the documents were temporary, and their final approval would wait until the following meeting in two weeks. They elected the officers of their new organization. In addition, they produced a list of twenty-four names of women who might serve as members of a Board of Managers. Ferris would write to each of these women requesting their voluntary service on the board, and a final list of names would be voted on at the next meeting. And they prepared a suggested constitution to be used by local missionary societies that wished to establish themselves as missionary societies auxiliary to the WBFM. It was reported in the first *Annual Report* that all of this business was accomplished at that first meeting on January 7, 1875.

Two weeks later, January 21, the women met for a second time. Members of the Board of Managers were identified and approved. The constitution and by-laws were approved, and, with this action, January 21, 1875, "was officially placed in the calendar of the Reformed Church as the Birthday of the Woman's Board of Foreign Missions."[8] In following years, "birthday" and "anniversary" celebrations would become highly anticipated annual events. Also agreed upon were a suggested constitution for local auxiliary societies, directions for forming mission bands for young ladies and mission circles for children, and a pledge for mission circles.

Each of these documents created by the women had far-reaching consequences. The constitution, which contained eight articles, and the by-laws, which contained eleven articles, formed the basic organizational structure. Changes would be made to the original documents to accommodate WBFM growth and expansion, but these foundational instruments continued to shape the life of the organization for seventy years.

Because the constitution and by-laws served the WBFM so well for so long, this study into the internal organization of the WBFM will rely upon a comprehensive and detailed examination of these documents.[9] The documents to be examined will include

(1) the constitution and by-laws;
(2) a suggested constitution for auxiliaries;
(3) directions for forming mission bands of young ladies;
(4) directions for forming mission circles for children; and
(5) a pledge for mission circles.

In the present chapter, I will examine those documents that focus on how the Board of Managers governed itself. In chapter five, the examination of documents

---

7. *ARWBFM*, 1875, 6-7.

8. Chamberlain, *Fifty Years*, 11.

9. Article 10 of the by-laws states the circumstance for dropping managers from board membership, and Article 11 explains the process for amending the by-laws. Because these two articles seem self-explanatory, no additional discussion of them will be presented.

3

Meeting of January 7th 1875.

Pursuant to a call issued by the Board of Foreign Missions and in accordance with a resolution of the General Synod, adopted in June 1874, twelve or thirteen ladies met in the Lecture Room of the Ref' Dutch Church corner of 5th Ave & 29th St, N.Y. City at 11 A.m. The Rev Dr Ferris, Corresponding Sec'y of the Board of Foreign Missions opened the session with prayer. The day was an extremely unpleasant one. — Rain was falling rapidly, and froze as it touched the side walks, so that it was very difficult to traverse the streets. Yet the ladies present had come from Hackensack N.J. Brooklyn L.I. Yonkers. Millbrook, Saugerties N.Y & Belleville N.J.

Rev Dr Ferris was requested to preside.

The following were adopted as articles of a temporary Constitution.

This Society shall be called The Woman's Board of Foreign Missions of the Reformed Church in America.

There shall be a Board of Managers consisting of twenty-four Members who shall elect the Officers of the Society.

It was resolved, That these articles shall continue in force until the Managers shall present a complete constitution, which they are requested to do as soon as possible.

First page of the minute book of the WBFM

will focus on how the Board of Managers developed its constituencies. Essential aspects of the organization, not discussed within the framework of the foundational documents, will be dealt with topically in chapter six.

Following acknowledgment in Article 1 that the organization shall be called the Woman's Board of Foreign Missions of the Reformed Church in America, and "its central point of operations shall be in the City of New York," Article 2 of the constitution states:

> Its object shall be to aid the Board of Foreign Missions of the Reformed Church in America, by promoting its work among the women and children of heathen lands, and for this purpose it shall receive and disburse *all* money which shall be contributed to this society, subject to the approval of the Board, in the appointment of missionaries supported by this association, and in fixing their locations and salaries. To the furtherance of this end, it shall also endeavor to organize similar associations in *all* Reformed Churches, and these associations shall bear the name of Auxiliary Societies to the Woman's Board of Foreign Missions of the Reformed Church in America, and shall report their work to this Board at such times as the by-laws may direct.[10]

The role of money within the WBFM, how it was collected, recorded, and disbursed, and how it was used by the organization is worthy of an essay all its own and lies beyond the scope of this present history. Given the cultural assumption of the times that moral rectitude was the special gift of women, it was believed that honesty in dealing with money could be expected from women. Money was thought to be safe with these women, and the WBFM officers and board members became the literal "trustees" of the money of the organization. Their job was to serve as a conduit through which the money would safely pass on its way to the urgent work of missions. *All* pennies and *all* dollars contributed to the organization would find their proper place in the accounting ledger, and a proper record would be made, especially for those whose pennies and dollars were received.

In the *First Annual Report*, it is impressive to note:

> Next, we would remind them, that hereafter, in the missionary operations of our church, women are to be bearers of the comforts of our most holy and blessed faith to their fellow women; that *every penny* dropped into the missionary box by the baptized babe of the American Christian mother, may go through the hands of mothers and daughters, to sustain the schools in which the waifs of heathendom are gathered and taught the sweet story our nurslings lisp before they can tell their right hand from their left.[11]

The women who composed the WBFM and Women's Board of Domestic Missions (WBDM) would throughout their histories remain extremely sensitive and attentive

---

10. *ARWBFM*, 1875, 17. Author's emphasis.
11. *ARWBFM*, 1875, 6. Author's emphasis.

to their commitments to be "trustees" and faithful stewards.[12] Administrative costs were always kept as low as possible, as part of this faithful trust in the money management of WBFM and WBDM women. Paying interest to service debt was taken very seriously, and it was not viewed as good stewardship in light of this commitment.

When the General Synod of 1874 voted to establish the WBFM, it did so stating expressly "with auxiliary associations in all those Churches where it is practicable...."[13] It is significant to note that in their constitution, the women of the WBFM state their intention to have auxiliaries formed in *all* RCA congregations—practicable or not. From the start, the WBFM's goal was 100 percent involvement in all Reformed Church congregations, and if the number of auxiliaries amounted to less than this, organizational leaders wanted to know why.[14] Because all of this was God's doing, it was improbable that any Christian woman in any congregation could or would turn down such an appeal. The fault would lie not with the women in the congregations; the fault would lie with how well the organization was run.

Article 3 of the constitution stipulated that anyone paying one dollar annually either to an auxiliary or to the treasury directly shall be considered a member of the WBFM. Additionally, "the payment of twenty-five dollars by one person, at one time, shall constitute a life membership."[15]

It is difficult to gain a sense regarding the value of money in 1875. The WBFM membership fee of one dollar per person per year doesn't feel like a lot of money in today's terms. Figured for annual inflation increases, however, one dollar in 1875 is roughly equivalent to $16.39 in 2002. Similarly, a life membership of $25 in 1875 equates to $409.84 in 2002. Although a $1 membership fee continued at least through 1916, the $25 life membership fee remained in place through 1939 and beyond. For many RCA women these fees were a consideration and a cause for saving pennies. Pennies were important.

Life memberships in the WBFM served several purposes. The income from life memberships added to the treasury, and this made a difference, especially in the

12. In the Executive Committee minutes of the BFM dated November, 1955, this concern as trustees continues to be present. The minutes read:

Miss Ransom reported that she had met with Mrs. Wagner, Chairman of the Sewing Guild. There is $25,000 in the Sewing Guild Fund to disburse. Because the treasurer is anxious to have this fund in the budget, a problem arises as to how this money should be divided and how it is going to be used, for it would be breaking faith with the women if not used in the way in which they were told. It is hoped by next year that there will be recommendations so that all problems may be ironed out.

BFM Minutes, November, 1955, 154.

13. *MGS*, 1874, 142.

14. Following the WBFM decision in 1881 to appoint two members from each classis to visit all the churches in each classis in which auxiliaries had not yet been established, it was reported in 1882, "From some of the Churches reasons were received why societies could not satisfactorily be formed for the present; in others, encouragement was given that the subject would be considered in the near future, when they would become co-laborers with us, and rejoicing with us at the progress attained by the Divine blessing, since the first appeal was sent forth in faith and prayer, for the aid and hearty co-operation of the congregations in the communion of our Church." *ARWBFM*, 1882, 17.

15. *ARWBFM*, 1875, 17.

early years when local auxiliaries were still in the process of being established. Additionally, using such a method for raising money for the treasury provided a means for honoring or memorializing a family member or friend. Honorees could be either female or male, and a list of the names of life members was routinely included in the annual printed report. During the early years of the organization, two lists of life members appeared in the annual reports—a list of new life members added in each specific year and a list of life members from all the years combined. This worked well until 1893, when the total number of life members took up twelve and one-half pages in the *Annual Report*, and the task of identifying deceased members in the listing became an impossible task. Beginning in 1884, only the names of new life members were published annually.

Life memberships added another dimension to the organization. The number of life memberships added each year could be counted—thereby serving as one means for showing organizational growth. It was extremely important to show growth as a sign of health and progress. Life memberships continued to serve as a means for honoring women, especially through 1960, which is the end of the history here undertaken.[16]

The management of WBFM business was spelled out in Article 4 of the constitution and Article 1 of the by-laws. The business of the organization was to be conducted by a Board of Managers. Members of this Board of Managers numbered thirty and were elected each year at the annual meeting. Following their election, they were to meet on the first Tuesday to organize and to elect officers. Those officers included a president, two vice-presidents, a recording secretary, two or more corresponding secretaries and a treasurer. Members of each new Board of Managers were to elect not more than twelve honorary vice-presidents. They were to appoint corresponding members as needed, and they were also given authority to fill vacancies occurring in their body in the year.[17] Regular meetings of the board were scheduled to be held four times a year—on the second Tuesdays of February, May, August, and November, "at eleven o'clock A.M., at such place as they shall appoint." A quorum consisted of seven members, and the president could call a special meeting of the body upon the request of five members.[18]

To conduct necessary business between stated meetings of the Board of Managers, Article 5 of the constitution established an Executive Committee. It was composed of the officers (president, two vice-presidents, the recording secretary and the corresponding secretaries and the treasurer) plus two other members of the Board of Managers, all of whom were elected annually. Article 2 of the by-laws specified that members of the Executive Committee should meet once a month to conduct their business. Most of these meetings took place in members' homes.

---

16. Eventually honorary memberships would be added as a means to honor individuals. Gifts of $50 would provide this recognition.

17. Article 4 of the constitution as found in *ARWBFM*, 1875, 17.

18. Article 1 of the by-laws as found in *ARWBFM*, 1875, 18.

The Board of Managers continued to serve as the primary source for the direction and the conduct of business for the WBFM until the turn of the century. By 1899 it was found that the work of the organization had so greatly increased that the Board of Managers needed to meet five times a year instead of four. The Board of Managers was henceforth to meet annually in October, December, February, April, and May. Executive Committee members were broadened to include the *ex officio* membership of the editor of the *Missionary Gleaner* and the editor of any other publication issued by the board.[19] The constitution was also changed to allow the annual appointment of twelve or more honorary vice-presidents.[20]

As the number of auxiliaries increased and the mission task was broadened to include young women, more and more women became leaders in their local organizations and in their classical unions. How to invite their participation as leaders at the national level became the question, and this question was made difficult by the need legally to change the organization's Articles of Incorporation. This reached its final accomplishment, however, at the annual meeting May 14, 1918, when approval was given for a board of seventeen directors to assume the corporate legal power previously held by the thirty managers. This Board of Directors would include the officers and secretaries of the organization. According to the minutes of April 3, 1918, it was decided that "the word Directors be used with regard to members of the Executive Committee."[21] The number of members of "the board," as it was now called, was raised to "not more than sixty-five active members."[22] To the officers were added four vice-presidents representing each of the four particular synods,[23] the new position of editorial and educational secretary,[24] and the position of assistant treasurer. In recognition of the problem of distance and travel for board members not living in the East, board meeting attendance was changed to be less limiting. "Members of the Board, except where distance prevents, absenting themselves from five consecutive meetings of the Board without reasonable excuse shall be considered having resigned and shall be so notified."[25]

---

19. Articles 1 and 2 of the by-laws as found in *ARWBFM*, 1899, 98.

20. Article 4 of the constitution as found in *ARWBFM*, 1899, 97.

21. WBFM *Minutes*, December 11, 1917, 182.

22. WBFM *Minutes*, April 9, 1918, 202.

23. The four particular synods included New York, Albany, Chicago, and New Brunswick.

24. From November 1883 to January 1918, the *Mission Gleaner* served as the publication vehicle for the WBFM. In 1917, however, the editor of the *Mission Gleaner* resigned, and "in this day of combinations towards greater efficiency" (1918 *ARWBFM*, 15) the periodical ceased publication under the name *Mission Gleaner*. A new joint publication of all the mission boards began under the name, the *Mission Field*. At this point, the WBFM created a new position, editorial and educational secretary. It was the job of the editorial and educational secretary "to edit the department of the Woman's Board of Foreign Missions in the *Mission Field* and to use the Denominational Papers in the interests of the Woman's Board; to promote the work of the Board in conference with the Committee on Publication in collecting material and preparing leaflets and such other publications as may be approved by the Board; to represent the Woman's Board of Foreign Missions on such Committees as would properly belong to the office. Also to promote the interests of the Board by speaking, when possible, and not conflicting with the regular work of the office." WBFM *Minutes*, March 6, 1918, 193.

25. WBFM *Minutes*, March 6, 1918, 205. According to Article 10 of the original by-laws, managers missing three successive meetings without giving notice were considered resigned.

At this time the task of the organization had grown so large and demanding that additional leaders were needed to accomplish the work. Although standing committees were already instituted in 1902, the work of these standing committees was broadened and would continue to broaden throughout the life of the WBFM.[26]

An annual meeting of board members and the organization membership was to take place the second Tuesday each May in New York City, according to Article 6 of the constitution. At the annual meeting, managers updated the membership on "the operations, conditions, and prospects" of the organization. The election of new managers for the upcoming year also took place.

Annual meetings grew to become large and festive occasions. For the first ten years, annual meetings were held in the chapel of the Marble Collegiate Church. As attendance grew, creating the need for additional space, meetings began to be held first in the chapel and then in the sanctuary at St. Nicholas Collegiate Church on Fifth Avenue at 48th Street.[27] Both women and men composed the gathered group. Women traveled considerable distances to attend annual meetings, and many pastors were in regular attendance.

As reported in the WBFM *Minutes,* early annual meetings were conducted entirely by men. From devotions, to all reports prepared by the organization's officers, to the worship leaders and speakers of the day, men provided the leadership. At the first annual meeting in 1875, the Reverend David Inglis of the Brooklyn Heights Church was a guest speaker. It was memorably recorded in Mary Chamberlain's fifty-year anniversary history:

> Apparently there was still a lingering fear in the Dutch Church that "the ladies were stepping out of their proper sphere." Dr. Inglis expressed the opinion that they could give "their spare moments" to this work. "Home duties need not conflict."[28]

It was also noted in the minutes of that first annual meeting:

> Rev. Mr. Steele of Newark also addressed the ladies telling how much might be accomplished by interesting all the church members and let each one do and give her share.[29]

It took some years, but changing times eventually brought changing attitudes toward the leadership of women at the annual meetings. In 1884 Miss H. F. Winn of

---

26. At this time, these standing committees included the Nominating Committee, the Finance Committee, the Committee on the several Missions, the Young Woman's Committee, the Joint Advisory Committee on Young Women's Work, the Missionary Candidate Committee, the Publication Committee, the Sewing Guild Committee, and classical committees. Eventually several additional standing committees, including a Hospitality Committee, would be added.

27. In 1949 St. Nicholas Collegiate Church, located at Fifth Avenue at 48th Street, was sold to the Standard Oil Corporation. The church was torn down to make way for the Standard Oil Building, which occupies the property presently.

28. Chamberlain, *Fifty Years,* 16.

29. WBFM *Minutes,* May 11, 1875, 35.

Yokohama, Japan, spoke, the first woman to speak at an annual meeting. "Very modestly and beautifully she told the story of life in Japan from a missionary point of view, giving a rapid sketch of the work carried on in the Isaac Ferris Seminary."[30] As missionaries and their wives returned home on furlough, they would be invited to attend annual meetings, and the men would be invited to speak.[31] At the annual meeting in 1895, Amelia Van Cleef, the new president, presided and read the scripture lessons, the first time a woman read the scriptures at an annual meeting. At the same meeting, Miss Mary Katherine Scudder, from the Arcot Mission in India, and Mrs. Wellington White, formerly of China, spoke. Having unmarried women missionaries and the wives of missionaries serve as speakers brought a special sense of pride to the women.[32] At the 1896 annual meeting it was reported, "An innovation this year was the reading of the Annual Reports by the Corresponding and Foreign Corresponding Secretaries."[33] The innovation was that in place of men, women for the first time read in public their own written reports, something that had not happened before this time. In 1897, for the first time at an annual meeting, the treasurer herself announced the receipts for the year.[34] And at the 1898 annual meeting, "Mrs. A. A. Raven led the closing devotional service, in which Mrs. Gowan, Mrs. Goodlatte, Mrs. Burrell and others took part,"[35] another first for the women.[36]

According to the constitution, the annual meeting "shall be held...in the City of New York." This it was until 1903, when it was held at the First Church in Albany with eleven hundred people reported to be in attendance. In 1906 the annual meeting was held in Kingston, New York, at the First Reformed Church. Given the large attendance at these annual meetings, arrangements for travel and housing at out of town meetings demanded tremendous planning by the women.

---

30. *ARWBFM*, 1884, 6.

31. One recognized that change was in the making when the *Annual Report* of 1892 reported that Miss Olivia H. Lawrence during that year had traveled 2,835 miles and visited forty-three churches on behalf of the WBFM, "and one pastor who had said that he never wanted to see a woman in his pulpit, after listening to an address made by her, said, 'My pulpit will always be open to Miss Lawrence. God has been pleased to bestow his precious blessing upon her labors'" (25).

32. The *Mission Gleaner* was the bimonthly periodical of the WBFM and was published 1883-1918. In the July-August 1895 issue, the *Mission Gleaner* reported:

We were glad to see a departure from the custom of the last few years, in the platform on which were gathered the managers of the Board, and on consulting the dainty program provided, to find that it was quite emphatically a "*woman's* meeting," two of the three speakers being women. Not that we wished to shove the men out into the cold and rain—perish the thought! for we could not do without them; but when there *are* women, able and willing to speak, and with a direct message *from* women *to* women, let us hear them.

Mission Gleaner, vol. XII no. 5 (July-August, 1895). Italics are original.

33. *ARWBFM*, 1896, 4.

34. *ARWBFM*, 1897, 4.

35. *ARWBFM*, 1898, 5.

36. With regard to WBFM women in the western churches, the *Annual Report* of 1919 notes, "At the mission-fest in Grand Rapids last summer the Vice-President gave a brief review of the fields under the care of the Woman's Board, the first time that this work has been given a place in the mission-fest program" (56).

The constitution duly provided in Articles 7 and 8 for special board meetings and changes to the constitution. Special board meetings could be called at any time by the president upon the request of the managers, and changes to the constitution might take place by a two-thirds vote of the membership at any regular board meeting.

In Article 4 of the by-laws, reference was made to the election of honorary vice-presidents, who were to be selected annually by the Board of Managers to serve for the period of one year. Within the WBFM organization, these honorary vice-presidents occupied a special place—a place where the work of church women received acknowledgment and respect. It was a place of honor.

Honorary vice-presidents also had a job to do. As stated in the WBFM *Minutes* of March 9, 1875, "The duties of the latter [honorary vice-presidents] were to exert their influence in the churches and section of the country where they reside."[37] These honorary vice-presidents functioned in the capacity of lightning rods. They were women who had demonstrated interest and energy and commitment to the cause. They were known to be active and bold on behalf of the gospel message, and they would not be satisfied with anything less than the total involvement of all church women in the cause of foreign missions.

The use of honorary vice-presidents was a masterful stroke of political strategy. It is not possible to know whether their use was intended to be a strategic effort. But the effect became clear almost immediately. These women were well known in Reformed churches that were located beyond the immediate New York City area, in places where churches needed women's auxiliaries to be established. They would throw themselves into the work on behalf of the new WBFM. Their support was guaranteed.

Article 5 of the by-laws reads:

> The Treasurer shall receive and hold, and keep an account of, all money given to the Board, and shall disburse it as the Managers shall direct. She shall report the state of the treasury at each regular meeting of the Executive Committee, and make a quarterly report to the Managers. Her annual report shall be examined by an auditor appointed by the Managers.[38]

From this description of the treasurer's position, the job of the treasurer would appear to be a rather straightforward, simple, routine, standard task. Certainly the job would not extend beyond the application of routine accounting practices and the usual work of reporting balances at stated intervals. Such was hardly the case.

From the first year of its organization to the last, the names of individual donors and amounts contributed to the WBFM were recorded and printed in each annual report. Regardless of the size of the contribution, all contributions were so noted. This practice had the subtle effect both of advertising and encouraging the financial support of individual donors. It was also a means whereby donors of the smallest

---

37. WBFM *Minutes*, 1875, 23.
38. *ARWBFM*, 1875, 18.

contributions would be recognized to the same degree as donors of more substantial gifts. As Mary Chamberlain has noted,

> Mrs. Sturges, the honored first President of the Board, besought the women not to despise the day of small things. She reminded them that they should be grateful for the dollars, thankful for the small sums which found their way so timidly into the treasury in those early days.[39]

Over the years, many gifts of twenty-five cents were recorded, along with small, uneven amounts obviously coming from upturned piggy banks of children. All donations were valued equally, and that value was communicated by listing the names of all contributors.[40]

From the beginning of the WBFM, some contributors designated how their contributions were to be allocated. For example, the Woman's Missionary Society of the First Reformed Church in Hackensack, New Jersey, in 1875, contributed $200, of which $50 was to go for the seminary at Chittoor (India); $50 was intended for the girls school in Amoy (China); $50 for the girls school at Vellore (India); and $50 for a class for nurses at the dispensary at Arcot (India).[41] By encouraging contributors to designate their gifts, "not as a mere commercial means of securing the salaries but to establish a close personal relation between the Missionaries and the home-folk,"[42] contributors quickly developed a sense of involvement and ownership of a particular aspect of the mission task. Interest grew as gifts were contributed, and the demand for information about a particular mission situation or specific missionary personnel grew proportionately. With growing interest, contributions increased, and one can quickly see how the "simple, routine, standard" task of the treasurer quickly became a very complex process.

From such contributor designations, the managers either consciously or unconsciously realized how important a sense of interest and ownership was to individuals and local groups. Soon the costs to support a specific missionary or student or to underwrite a specific project or program became identified by the managers and used to encourage individuals and church groups to greater involvement. In 1879 the home corresponding secretary wrote:

> We would earnestly recommend to the Auxiliaries that some specific object be decided upon, and the efforts devoted to it year after year. The work would then be regular and systematic, rather than an excess for one school, and the rest, perhaps embarrassed, and *vice-versa*. If this course were pursued, Synod's Board would be able to know more definitely what could be depended upon and what was provided for.[43]

---

39. Chamberlain, *Fifty Years*, 16.

40. It is believed that the largest legacy received by the WBFM was $32,500 received in 1910 from Miss Jane A. Gopsill. Figured for inflation, this figure in 2002 would stand at $625,087.32.

41. *ARWBFM*, 1875, 8.

42. *ARWBFM*, 1921, 56.

43. *ARWBFM*, 1879, 15. Italics in original.

Educational Work & Special Objects.

GIRLS' BOARDING SCHOOL, AMOY, CHINA.
Support of pupil, $20.00 each.

GIRLS' BOARDING SCHOOL, SIO-KHE, CHINA.
Support of pupil, $20.00 each.

FERRIS SEMINARY, YOKOHAMA, JAPAN.
Support of pupil, $60.00 each.

JONATHAN STURGES SEMINARY, NAGASAKI, JAPAN
Support of pupil, $40.00 each.

GIRLS' BOARDING SCHOOL, MADANAPALLE, INDIA
Support of pupil, $30.00 each.

SEMINARY FOR GIRLS, VELLORE, INDIA.
Support of pupil, $30.00 each.

THIRTEEN (HIGH CASTE) GIRLS' SCHOOL, INDIA.
$150.00 average cost for each school.

MEDICAL WORK,
NEERBOSCH HOSPITAL, SIO-KHE, CHINA.
Forty beds, $35.00 each.

Dr. Otte.

Costs for mission work from the *Mission Gleanor*

As contributions from individuals and from local missionary societies increased, so did the designations for their gifts. What might be described by some as an accountant's nightmare was handled with grace and perseverance by the woman who volunteered her time as treasurer.[44] As provided by the constitution, the books were audited annually, and for the first twenty years of the WBFM's life, the auditor was the Reverend Talbot W. Chambers.[45]

The by-laws provide for a recording secretary in Article 6. She "shall keep a full record of the proceedings of the Executive Committee and Managers, which shall be read for correction at the close of each meeting, and she shall give proper notice of special and stated meetings."[46] Cautious to safeguard their decisions and actions, they required that the record of each meeting be written and agreed to by the end of each meeting. This requirement demanded a recording secretary with skills in both listening and writing. The leaders were taking no chances.

The last two articles of the constitution, Articles 7 and 8, articulate actions that may be taken largely in response to the question, what happens if we want to change? In Article 7, it is stipulated that the president may call the managers to a special meeting upon the managers' request, which seems to reflect the placement of great trust in the judgment of the president. Article 8 takes care to provide how the constitution could be changed, if necessary. The Board of Managers may alter the constitution at any regular meeting of the board by a two-thirds vote, provided a notice of the suggested change had been circulated previously among board members. This concludes the articles as specified in the constitution.

---

44. From the time of its inception in 1875 to 1896, the treasurer of the WBFM was Anna J. E. Donald (Mrs. Peter). Only one time in her twenty-one years of serving as treasurer did she use her given name in an annual report, and that was in 1895. When she retired in 1896, her resignation was described this way:

> At the beginning of the year we met with a new experience, for of all the changes that had occurred in our Board during the 21 years, the office of Treasurer had remained the same. The name of Mrs. Peter Donald was so interwoven with our existence that it seemed a part of it, but sickness came and a pressure of other cares made it impossible for her to bear the burden longer, and we were obliged to accept her resignation. Of her long, faithful service for our Board there can be but one expression, that of sincere, heartfelt gratitude.

Anna Donald remained a manager of the WBFM through 1905 and died sometime the following year. *ARWBFM*, 1897, 5-6.

45. From 1875 through 1895, Talbot W. Chambers, pastor of the Middle Collegiate Church, served as auditor for the WBFM. His wife, Louise Frelinghuysen Chambers, was one of the original organizers of the WBFM and served on the WBFM Board of Managers from 1875 to 1892. Following his wife's death June 2, 1892, Chambers continued as auditor for three additional years. As auditor, he was followed by the Reverend Edward B. Coe, pastor of the St. Nicholas Collegiate Church.

46. The original constitution stated that the recording secretary was to record "the proceedings of the Board and Managers." This oversight was corrected in 1878, when the constitution was changed to read, "the proceedings of the Executive Committee and Managers."

Chapter 5

Developing Constituencies

Not until all Christian women have learned that the Cross of Christ is not
to be sung about, nor wept over, nor smothered in flowers; that Our Lord
never commanded us to cling to that Cross, but to carry it; the work of the
Missionary Society will not be done nor its warfare accomplished.

Olivia H. Lawrence
Home Corresponding Secretary
ARWBFM, 1904, 15

Beginning with Article 6 of the by-laws, the primary focus of the by-laws shifts to
the work of the foreign corresponding secretary, the home corresponding secretary,
and an annual report. We shall now identify and examine the offices and
responsibilities of these officers. An examination of the annual report and how it
served WBFM members and constituencies will follow.

Article 6 of the by-laws spells out the responsibilities of the corresponding
secretaries for the foreign field. Those responsibilities include "conducting the
business of this Board with the Board of Foreign Missions, and also with the
Missionaries, Teachers, and Bible-readers supported by this association. They shall
prepare the annual report of the Managers; and missionaries supported by this
association shall report to them."

One can immediately foresee that the responsibilities of the "foreign secretaries,"
as they came to be called, might be managed without undue difficulty when the
missionaries were few in number. But once that number began to rise, corresponding,
helping meet the needs of the missionaries overseas, coordinating furloughs and

travel, handling emergency situations, and communicating the results of missionary work to the home front entailed a tremendous amount of correspondence, care, and planning.

When the WBFM was established in 1875, there were thirty-one BFM missionaries in the foreign field.[1] Of this number, fifteen were men, eleven were married women, called "assistant missionaries," and five were unmarried women, who were also called "assistant missionaries." It would take time to develop auxiliary support on the home front before the WBFM could assume financial responsibility for the existing sixteen women missionaries and their work with women and girls, much less fund and send out "their own" women missionaries.

But the WBFM became impatient. In 1878 WBFM women responded to pleading from women missionaries and sent to Japan two teachers who were sisters, Elizabeth T. and Mary J. Farrington, "formerly of Newburgh, now of Fishkill Village."[2] One of the sisters became ill, and unforeseen circumstances "not of their making" forced their return after one year.[3] This proved a learning experience for the WBFM. From this point on, the Woman's Board delayed in sending out missionaries of its own and focused on providing "additional grants of money to each of the missions for their greater comfort or efficiency."[4] Beginning in 1881, the WBFM was able to "redeem our pledge made to Synod's Board at the beginning of the year, viz., the payment of $5,500 for the support of the three Seminaries for girls, at Amoy (China), Yokohama (Japan), and Chittoor (India), and the two Caste-girls' schools at Vellore (India)."[5]

In 1875, two women served as foreign secretaries. Each of the original secretaries, Gertrude L. Vanderbilt and Mary Virginia Payson (Rev. Edward Payson)[6] served for

---

1. The following men were included: In China, the Revs. John Van Nest Talmage, Daniel Rapalje, and Leonard W. Kip. In India, the Revs. Ezekiel C. Scudder, M.D., and John H. Wyckoff; Jared W. Scudder, M.D.; John Scudder, M.D.; Enne J. Heeren; Jacob Chamberlain, M.D.; Henry Martyn Scudder, Jr., M.D. In Japan, the Revs. Samuel R. Brown, James H. Ballagh, Henry Stout, Charles H. H. Wolff, and Guido F Verbeck.

The following married women "assistant missionaries" were included: In China, Mary E. (Van Deventer) Talmage (Mrs. John Van Nest) and Helen (Culbertson) Kip (Mrs. Leonard W.). In India, Sophia (Weld) Scudder (Mrs. John), Charlotte (Birge) Chamberlain (Mrs. Jacob), and Aleida (Vennema) Heeren (Mrs. Enne J.). In Japan, Elizabeth Goodwin (Bartlett) Brown (Mrs. Samuel R.), Margaret (Kinnear) Ballagh (Mrs. James H.), Mary E. (Kidder) Miller (Rev. E. Rothsay), Elizabeth (Provost) Stout (Mrs. Henry), L. (Buboc) Wolff (Mrs. Charles H.), and Marie (Manlon) Verbeck (Mrs. Guido).

The following unmarried "assistant missionaries" were included: In China, Helen Van Doren and Mary E. Talmage. In India, Martha J. Mandeville and Josephine Chapin. In Japan, Emma C. Witbeck. *MGS*, 1875, 5-10. All women missionaries at this time were considered "assistant missionaries," reflecting the culture of separate spheres in which they lived.

2. *ARWBFM*, 1878, 7.

3. *ARWBFM*, 1880, 8.

4. *ARWBFM*, 1883, 8.

5. *ARWBFM*, 1881, 7-8.

6. The Reverend Edward Payson Terhune was a member of the Rutgers College Class of 1850. He died May 25, 1907. According to biographical notes on Terhune's life, which were collected by John H. Raven and presented at the meeting of the Rutgers College Alumni, June 17, 1908, "In 1856 he married

two years, after which J. H. Polhemus and Charlotte Duryee (Rev. William R.) would become the foreign secretaries. Polhemus served for six years. Beginning in 1881, Charlotte Duryee would serve alone as the foreign secretary, and she would serve in this capacity until her untimely death in 1885.

It was difficult, if not impossible, for one person to fill the monumental shoes left vacant by Charlotte Duryee's death. In 1887 the foreign work was divided into three foreign fields: China, India, and Japan. In 1890 each field began to be overseen by a separate foreign secretary, and after the BFM developed a mission in Arabia in 1889, a fourth foreign secretary was added. Eventually, each of the foreign secretaries would be aided by members of a standing committee, after standing committees became established in 1902.

Because it would take time for the establishment and growth of local auxiliaries to support and finance the mission task, the foreign secretaries began their work by communicating with women missionaries already in the field. The early letters from home were supportive, prayerful, and filled with questions. In response, the letters from the foreign field seemed to delight in relating to appreciative audiences the details of missionary lives and descriptions of the native women and their situations. In a nine-year statement of WBFM work, written by Gertrude L. Vanderbilt,[7] the

---

Miss Mary Virginia Hawes, of Richmond, Va., who is very widely known as a writer under the name "Marion Harland." *Biographical Notes of the Graduates of Rutgers College* (New Brunswick: n.d., n.p., ca. 1908), 6.

7. No biography on the life of Gertrude Lefferts Vanderbilt has yet been written. She was one of the original organizers of the WBFM and served as one of the first foreign secretaries. Throughout her life she was actively involved as a WBFM leader and was always ready and willing to step into demanding positions and to assume heavy responsibilities in times of special need. She was a gifted leader and lifetime volunteer on behalf of the WBFM. Following her death January 5, 1902, the WBFM remembered her this way:

Mrs. Vanderbilt had a great love for human kind, as shown in her benevolences which began in her immediate neighborhood, *her* "Jerusalem," reached to then farther off Brooklyn, extended to the western borderlands of our country, in domestic missions, and crossed the seas to the nations beyond. It was in this department,—foreign missions –that we knew her best. To the work she gave her labor and influence unstintedly. We highly prized her conservative wisdom. Mrs. Vanderbilt though decided in her opinions, expressed them gently, and with due consideration for the views of others, and was always open to conviction. When she *voted* for a measure or a new departure her associates were assured that it must be a good one.

With a well furnished mind and fine literary ability she rendered ready and efficient service with her pen in leaflets and papers for conferences, and for our periodicals (*Mission Monthly*, etc.). It was she, who in a great emergency prepared the Annual Report for 1885, when the beloved Foreign Corresponding Secretary, Mrs. Charlotte W. Duryee was called from her earthly labors.

Mrs. Vanderbilt was highly gifted with intellectual qualities, a strong personality, a noble loving heart, and a most winning manner. We could not but be conscious that surrounding her was the atmosphere of saint-hood, which was the evidence of her entire consecration to her God and Saviour. We loved and venerated her, and shall miss her prayers and vital concern for our work.

May the Lord whom she served, provide many such richly qualified women to conduct the business, and carry on the work of our Woman's Board of Foreign Missions.

Written by a committee composed of Amelia Van Cleef, Matilda Cobb (Rev. Henry), and Anna Donald. *ARWBFM*, 1902, 17-18.

report read:

> There are certain things which cannot be weighed in scales, nor adjusted in their length and breadth to any earthly measurement. We cannot, therefore, prepare a balance-sheet by which to show the relief afforded by our ladies to our sisters toiling in distant lands. In a womanly way we have offered many kindly words of sympathy, and assurances that they are not forgotten by friends at home; and they write to us in reply that our prayers for them, and our sympathy with them have been the means of encouragement and cheer in their hours of loneliness, amid strange faces and unfamiliar tongues. From Vellore one of our missionaries writes: "It is a comfort to know that a band of earnest workers at home are joining their efforts and prayers with ours in behalf of the work we are trying to do here."[8]

By the end of the fourth month of its organization, WBFM managers reported, "The first task, then, to which our Board addresses itself, is to bring the needs of those we would help home to the minds and hearts of those whose co-operation we crave."[9] But, how could this happen when no basic information existed about the life and work of each of the mission stations? At once the women took stock of just what information about the missions was known. It was very little, and it certainly was not enough for the new WBFM women, who were serious about getting the available facts. The managers knew that:

> If the women of our Church were to be enlisted cordially in the work, it was essential that they should know where it was, by whom carried on, what were its important features, and what the cost of various departments. They must be brought into sympathy with the men and women who had gone to distant lands to tell the old, old story of Jesus and His love. The converts must cease to present themselves as vague and unreal phantoms of the imagination, and become to them flesh and blood, human beings with like passions and like immortality with their own.[10]

Thus the managers immediately set to work to prepare a manual of missions. The introduction to the manual reads in part:

> This Manual of Missions is the outgrowth of necessity. We looked about us, and finding only fragmentary details in the files of our religious papers, while it was inconvenient to apply to our Secretaries for each item as we wanted it, we decided to prepare an adequate book of reference. We have had, in its compilation, the generous help of those who were best able to speak on the subjects they have

---

8. *ARWBFM*, 1884, 23.

9. *ARWBFM*, 1875, 6.

10. *A Manual of the Missions of the Reformed (Dutch) Church in America*, issued by the WBFM, ed. Margaret E. Sangster (New York: Board of Publication of the Reformed Church in America, 1877), ix.

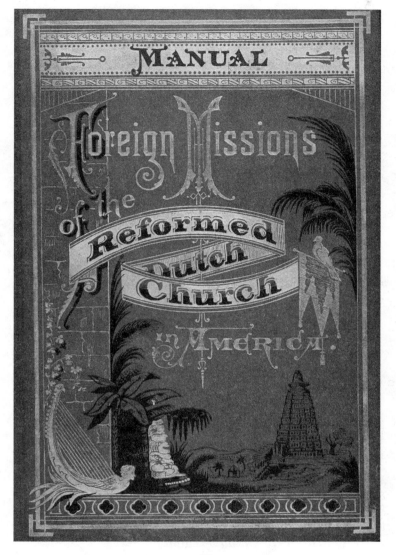

Cover of the *Manual of Foreign Missions*

undertaken. We have divided it, so far as practicable, into topical sections, properly indexed, so that information desired may be readily found. We have given it an attractive form and dress. Its beautiful illustrations, clear type, and appropriate cover, fit it to lie as an ornament on the family table, where one and another may often handle it lovingly.[11]

Margaret E. Sangster, whose pen name, "Aunt Marjorie," would often be signed to columns titled, "Aunt Marjorie's Corner," in the weekly issues of the *Christian Intelligencer*, was the editor of the book.[12] Margaret Sangster remained a highly involved member of the WBFM until the end of her life in 1912.

At this point one might ask how the managers, at this time in their organizational

---

11. *Manual of Missions*, 1877, ix.

12. For a description of Margaret Elizabeth Munson Sangster's life, see Una Ratmeyer, *Hands, Hearts, and Voices, Women Who Followed God's Call* (New York: Reformed Church Press, 1995), 176-78.

Mary Sturges
(First president of WBFM)

life, thought they would cover the cost of publishing a book such as this. After all, at the April 11, 1876, meeting of the Executive Committee, it was agreed "that a Manual be prepared with illustrations of different missionary stations and to be published under the auspices of the Board." There was, however, a further stipulation. The manual would be published "provided that the necessary funds are secured without drawing upon the Treasury of this Board, or the regular contributions of its auxiliaries for missionary purposes."[13]

At this point, Mary Sturges, the highly respected president of the WBFM from 1875 to 1894 and a woman of means, offered to cover the entire cost of the book's publication. A note in the introduction of the *Manual* reads:

> One final word: The cost of this undertaking has not come from the funds of our Board. We have not felt it right thus to use the contributions of our auxiliaries, nor to divert them from their legitimate channel. Our President, Mrs. Jonathan Sturges, with rare devotion to the good cause, and genuine missionary zeal, has herself assumed the expense of publishing this Manual. The thought which inspired it, was hers. She has watched every step of its progress with maternal solicitude, and her taste has supervised it from beginning to end.
>
> We send it to mothers and daughters. May they be stirred up, as they read its narratives, to larger efforts, to more entire consecration, and to willing self-denial, for the Kingdom and Crown of the Lord we and they love[14]

13. WBFM Executive Committee Minutes, April 11, 1876, 69.
14. *Manual of Missions*, 1877, x-xi.

Amelia Van Cleef
(President following Mary Sturges)

Mary Sturges and her husband, Jonathan, were prominent citizens of New York City, where Jonathan, a successful industrialist, served as an elder in the Collegiate Church. Mary and Jonathan Sturges were generous benefactors of many causes.[15] In covering the cost of publishing the *Manual*, Mary Sturges also provided for a complimentary copy to be sent to each new auxiliary formed.[16] This generous act provided the first major step in educating Reformed Church women in the structure and work of foreign missions.

Article 8 of the by-laws established the position of corresponding secretaries for the home field. Home secretaries, as they came to be called, had responsibility to

15. Nothing has yet been written on the life of Mary Sturges. A tribute to Mary Sturges was written by Margaret E. Sangster and appeared in "Aunt Marjorie's Corner" of the *Christian Intellingencer*, August 8, 1894. Her obituary notice, which appeared in the New York *Times* on July 31, 1894, is reproduced in Mary Chamberlain, *Fifty Years in Foreign Fields, China, Japan, India, Arabia: A History of Five Decades of the Woman's Board of Foreign Mission, Reformed Church in America* (New York: Abbott Press, 1925), 65. An obituary for Jonathan Sturges, who died November 28, 1874, appeared in the *Christian Intellingencer*, p. 8, and noted, "It is worth while of young men who are shaken by the contempt in which modern infidelity holds religious faith, to know that the cool head of one of the shrewdest practical men of our city has ever known, found commanding evidence on the side of the gospel. Nor could his faith, any more than his mercantile success, be set down to the weak side of a strong mind. Mr. Sturges was preeminently a thinker." At the June 11, 1878, meeting of the Executive Committee of the Woman's Board, "it was resolved that the Home and School about to be established at Nagasaki, Japan, should be called the Jonathan Sturges Seminary, after the husband of the President of the Board, Mr. And Mrs. Sturges having been among the most generous contributors to the fund" Chamberlain, *Fifty Years*, 33.

16. *ARWBFM*, 1886, 19.

"correspond with the churches, and propose the organization of auxiliary societies wherever it is possible to awaken an interest in the work for which this association is formed."[17] The work thus had three objectives: to correspond, to generate interest, and to organize local churches in supporting foreign missions. It was the job of the home secretary to carry out these responsibilities. How was this job accomplished?

The pioneer officers of the WBFM fully realized that the future of the organization rested on building a solid organizational foundation. This foundation rested on the active involvement and continuing support of local auxiliaries. For the first two and a half decades at least, establishing and building up local auxiliaries formed the major focus of the work of the managers and the home secretaries. Increasing the number of local auxiliaries was essential to the continued success of the WBFM. This need shaped the first step in creating an organizational system.

In the initial letter sent to the churches, local women were extended an invitation to establish an auxiliary. Such an invitation might be described as a "call to formation." The letter was accompanied by a suggested constitution, directions for forming "mission bands of young ladies," and mission circles of children, and a pledge to be used by the children.[18] Deciding to enclose a suggested constitution for women and the accompanying documents for young ladies and children with each initial call to formation proved to be ingenious.[19] Not only did these documents describe in very specific ways what the new WBFM wanted from local auxiliaries, but these documents "locked in" what could be expected from local auxiliaries. A pledge or commitment of a specific annual contribution was obtained from each local auxiliary. The creation of a local organizational structure was outlined, complete with officers, a listing of their respective duties, regular meeting dates, annual dues, and an annual meeting to elect officers and prepare an annual report. For younger women, who would form mission bands, similar expectations were noted plus individual dues of twenty-five cents yearly and an annual group commitment of twenty dollars. Children, who were encouraged to form mission circles, were expected to make an annual group contribution of five dollars and to receive a pledge from each child "to give one cent a week to the mission box, and to come together once a month to hear about missions, and to work for the cause."[20]

By forming women's auxiliaries in this manner, women, young women, and children were brought into an organizational system. In addition to the clear expectations of their financial support, women were expected to become active participants in very specific ways. Among other things, this active participation, for many if not most women, meant overcoming "the timid objection to read a letter in public or hold an office, to the best utterances of gifted and devout women."[21] It meant overcoming

---

17. *ARWBFM*, 1875, 18-19.

18. *ARWBFM*, 1875, 4.

19. See appendix for copies of these documents.

20. *ARWBFM*, 1975, 20.

21. Ellen C. Parsons, "History of Woman's Organized Missionary Work as Promoted by American Women," in E. M. Wherry, comp., *Woman in Missions: Papers and Addresses Presented at the Woman's Congress of Missions October 2-4, 1893, in the Hall of Columbus, Chicago* (New York: American Tract Society, 1984), 93.

ingrained inhibitions and learning to pray aloud in a group and acquiring other necessary leadership skills.

At the time the WBFM was organized in 1875, two women, Elizabeth M. Cumming (James P.) and Mary Myers (the Rev. Alfred E.), were elected home corresponding secretaries. These two women formed the first of a long line of distinguished home secretaries. For the life of the WBFM, the work of the home secretaries would be undertaken by two women and sometimes by a lone woman. As home secretaries in 1875, it was their initial responsibility to write a letter containing a call to auxiliary formation to each of the 490 RCA congregations then in existence. This must have been a Herculean task, given that the typewriter came into general public use only in the 1890s.[22] With no known copy of the 1875 letter of invitation either in the RCA archives or in any known congregational archive, it is not known if the original letter and its accompanying documents were handwritten or lithographed.[23] Just for the record, sending a letter weighing one-half ounce cost three cents in 1875.[24]

---

22. Having purchased the patents for the recently invented typewriter, John Thomas Underwood (1857-1937) founded the Underwood Typewriter Company, which beginning in the 1880s manufactured and marketed typewriters to the American public. The reliable Underwood No. 5 typewriter, one of the most successfully designed typewriters in history, appeared shortly before 1900. This machine and those similar to it introduced a new age in communication. John Thomas Underwood, the founder and owner of the company was an entrepreneur and soon became a successful businessman. His family, a remarkably pious family, came to the United States from England in 1873 and joined the Grove Reformed Church in North Bergen, New Jersey. Among John Thomas Underwood's four siblings was a younger brother named Horace Grant Underwood (1859-1916). From an early age young Horace knew he wanted to be a missionary, and to prepare for mission work he attended New York University and New Brunswick Theological Seminary, graduating from NBTS as a member of the class of 1884. Although initially wanting to go to India, and preparing himself for this with a year of medical training following his graduation from seminary, Horace felt called increasingly to Korea. He twice appealed to the BFM of the RCA to go to Korea, but denominational debt and limited available finances precluded the RCA from expanding its mission focus beyond China, India, and Japan. The Presbyterian Church, however, was encouraged to begin a new mission work in Korea with a gift of $6,000 from the Lafayette Avenue Presbyterian Church in Brooklyn, where John Thomas Underwood and his wife, Grace Brainard Underwood, were members. Horace Grant Underwood not only preached the gospel and established a large number of churches in Korea, of which the Saemoonan Presbyterian Church in Seoul [founded in 1885] was the first. He also founded the school that has become Yonsei University, its medical and dental schools, and the YMCA. A gift of $52,000 from his brother John Thomas enabled the purchase of land on which Yonsei University stands today. Horace Grant Underwood became a national hero of the Korean people. As part of his legacy, 20 percent of the NBTS student body today is Korean, and Laurel Underwood Brundage, the great-granddaughter of Horace Grant Underwood, serves as a member of the NBTS Board of Trustees. Lillias H. Underwood, M.D., *Underwood of Korea* (New York: Revell, 1918). For the above information I am also indebted to the Reverend Laurel Underwood Brundage and to Horace Grant Underwood (III) of Korea.

23. We do know that the WBFM used a lithograph machine to prepare circulars in 1880 when classical committees were formed. See Chamberlain, *Fifty Years*, 35.

24. From March 3, 1863, to March 2, 1883, the U.S. Postal rate was three cents per one-half ounce to all parts of the country. This changed March 3, 1883, to two cents per half-ounce, and in 1885 was further reduced to two cents per one ounce. This rate remained relatively stable until 1958, when it increased to four cents and thereafter slowly moved upward.

It is interesting to note that in the *First Annual Report* for 1875, which covers only four months of

A number of women's missionary societies already existed within individual congregations in the Reformed Church prior to the formation of the WBFM.[25] At the end of four months in 1875 (the end of the first reporting year), the home secretary reported that eight previously existing societies had become charter auxiliaries. They were joined by eleven newly formed auxiliaries for a total of nineteen auxiliaries. These charter auxiliaries and their dates of organization "as nearly as could be determined" were listed as:

First Reformed Church	New Brunswick, N.J.	1825[26]
Reformed Church	Bedminster, N.J.	1825-35[27]
Owasco Outlet	New York	1870[28]
Saugerties	New York	1873[29]
Flushing	New York	1873
Bronxville	New York	1874[30]

WBFM existence, the treasurer's report makes no record of a disbursement for any costs. In the *Second Annual Report*, a disbursement of $52.68 was made to cover the costs of "stationery, Printing Certificates [for life memberships] and etc." No mention is made of any postage costs. However, the total postage bill for 490 letters at three cents each would have reached only $14.70.

25. For a discussion of these missionary societies, see Chamberlain, *Fifty Years*, 13-14.

26. This list of charter auxiliaries is taken from *ARWBFM*, 1875, p. 5, and from Chamberlain, *Fifty Years*, 15. There is a discrepancy regarding the date when the First Reformed Church in New Brunswick officially became an auxiliary of the WBFM. The *ARWBFM* of 1878, p. 23, suggests that the actual date is 1878. "The following communication was received from this Church in November, 1878: The ladies' Missionary society of the First Reformed Church, New Brunswick, has never been recognized as an Auxiliary of the Woman's Board, yet it is in full sympathy with the work in which you are engaged, and if agreeable to your views would desire to be placed on your list. The organization has been in existence for upwards of fifty years, and has always contributed both to the Home and Foreign Boards of our Church."

27. Mary Chamberlain writes, "At Bedminster, N.J., there was, it is said, 'a very large and flourishing society of forty or fifty years' standing.'" Chamberlain, *Fifty Years*, 14.

28. In her fifty-year anniversary, Mary Chamberlain goes out of her way to point out the specific involvement of the Ladies' Missionary Society of the Reformed Church at Owasco Outlet, New York. She says,

That was, indeed, a missionary church. From its membership went out in 1859 Miss Caroline E. Adriance, first to Japan and later to the Amoy Mission. Miss Mary E. Kidder, afterwards Mrs. E. Rothesay Miller, went out from it to Japan in 1869. Its Pastor, the Rev. S. R. Brown, and Mrs. Brown went out as pioneer missionaries to Japan in 1859. This same church sent out Miss S.K.M. Hequembourg to assist Miss Kidder in 1872. Before going out to Japan in 1859 Mrs. G.F. Verbeck united with this church. The Ladies' Missionary Society had for years been accustomed to contribute to the work of the Amoy Mission in memory of Miss Adriance and to Ferris Seminary because of their interest in Miss Kidder.

Chamberlain, *Fifty Years*, 14. The Reformed Church in Owasco Outlet was known as the Sand Beach Reformed Church and was located just south of Auburn, New York. It was disbanded in 1997.

29. Mary Chamberlain simply notes, "In Saugerties there had been a woman's missionary society for many years." Chamberlain, *Fifty Years*, 14.

30. Notes Mary Chamberlain, "The ladies of the Bronxville Church organized, under the leadership of Mrs. Alfred E. Myers, a missionary society which antedated the founding of the Woman's Board." Chamberlain, *Fifty Years*, 14. This is the same Mary Myers (Rev. Alfred E.), who served with Elizabeth M. Cumming as the first home corresponding secretaries of the WBFM.

Church on the Heights	Brooklyn, N.Y.	1874
Flatbush	Long Island(Brooklyn)	1874
Adams Station	(Delmar)New York	1875
Yonkers	New York	1875
Marble Collegiate Church	New York City	1875
First Reformed Church	Brooklyn, N.Y.	1875
First Van Vorst Church	Jersey City, N.J.	1875
First Reformed Church	Newark, N.J.	1875
North Reformed Church	Newark, N.J.	1875
Reformed Church	Bergen, N.J.	1875
Reformed Church	Freehold, N.J.	1875
Reformed Church	Belleville, N.J.	1875
North Collegiate Church	New York City	1875[31]

During the second year of the WBFM's existence, the total number of auxiliaries grew to thirty-three; and, by 1880, the total had reached seventy-four auxiliaries.[32] This respectable growth in the number of women's auxiliaries was supported by receipts of $1,039 the first year, $4,539 the second year, and $13,456 in 1880. But the women hoped and prayed for more. Of the 510 RCA congregations in existence in 1880, 436 of the churches as yet had no women's auxiliary. Beyond New York and New Jersey, a women's auxiliary and a mission circle (called the "Buds of Promise") were established at the Reformed Church in Bushnell, Illinois, and joined the WBFM already in 1876.[33] In 1877, the women of the Second Reformed Church in Pella, Iowa, organized a women's auxiliary and a children's circle (called "The Little Workers,") and they were listed as new auxiliaries in 1878.[34] Auxiliaries in these two churches became the first WBFM auxiliaries beyond the East Coast.

The Board of Managers was greatly encouraged, however, by signs of growth in the "Western Church," as it was then known. It was reported, for example, that Mrs. M.S. Van Olinda of Holland, Michigan,

---

31. *ARWBFM*, 1875, 5. See also Chamberlain, *Fifty Years*, 15. It is puzzling that in her fifty-year anniversary history, Mary Chamberlain noted, "There is an unbroken record of the society in Glenville, N.Y., founded by Mrs. Phoebe G. Clowe on May 19, 1837." According to the 1895 WBFM list of auxiliaries and their dates of organization, First Glenville was organized in 1839. See *ARWBFM*, 1895, 60.

32. This number did not include the number of mission bands of young ladies and mission circles of children. These figures were reported in the *Annual Reports* only sporadically.

33. The pastor of the Reformed Church in Bushnell, Illinois, at this time was George E. Bodine, who served the Bushnell congregation 1874-1879. He was followed by George Sharpley, who served there 1880-1884.

34. The pastor of the Second Reformed Church of Pella, Iowa, at this time was Harvey R. Schermerhorn, who served there 1875-1879. He was followed by Cyrus Cort, stated supply 1881-1882; pastor Garret Huyzer, 1883-1885; Abram N. Wyckoff, stated supply 1885-1886; and then George Sharpley 1887-1892. It is interesting to note that after leaving the Bushnell Reformed Church in 1884, George Sharpley served for three years in the Congregational Church and then became pastor at Second Reformed, Pella. Following his years of service there, he was dismissed to the Presbyterian Church.

a lady inspired with zeal for the cause of Christ and ardent love for our branch of Zion has made a successful effort in this direction by a union of the three Dutch speaking Churches[35] with the Hope Church which is English, in forming an Auxiliary. Our correspondent called on these ladies and found them much interested in the missionary cause and ready to enter into the work. Three weeks were spent in visiting the different congregations; and after obtaining the approval and co-operation of the ministers, a meeting was held which resulted in the formation of an Auxiliary by the married ladies, one also by the young ladies, and a Mission "Band" and "Circle" by the children and youth. The exercises were conducted in both the Dutch and English languages, as many of the ladies present could not take part in the English.[36]

The *Annual Report* of 1886 goes on to note:

The evidence seems conclusive that the first advance in this new field of labor has been successful in its initiation. The question arises why more of these Dutch speaking Churches may not be brought into a closer fellowship and a more vital union with those at [sic] the East, claiming with them "one hope, one faith, one baptism." By a concerted plan and union with the English speaking churches they might have a part with us in conveying to those "who sit in the region and shadow of death," the blessed knowledge of the Gospel of Christ. May not this prove an opening whereby the cause shall gather strength and importance and a more perfect knowledge be gained of what these churches are able and willing to do in this department of work for the Master.[37]

In addition to the formation of an auxiliary in Holland, Michigan, an auxiliary was formed in the English-language congregation in Constantine, Michigan, in 1880. This congregation had been organized in 1843; its pastor in 1880 was John Walter Beardslee, Sr.

There seemed to be no encouragement for any organized effort, but at last one inspired with faith and hope offered to canvass the Church for this purpose and the result shows an evident and increasing interest in missionary work. There is a great want felt in these societies so far removed from a great centre where missionary intelligence and assistance is available as one of our co-laborers writes: "A live missionary is seldom seen here." The secretary of the Constantine Auxiliary

---

35. The 1886 *ARWBFM* makes clear that these churches included First (organized 1847), Second, which was known as Hope Church (incorporated 1862), and Third Reformed (organized 1867). In 1886, "it was thought recently, that the cause of Missions would be increased if each church had its own auxiliary, although the union had been perfectly harmonious. It was found that the hour was too short to conduct the exercises in both languages and have time enough for interpretation. It was also thought that this new movement would open the way for auxiliaries in Hollandish Churches."*ARWBFM*, 1886, 25.

36. *ARWBFM*, 1880, 19.

37. Ibid.

asks, "Why will not some of our missionaries now in this country make a tour of the Western Churches this coming season? If an interest could be awakened in the hearts of Pastors it would be easy to enlist the people. Something is needed to arouse the love and enthusiasm for the cause in which we all feel ourselves to be greatly lacking but for which we are praying.[38]

At the General Synod of 1880, the women of the WBFM were unquestionably affirmed. The Synod's Committee on Missions reported:

> The rapid increase of auxiliaries, as well as the interest manifested in their meetings, are prophetic of large and blessed results. It is the opinion of your Committee, that there resides among the ladies of our denomination a power which, when fully developed, will tell with mighty effect upon our foreign work, and it is to be hoped that new organizations will continue to spring up from year to year, until each Church in our Zion shall have an auxiliary, and each Sabbath-school its Mission Band.[39]

It was during the General Synod of 1880 that the decision was made to hold an annual missionary conference "for the purpose of diffusing information, and creating a deeper and more general interest in all the missionary operations of our Board."[40] In November, the first denominational missionary conference took place in Poughkeepsie, New York, and the women were there to listen. According to Mary Chamberlain's fifty-year history:

> On the second day of the conference an informal meeting was held by the delegates of the Woman's Board and other women drawn together by their interest in missions. Mrs. Martin (Mrs. E. Throop Martin from Auburn, New York) was there and again[41] spoke very earnestly of the importance of interesting in our work the women of *every* church....To bring this about she proposed the following plan which was afterward adopted by the Board. Two women were to be appointed in each Classis who were to endeavor to arouse a missionary spirit and to establish societies auxiliary to the Woman's Board in all the churches in the Classis in which they did not already exist.

This plan was utterly brilliant! The plan was built upon the use of the existing structure of classes, and women as well as men in the church commonly understood the relationship of churches to one another within a classis.

---

38. Ibid.

39. *MGS*, 1880, 569-70.

40. *MGS*, 1880, 570.

41. According to Mary Chamberlain's history, Martin, who was an honorary vice-president of the Woman's Board, had earlier, on April 13, 1880, made the suggestion to the Executive Committee that "classical meetings for women be held in connection with the Church meetings of Classes, similar meetings having been successful in a sister Church held in connection with Presbyterial [sic] meetings." Chamberlain, *Fifty Years*, 35.

In 1881, the home secretary reported that within a year, the managers had established a plan, prepared circulars of explanation, corresponded with potential classical committee members, and produced a complete list of the new classical committee members for their 1881 *Annual Report* with the final words, "We rejoice to be able to report that in nearly all of the Classes, arrangements have been perfected for carrying forward this work; most of the ladies receiving the appointment having accepted, and are about to commence an active prosecution of the work."[42] The entire plan was activated in one year's time.

It is important to observe that within seven years of its organization, the home secretary estimated that a hundred percent of all RCA congregations had been contacted either in person or in writing.

> The Board feels assured that the Churches in our denomination have been visited, where this was possible, or the Pastors addressed in writing, on the subject.... We have reason to believe that the number of auxiliaries organized during the year has been increased by this means.

---

42. *ARWBFM*, 1881, 14.
Women serving as members of the first classical committees include:
Classis of Albany: Mrs. Mary Pruyn and Mrs. S. R. Brown
Classis of Bergen: Mrs. Wm. Williams, and Mrs. John Van Deventer
South Classis of Bergen: Amelia Van Cleef and Charlotte Duryee
Classis of Cayuga: Mrs. E.T. Martin, Mrs. E. Van Slyke, and Mrs. Isaac Hartley
Secundi: Miss Caroline Gridley and Miss Katharine Brayton
Classis of Geneva: Mrs. H. P. McAdam and Mrs. D. C. Wheeler
Classis of Greene: Mrs. J. P. Thompson and Miss L. Lusk
Classis of Holland: Mrs. M. S. Van Olinda
Classis of Hudson: Mrs. Ezekiel C. Scudder
Classis of Illinois: Miss M. L. Morris
Classis of Kingston: Mrs. James Demarest, Jr.
North Classis of Long Island: Margaret E. Sangster and Miss E. R. Hallock
South Classis of Long Island: Gertrude L. Vanderbilt and Mrs. Remsen Bennett
Classis of Michigan: Mrs. J. W. Beardslee and Miss P. B. Chamberlin
Classis of Monmouth: Mrs. I. P. Brokaw
Classis of Newark: Mary Cushing and Mrs. Wm R. Taylor
Classis of New Brunswick: Miss M. A. Campbell and Mrs. J. C. Elmendorf
Classis of New York: Louise Chambers, Anna J. Donald, Miss E. Bergen
Classis of Paramus: Mrs. C. S. Hageman and Mrs. M. B. Smith
Classis of Passaic: Mrs. James Kemlo
Classis of Philadelphia: Mrs. John Lefferts
Classis of Poughkeepsie: Mrs. J. Elmendorf and Mrs. C. H. Polhemus
Classis of Raritan: Mrs. John H. Smock and Mrs. H. V. Voorhees
Classis of Rensselaer: Mrs. John Steele
Classis of Saratoga: Miss Anna Lansing and Mrs. Aberdeen Curtis
Classis of Schenectady: Miss Francis C. Paige and Miss Cornelia Boardman
Classis of Ulster: Mrs. Joseph Scudder and Mrs. Stephen Searle
Classis of Westchester: Mrs. David Cole and Elizabeth M. Cumming
ARWBFM, 1881, 15-17.

From some of the Churches reasons were received why societies could not satisfactorily be formed for the present; in others, encouragement was given that the subject would be considered in the near future....[43]

The Board of Managers recognized that "the great working force behind our Board are our Classical Committees," and the *Annual Report* of 1904 notes:

The motto of Mrs. Charles Spurgeon, "Just do a thing, don't talk about it," is applicable to these women who are the link between the Board and the Societies. With an undismayed faith, and loving, persistent effort this corps of efficient workers has quietly and steadfastly cared for the work in each Classis. One, has introduced a Missionary Book Club; another, written fifty-four letters to her auxiliaries; while a third, in the sorrow-shadow of the home circle, sent her message to the special committee meeting; she mourns not without hope, and her heart yearns over the countless Christless mothers and widows who have not The Comforter. Profoundly grateful are we for women like these whose interested lives wield an influence beyond their ken as they "magnify their office."[44]

Not only did the work of classical committee members include enlisting women in each classis in the missionary cause. These women recognized that the work of classical committee members placed women in relationship with one another, which meant they were increasingly in a position to help one another.

Our Classical Committees are conspicuous for their quiet, unobtrusiveness, intent on faithful service, and we rest more year by year, upon their dependableness. Their correspondence reveals the personal sacrifice of those in rural districts to create and maintain interest. More and more we need to know each other's problem and to share in its solution.[45]

Beginning with the *Annual Report* of 1893, classical committees regularly communicated to the home secretary the progress of their work, and almost all of these reports found their way into the *Annual Report*. Sometimes classical committee members could be extremely realistic—much in the tradition of reporting the results of one's annual health examination, and, of course, this information was disseminated to all WBFM auxiliaries.

It wasn't long before these behind-the-scene, "silent workers"[46] recognized the value of having all the auxiliaries within a classis meet together for classical conferences—

43. *ARWBFM*, 1882, 17.
44. *ARWBFM*, 1904, 10.
45. *ARWBFM*, 1909, 10.
46. The "silent workers" were recognized frequently and referred to with great respect. Of all the participants involved in the work of classical unions it was said, "We have too the silent workers, who have given time, talent and strength in speaking whenever a call has come from a Church, Society or Convention. They would not wish their names recorded here, but they are known and honored throughout the entire Church." *ARWBFM*, 1902, 10.

to receive "missionary intelligence,"[47] to become inspired, and to form stronger bonds in pressing forward with the work of missions. In 1883 the Woman's Classical Missionary Association of the Classis of Cayuga, the first of the classical unions, reported on its April 10 meeting in Utica, New York:

> Hereafter the meetings will be held in the autumn, as the weather and facilities for traveling are very much better at that season of the year. It may not be uninteresting to know that such was the desire to attend this meeting by two members of Classis and their wives, that they walked eight miles through the snow to the railroad station, it being impossible to drive, and two others walked twelve miles—a comment on those who will not walk across the street to attend a missionary meeting.[48]

The following year, the Ladies' Classical Missionary Association of the Classis of Newark also met, and with these two meetings began the formation of women's classical unions throughout the denomination. By 1904, the *Annual Report* noted that "Classical Unions existed in all but one of the Eastern Classes and four Western."[49]

As with the work of classical committee members, reports of classical union meetings were submitted to the home secretary and published in the *Annual Report*, thus enabling women throughout the denomination to be in closer touch with the experiences of other women miles and miles away. By using the opportunity of classical union gatherings, auxiliary members practiced their leadership skills, and "women who have felt that they had no gifts for public service, have come to the front as strong, efficient leaders and an inspiration to others."[50] By reporting the number of attendees at classical union conferences, women gained an additional sense of growth and progress. Women's classical union gatherings, "these feast-days of Gods [sic] working women"[51] brought women together to be strengthened in the cause. Indeed they were. "There is nothing so satisfactory in all this world as the companionship we feel with "the children of the Kingdom."[52]

As Article 8 of the by-laws had specified, it was the responsibility of the home secretary to correspond, to generate interest, and to organize women in local churches in support of foreign missions. By the end of 1881, just six years after their formation, the WBFM organizational structure was fully organized and operational.

As indicated on the following graphs,[53] growth in the number of women's auxiliaries increased steadily, and, by the turn of the century, the number of auxiliaries

---

47. "Missionary intelligence" was a commonly used term referring to any information or knowledge pertaining to the lives and the work of the missionaries and/or their constituencies.

48. *ARWBFM*, 1883, 18.

49. In 1904, there were a total of thirty-four classes in the denomination.

50. *ARWBFM*, 1901, 14.

51. *ARWBFM*, 1904, 11.

52. *ARWBFM*, 1904, 11.

53. For the broadest and most inclusive data of all women's foreign missionary societies in the United States and Canada, see Helen Barrett Montgomery, *Western Women in Eastern Lands* (New York: Macmillan, 1910) n.p.

approximated the number of existing RCA congregations. The number of auxiliaries continued to grow as the women's mission movement gained in size and strength in the twentieth century. It must be remembered that these figures reflect only the number of married women's auxiliaries. They do not include the number of mission bands and children's circles, which were attached to local women's auxiliaries; nor do these figures reflect auxiliary organizations later established such as the Young Woman's Branch, founded in 1901, and the Crusaders, a mission-focused organization for boys and girls, begun in 1903. Figures showing the total number of women's auxiliaries, mission bands, and children's circles, plus those named above, were reported only sporadically, but in 1924 the total number of organizations was reported to be 1,124, with 730 women's auxiliaries alone reported for the same year.

WBFM giving reflected the growth pattern of the auxiliaries. Annual giving steadily rose over time, and, except for the years of severe economic depression in the early 1930s and years when major RCA fund drives were undertaken, the WBFM routinely met its budgets and the high income expectations necessary to underwrite the cost of ever-increasing WBFM involvement in the foreign mission effort.

The success of the WBFM in establishing local auxiliaries, generating interest in foreign missions, and growing its financial base was striking. With the creation of classical committees and classical unions, the basic organizational structure of the WBFM in 1881 was complete, functioning well, producing interest in missions among the women and children of the church, and, of course, producing income receipts.

The slow steady growth in WBFM income receipts was moving in a direction opposite from the erratic, boom-and-bust pattern that the General Synod treasury seemed to be following in the early 1880s. As noted in chapter 1, the General Synod's failure to establish an effective organizational system for supporting foreign missions contributed in a major way to the synod's financial problems, and the financial situation only worsened as time wore on.

It doesn't take much imagination to foresee that in time tension would arise between the growing financial base of the WBFM and the General Synod's exasperating whipsaw pattern of deficits. This deficit pattern seemed to suffer endlessly from uncontrollable currency fluctuations, rising and falling national economic conditions, and, perhaps worst of all, with the seemingly half-hearted response of church members to the call to support financially the work of foreign missions.

The tension between WBFM women and the synod's BFM became noticeable in 1881, when the General Synod conducted a major fund drive to retire the synod's mounting debt. WBFM leaders were sympathetic with this effort and encouraged auxiliaries to participate in retiring the synod's debt. This auxiliaries and individuals did, and the *Annual Report* for 1881 notes:

> The Foreign Mission work of our beloved Church has come to the front grandly during the past year. The special feature of the work has been the payment of the debt so long and so heavily resting upon Synod's Board. As fellow laborers we rejoice with them.
>
> We are proud that the first contribution to this end was made through a society

INCREASE OF WBFM AUXILIARIES AND RCA CONGREGATIONS, 1875-1900

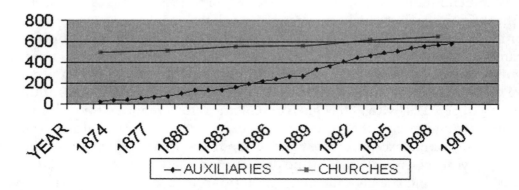

In 1898, the Annual Report of the WBFM noted: "There are but few churches now where we have not Auxiliary Societies, the exception being in our smaller Churches where the struggle is to live. These societies now number 538, with an approximate membership of 12,000" (ARWBM, 1898), 8.

MISSIONARIES: MEN, MARRIED WOMEN, UNMARRIED WOMEN

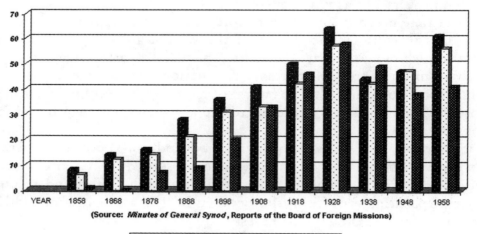

(Source: *Minutes of General Synod*, Reports of the Board of Foreign Missions)

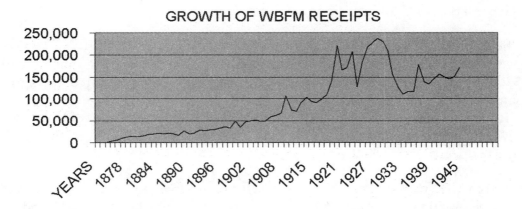

GROWTH OF WBFM RECEIPTS

Receipts include gifts for current operations, gifts of endowment principal and investment income arising from mortgages held by the WBFM, bonds, and cash deposits.

auxiliary to the Woman's Board, that of the Second Church of New Brunswick; and that the next to enter the lists were the ladies of the Second Church of Tarrytown. We know too that, both through individual subscriptions and by bearing the burden of collecting in many of the churches, much was accomplished through our auxiliaries; although the Woman's Board deemed it unwise, by any separate action of its own, to interfere with the very efficient plans of the committee of gentlemen nominated at Poughkeepsie.[54]

In spite of the encouragement of auxiliary leaders to auxiliary members to contribute to the reduction of the synod's debt, which initially was believed surely to impact the contributions of auxiliaries to the WBFM, the managers were still able to keep their pledge to provide $5,500 to the BFM. In addition, they gave two extraordinary gifts: $250 for Dr. Chamberlain's work in India and $1,000 from a specified fund to begin construction of an academic building for girls in Madanapalle, India. This was accomplished with WBFM annual receipts for 1881 amounting to $12,989.23, which were down only $466.40 from total receipts of $13,455.63 the year before.[55]

---

54. *ARWBFM*, 1881, 7.
55. These figures are taken from the audited figures in the *ARWBFM*, 1880, p. 45, and *ARWBFM*, 1881, p. 43. They are at variance with the figures reported in the BFM report in the *MGS*, 1881, p. 54, which lists WBFM receipts of $8559.75 for 1881 and $8720.55 for 1880, a decrease of only $170.80. The difference in figures most likely reflects the omission of a separate fund, called the Nagasaki Fund.

Initially, General Synod's 1881 fund drive to retire its debt appeared to be successful. The General Synod Committee on Missions reported:

> The responsibility was recognized, and the result is before us. Of the sum raised, over $86,000 was contributed by and through our church organizations, or nearly $20,000 more than was ever before realized from the same source during the same period.
>
> It has been a generous, general and systematic offering to the Lord.
>
> We have also secured, as we trust, a broader as well as a more certain base of future operations.[56]

Although the fund drive proved successful, contributions the following year plunged below 50 percent of the 1881 level of giving. At the 1882 General Synod, the synod's Committee on Missions lashed out at the churches saying:

> The number of churches in our denomination in this country, is 485.
>
> An examination of the list of churches contributing to the Board of Foreign Missions during the past year, shows that of this number 128 churches, reporting 6,718 families, and 9,955 members, gave *not one cent* toward spreading the Gospel in heathen lands.
>
> That is, *more than one fourth* of the churches of our denomination bore no part whatever during the past year in the work of extending the Redeemer's Kingdom in the dark places of the earth.
>
> Their members may have sung
>   "Fly abroad thou mighty Gospel,"
> but they gave nothing to make it fly.[57]

The anger of the committee could scarcely be contained. Someone had to be blamed. The committee in its frustration pointed its finger at pastors, and in the process edged toward blaming the WBFM as well.

> Some churches report contributions through their auxiliaries to the Woman's Board of Missions, but little or nothing from the church itself. The Woman's Board is doing a great and noble work, but it was never designed to relieve pastors, and church officers, and congregations, from their own proper personal responsibility. Its purpose rather is, to supplement the endeavors of the churches, and to increase the contributions to the work of missions, by interesting the women of our Church in this great cause, and thus stimulating enthusiasm, and soliciting aid which might not otherwise be procured.
>
> It is to be hoped that our *pastors* will feel more deeply their responsibility in the work of Missions. When a church does not manifest interest in this great cause, and sends no contribution to its support, the fault, in the great majority of

---

56. *MGS*, 1881, 766.
57. Italics in original. *MGS*, 1882, 138.

instances, is *with the pastor*. He can at least, present the cause to his people, and afford them the opportunity to contribute of their substance to aid in carrying on the work. He can at least send an offering himself, and thus discharge his own individual responsibility, and remove the church under his charge from the list of non-contributors.[58]

This act of finger pointing was carried one step further the following year. In its annual report to the synod, the BFM routinely had a small section in each report on the work of the Woman's Board. After noting WBFM growth for 1883 and thanking the women for their donation of $8,762.22 and pledges of $2,000 and $2,500 to specific BFM projects, the BFM seized the opportunity to charge WBFM women with overstepping their bounds. In other words, the BFM charged that WBFM women had stepped out of their sphere. The report said:

> These services and pledges justly merit, as they have always received, the thankful recognition of this Board and the appreciation of the churches.
> This Board has certainly no disposition to detract from the value of these services, or to disparage or discourage the godly zeal and earnest efforts of the members of the Woman's Board and its auxiliaries, which are worthy of all praise. But, with a deep sense of its importance, we would call the attention of the Synod and the Church to the fact that, notwithstanding the large and constantly increasing receipts of the Woman's Board, there has been almost no increase in the average contributions of the Church to the foreign work since the organization of that Board. It was organized in 1875. The average receipts of this Board for the eight years preceding were $65,263.06. For the succeeding eight years the average has been $66,208.01, and that notwithstanding the fact that in the year 1880-81 the Church lifted a debt of more than $30,000 from the Treasury of the Board.
> These figures can be interpreted by us in only one way. We can only read them as showing that the willing and successful activity of the auxiliaries of the Woman's Board has been suffered, by many of our churches and their officers, to supplant instead of supplementing the activity of the churches themselves by their accustomed methods, through the instrumentality of pastors, and by means of church collections. We do not believe for one moment that this is to be laid at the door of the Woman's Board. We are sure that no such result is desired by it. We are quite as sure that no such result was contemplated by the General Synod when, in 1874, it recommended "the organization of a Woman's Missionary Society, with auxiliary associations in all those churches where it is practicable, in the work of which our Board shall fully sympathize and co-operate." But we submit that it presents a case requiring to be brought to the notice of the Synod, in order that the work which properly belongs to pastors and to churches may not be left for faithful women to perform, while their labors are left free to advance the special work for women which they have so earnestly sought and heartily embraced.[59]

58. Italics in original. *MGS*, 1882, 138-39.
59. *MGS*, 1883, 6-7.

Matilda Cobb

The women pressed ahead with their work. The year 1883 was a busy one for the WBFM. It was earmarked by the publication of the first issue of a new bimonthly missionary magazine called the *Mission Gleaner*.[60] Its editor was Matilda Van Zandt Cobb.[61] It was especially memorable that at the WBFM annual meeting of 1883, a woman presented an address for the first time. For this same annual meeting, a

60. The *Mission Gleaner* was designed primarily to disseminate "missionary intelligence." It began publication in November 1883 and continued until 1917. See Reneé House, "Women Raising Women," in Reneé House and John Coakley, eds., *Patterns and Portraits, Women in the History of the Reformed Church in America*, The Historical Series of the Reformed Church in America, no. 31 (Grand Rapids: Eerdmans, 1999), 103-18.

61. Matilda Van Zandt Cobb (1840?-1910) was editor and business manager of the *Mission Gleaner* from 1883 to 1906. She was also a charter member of the WBFM, served as WBFM vice-president and as president for one year (1900-1901), and was always involved in promoting the work of missions. Ratmeyer, *Hands, Hearts, and Voices*, 4-5. Matilda Van Zandt Cobb was married to the Reverend Henry Nitchie Cobb, who at the time of the founding of the WBFM in 1875, was a member of the BFM. In November, 1883, Henry Cobb became secretary of the BFM, a position he held until his death April 17, 1910. Given Cobb's position as secretary of the BFM in 1883 and the text of the BFM report of 1883, one might suspect some spirited dinner conversation in the Cobb home in 1883 concerning the role of the WBFM. Over time, however, WBFM leaders grew to appreciate Henry Cobb, and upon his death noted in a letter to Matilda Cobb, "The hearts of the Board of Managers of the Woman's Board of Foreign Missions are griefstricken [sic] at our loss in the departure of dear Dr. Cobb. It is an irreparable loss; we may not hope to see his like again. He has been our benign counsellor [sic], guide

The *Mission Gleanor*

---

and sympathizing friend, ever patient and courteous. We loved him and will hold his name precious in memory." Chamberlain, *Fifty Years*, 188. For the WBFM to have chosen the words "we loved him" clearly breaks away from common usage in the language of the time. In the *Annual Report* of 1908, the WBFM records its sense of loss this way: "During these years we have realized in fullest measure the readiness with which he has always 'helped those women,' who have relied upon his counsel and judgment, as we have labored together; and to-day we 'thank God upon every remembrance of him for his fellowship from the first day, until now....'" *ARWBFM*, 1908, 12.

hymn text was written especially for the occasion by Margaret E. Sangster, although the hymn text was read aloud not by the author, but by the preacher of the day.

When the synod of 1885 met and projected an 1886 budget of $100,000, which included a debt of $8,500,[62] the women were again approached and asked to aid in funding this $100,000 budget beyond their annual pledge of $5,500.

The following response by the WBFM Board of Managers is recorded in the 1885 *Annual Report* of the WBFM:

> The Woman's Board has deeply sympathized with the efforts of Synod's Board to lift the debt which rested so heavily upon it during the past year. In November, a communication was received from the Secretary of that Board, stating that at the Conference held at Kingston in the interest of foreign missions, and with special reference to the liquidation of the debt, the following "Resolution" which formed a part of the report of a committee, was adopted:
> *Resolved:* – "That the Woman's Board which has responded so nobly in the past, be earnestly requested to supplement their present efficient aid by special endeavors suited to the existing emergency."
> This important matter was duly considered by the Woman's Board, and the following resolution unanimously adopted:
> *Resolved:* – "That the Classical Committees be requested to write to the several auxiliaries in their churches, urging them to unite in a special season of closet prayer, at the twilight hour of the last Sabbath of the year, with reference to the present financial emergency of Synod's Board."
> This resolution was communicated to the Classical Committees, and many sympathetic responses were received from friends and colaborers [sic] in the cause.
> It was an inspiring thought that at the twilight hour of holy day a concert of petition was ascending to the Mercy seat for a baptism of the spirit that the Kingdom of Christ might be advanced, and God's people led to give of their substance that the burden of debt might be lifted. The hallowed hour appealed to us in an especial manner, for we knew that:
>
> In many a secret chamber,
> In many a heart unknown,
> In town, and village, and country,
> The links of that wonderful zone,
> Were silently, steadily forming,
> As borne on the evening air,
> To our "Father in Heaven" uprising
> The voice of the hour of prayer.[63]

To this response by the women, there could be no argument. No one could argue

---

62. *MGS*, 1895, 752.

63. Using a poem or hymn text to underscore such a message as this was not uncommon at the time. *ARWBFM*, 1885, 24.

with prayer as an answer, although the BFM and the General Synod might have hoped for a more tangible outcome.

Trying to defend themselves as best they could against the BFM charge of stepping out of their sphere, WBFM women at the time had also to contend with their own grief, caused by the untimely death in that same year of Charlotte Duryee,[64] their beloved friend and colleague, who had served for eight years as WBFM foreign secretary. Inasmuch as it was the responsibility of the foreign secretary to prepare the report of the Board of Managers for the *Annual Report* and the BFM, the death of Charlotte Duryee left this task unfinished.[65] Into the breach stepped two stalwart and ever-faithful WBFM women. Gertrude Lefferts Vanderbilt, serving as one of the two vice-presidents at the time, pulled together the managers' report. Margaret E. Sangster, known to many by her pen name, "Aunt Marjorie," which she used in her *Christian Intelligencer* column, and a member of the Board of Managers, became the temporary foreign secretary and wrote the foreign secretary's report.

Margaret Sangster's foreign secretary report for 1886 responds directly to the BFM's charge from the year before. She says:

> Insisting that ours is woman's work, far be it from us to interfere with or subtract from the beneficence of the church at large. No annual collection for the Board of Foreign Missions should in any church be smaller, because in that church there exists an Auxiliary Society of the Woman's Board.
>
> Coming with the children's pennies dropped into their little boxes, with the fruits of small house frugalities the larger gifts of unobtrusive love, the Woman's Board lifts no responsibility from the shoulders of men; proposes only in its modest way to assist in the education of its own sex.
>
> The mother with her babe, the forlorn little girl, despised and enslaved from her birth, the maiden with life beckoning her frowningly to narrow drudgery, or idle dreams, each in her place is the object of our care. By the brightness of our homes, we measure the obscurity of theirs, and our endeavor is to bring to our sad-browed sisters, the dawn of a new day.
>
> A delightful part of our work, is in the impulse it gives in the education of our own children. Many of the streams flowing into our treasury are swollen by tiny

---

64. Charlotte Duryee died March 9, 1885, and reference to her extraordinary place among WBFM women both on the home front and in the foreign field is noted in Chamberlain, *Fifty Years,* 43.

65. Charlotte Duryee was extremely beloved by RCA church women, both by women serving in the foreign field and by her many women friends at home. In their memoriam, the WBFM said of Charlotte Duryee:

She was greatly beloved by those with whom she was associated, for she had the rare power of drawing friends towards her with an unusual strength of affection. The missionaries with whom she corresponded looked upon her as a personal friend, and were eager to receive her words of encouragement and cheer. Her judgment could ever be relied upon, and her sympathy was unfailing; this made her a great power for good in the mission work of the church. *ARWBFM,* 1885, 17.

In her honor, the Bible School in Amoy, China, which was begun in 1878, was named the Charlotte W. Duryee Bible School. See Chamberlain, *Fifty Years,* 22-23.

Margaret Sangster

rills from bands of little helpers, and we rejoice in the trend, which the Woman's Board, through its Mission Bands and Circles is giving to a host of youthful lives.

That we may be helpful rather than hindering, we deprecate being anywhere regarded as a substitute for the church itself. Ourselves auxiliary to Synod's Board, we are limited to a single department.

If we have any real sphere, any definite vocation, sphere and vocation are crystalized in one word, *plus*. We are plus the efforts of husbands, fathers, and sons, bringing with them our personal offerings to the treasury of the Lord.[66]

Margaret Sangster articulated a clear statement of where church women recognized themselves to stand in the Reformed Church and in the culture of that time. But she also implied that WBFM women knew clearly where they *needed* to stand to be faithful to their faith, which found expression in their organizational commitments and in the documents of their organizational formation.

For the moment, the issue was brought to conclusion—with Sangster having the last word on behalf of WBFM women. Contributions and income to the WBFM treasury would continue to rise over time, and the mission work of the WBFM continued to expand. The tension caused by the perception of women stepping out of their sphere, however, would remain a continuing issue.

---

66. Italics in original. *ARWBFM*, 1886, 8-9.

Annual reports were constitutionally mandated for the foreign secretary (on behalf of the managers), for the treasurer; and in Article 9 of the by-laws, "Auxiliary societies shall be required to make an annual report to the Managers through the Corresponding Secretaries, on or before the first Tuesday in April."[67] Because the fiscal year of the denomination ran May 1 through April 30 at the time (presumably reflecting its need to report to the General Synod later in the spring), WBFM reporting dates needed to coincide with the BFM schedule to report to the General Synod. Once submitted to the BFM, the WBFM report would be edited and freely abbreviated by the BFM and then appear in its report under the simple title, "The Woman's Board." For its own use, a much more extensive WBFM annual report needed to be written, printed, and prepared for distribution to all WBFM auxiliaries by the second Tuesday in May (the date mandated by the constitution for the official conduct of WBFM business). This timetable appears to have worked well for all concerned.

Issuing an annual WBFM report served several purposes. The report served as a tool for WBFM accountability. It became a kind of balance sheet, which measured the work and documented the progress accomplished during the year. Numbers were reported—the number of new auxiliaries and of new life members, the number of baby roll enrollees for the year and *Mission Gleaner* subscribers, numbers of publications, of letters written, of boxes sent, of miles traveled, and of course numbers and amounts of contributions and legacies received.

The report articulated special needs and projects in the field, and it shared the struggle of the managers to make decisions and to prioritize the work to be undertaken. The annual report clarified where things stood from one year to the next from the perspective of the Board of Managers. It also suggested the future direction of the work and how the managers hoped to achieve success.

WBFM annual reports served a second purpose. They communicated "missionary intelligence." The 1878 *Manual of Missions* provided fundamental information about missions. It was followed over the years by a variety of educational publications, including the WBFM journal, the *Mission Gleaner*. At the center of this missionary intelligence stood the foreign secretary. Each of the fields (China, India, Japan, and, after 1894, Arabia[68]) submitted an annual report to the foreign secretary, and originally these reports were published separately from the WBFM annual report and used as programs for local auxiliary meetings. In 1919 that practice changed. Field reports began to be included in the WBFM annual report, and in 1919 the

---

67. *ARWBFM*, 1875, 19.

68. According to Paul Armerding, "In 1889, the Arabian mission was organized by three New Brunswick Seminary students and a professor. James Cantine sailed from New York to Basra (in present-day Iraq), the mission's first station. In 1894 the independent Arabian mission was put under the administration of the Reformed Church in America's Board of Foreign Missions." Paul Armerding, "A Doctor for the Kingdom," *Church Herald*, December, 2003, p. 11. In 1896, the WBFM assumed support for Amy Zwemer, missionary wife of Samuel Zwemer, one of the three New Brunswick Seminary students who originally organized the mission in 1889. Amy Zwemer was the first missionary wife to serve in Arabia. "Miss Elizabeth DePree, who later became Mrs. James Cantine, was the first unmarried lady-missionary to go to Arabia (1901)." *ARWBFM*, 1919, 35.

"facts and figures" for the years 1874-1919 were included, along with maps for each geographical mission region, to provide a basis for future study. These facts and figures included such things as population, number of Christians, language, climate, etc. for each of the fields. The foreign secretary could be counted on to have her finger on the pulse of immediate missionary activity and missionary intelligence. The report of the foreign secretary, contained in the annual report, served as a trustworthy update of missionary activity. Because the annual report was circulated to all of the auxiliaries,[69] the managers could assume that each year's data and updated missionary intelligence were received safely in the hands and hearts of local auxiliaries. Local auxiliaries could feel a sense of "being there" and "on top of things."

Not only did the WBFM annual report function as an accountability tool and a means to transmit missionary intelligence, but it also served as a family newsletter. Everyone loves to receive a newsy letter from home. Generally speaking, letters from home are comforting. They tend to affirm one's worth and one's place in the family, to generate a sense of belonging. WBFM annual reports functioned in this capacity by making the mission effort the "home" of each auxiliary. Annual reports routinely notified auxiliary members of certain objective data. The names and addresses of the officers and managers began each annual report, along with the names of the honorary vice-presidents and where each one lived. Over time these names became familiar, and they began to take on the feel of family. Names were important, and when a member of this family left office or died, it was so noted in the annual report.

At the beginning of the annual report, members were always provided a quick review of the annual meeting—not dissimilar from being given a rundown of a family reunion. They were told when and where the annual meeting was held, how many attended, who the worship leaders and speakers were, what the texts and topics included, and, of course, appropriate thanks to the women of the local church, who cooked and provided hospitality for the meeting. Providing hospitality for out-of-town meetings, especially, required a great deal of planning and care.

Following the review of the annual meeting appeared the report of the foreign secretary. The foreign secretary reviewed the reports received from each field and the most recent correspondence. Interwoven in each of the field reports were comments, actions taken, and the managers' plans for the future.

Next followed the report of the home secretary, whose job included increasing interest in missions among the women of the church as well as increasing the number of auxiliaries. For the first twenty years of its institutional life, the home secretary's report included all the reports of all the local auxiliaries. From 1875 to 1890, the reports of local auxiliaries were edited by the home secretary. This practice changed in 1890. The home secretary noted:

> In presenting the struggles, hopes and successes of our faithful auxiliaries we have departed a little from the plan heretofore adopted, and instead of telling of their achievements have let them describe their work and their deep interest in it,

---

69. See *ARWBFM*, 1886, 5.

through their own secretaries, making only such unimportant omissions as a proper regard to space would seem to require. In this way individuality is given to our working associations, and our auxiliaries each speaking in its own way, to one common audience upon one common subject come to feel more and more that they are all parts of one great whole, and animated by the same desires they are thus drawn closer together and together enjoy that blessed Communion in Holy things which only God's children can know.

Thus we have gone on, Board and helpers, working together in God's field during the past year, experiencing its joys and feeling its sorrows.[70]

This practice of including all local auxiliary reports, especially using the author's own text, with her name at the end, had a transforming effect on rank-and-file auxiliary members. It gave value to who they were and what they were doing. In these local auxiliary reports, individual church women and their local missionary groups were given names and voices. They were given places in the WBFM family. The fact that someone—anyone—was interested in them and for them in their little corner of the world was for most church women different from anything they had known previously. Beyond a newspaper announcement of marriage or an obituary notice, women's names simply did not find their way into print very often. Seeing their names or their auxiliary's name in print was entirely new for most women. In the annual report, what they were doing was recognized as important, and how they went about their individual yet united tasks of doing the Master's work was meaningful and significant. Clearly, local women and their work were valued, especially by other women, and bonds of friendship among women across the denomination were established and nurtured.

For better or worse, the number of local auxiliary reports grew as the auxiliaries increased in number, which meant that WBFM annual reports became increasingly massive! To solve this problem, it was determined that a new means had to be found for communicating the work of local auxiliaries. The year 1894 became a transition year, and although individual reports from local auxiliaries were included, they were listed by classis. In addition, there was a classis list that included the names of the churches, each auxiliary's name, membership figures and contributions, plus the name of the secretary submitting the information.

In 1895, it was decided that the home secretary's report would change to "the blank system."[71] The blank system eliminated the narrative portion of local reports and listed churches with auxiliaries by classis, with considerable accompanying information. Dates of auxiliary organization were noted, membership figures and contributions for each auxiliary and each church's Sunday school, numbers of subscriptions to the *Mission Gleaner*, and the names and addresses of classical

---

70. *ARWBFM*, 1890, 25.

71. Exactly why it was called "the blank system" is never explained clearly. Presumably it referred to the kind of objective, "fill-in-the-blank" information that the national organization was requesting from local auxiliaries as opposed to subjective, narrative information.

committee members and missionary union officers. This new way of reporting had its good points, for it contained much objective data, which were easy to tabulate and report. It had the effect of sharing information quickly and showing at a glance how individual auxiliaries were doing. But increased growth also meant a change from the good old days of local reporting. Looking back in 1901, the home secretary noted:

> We miss the bright, chatty letters from our Societies and Mission Bands since the inauguration of the Blank System, some even failing to answer the necessary questions upon them. This is a cause of sincere regret, for we covet the messages from our dear home workers who are like children of one family circle.[72]

The blank system did not always gather the same information. It is significant that in 1899, and for this year only, auxiliary secretaries were asked to submit the number of women in their respective congregations. Of course not all auxiliaries complied with this request, perhaps because they did not have this piece of information conveniently at hand, but many auxiliaries did comply. It was the first and only known time that a count of women in each congregation appeared in any record.[73]

In addition to the reports of local auxiliaries, the home secretary included in her report a variety of themes, which appeared on a regular basis. Believing that God hears and answers the cries of God's people, prayer, the lifeline in the life of the entire church, became a passion for church women. In "closet prayer" women prayed alone and in private, but women had also to learn to pray aloud and to pray in public. It was both their individual and their group responsibility to pray and to pray "without ceasing." Church women also were encouraged to pray intelligently. This meant studying and learning about the needs of missionaries and their situations and about the differing cultures of women and children in foreign lands. In the home secretary's report, as in the report of the foreign secretary, prayer needs were made known, and these prayer needs presumed knowledge of the mission work and of the missionaries and their needs. In this way, prayers for the spread of the gospel in foreign lands became personal. By the time of the *Annual Report* in 1900, it could be said:

> A very encouraging feature in many of these Societies is the intelligent study of our Mission work. It is very seldom now that we hear persons asking how long the Scudders have been in China, or the Chamberlains in Japan.[74]

At the annual meeting in 1898, the speaker was Amy Zwemer (Rev. Samuel), missionary wife to Arabia. She spoke on "the why and how" of prayer. In her presentation she explained:

> There are four reasons why we should pray for missions; first, because missions are the fulfillment of Christ's last command, repeated in each of the Gospels,

---

72. *ARWBFM*, 1901, 10.
73. That is, the only record of these figures known to the denominational archivist and the author.
74. *ARWBFM*, 1900, 10.

emphasizing the fact that His redemption was for the *whole* world. Second, because missions prepare the way for Christ's second coming; we all desire that event, let us hasten it. Third, God's word promises the heathen and Mohammedans to Christ, we must win them for Him. Fourth, and greatest, prayer for missions is a personal work given us by Christ, Matt. 9: 37, 38.

How shall we pray? First, study God's Word as to duties, motives, methods and results. Our motive should be the glory of God, the methods and results we may learn in the Acts of the Apostles, and in many places in the Old Testament. Then upon knowledge, use the Prayer Calendar, read the *Gleaner* and *Mission Field*, and look for answers, –they may be published in reports or periodicals. Look to see what God's grace achieves. Third, pray that your missionaries may love the people among whom they labor, repugnant though their lives may be. Ask that God may make His missionaries channels for His love. Pray that your missionaries may work from above, not from beneath, that God's grace may lift them higher and higher. Then, when treasuries are low, and difficulties multiply, be "anxious for nothing," and "the peace of God, which passeth all understanding, shall keep your minds and hearts through Jesus Christ.[75]

For both the home secretary and the foreign secretary, writing in the annual report about the problems of missionary women and the native people with whom they interacted served to acquaint women on the home front with the burdens and hardships of mission life. Life for a married female missionary was especially difficult, inasmuch as she had to bear and to raise children, run a house, and support the work of her husband by investing herself in the work as well. At the WBFM annual meeting in 1900, Sara Couch, a missionary to Japan, spoke about "some of her experiences in mission work, telling of the necessity for being ready for any emergency, and for patience under continual interruptions. No part of a missionary's time can be called her own, Sunday being the hardest day of the week."[76] The same must have been true for married women missionaries as well.

In addition to coping with hardships from natural disasters, missionary women had to cope with family illnesses and the myriad illnesses of those to whom they were ministering. In 1919, the report from India noted:

> Plague, cholera, smallpox, influenza, and famine have ravaged the country, leaving the natives in pitiable condition.
> More pitiable than physical famine is the cry of a soul-hungry people for the

---

75. *ARWBFM*, 1898, 5-6.

76. *ARWBFM*, 1900, 7. Miss Sara M. Couch served as a missionary to Japan 1892-1946 and died in Nagasaki, Japan, January 27, 1946. For more on the life and witness of Sara Couch, see Jennifer Mary Reece, "The Education of Miss Sara Couch: The Preparation of Women for Foreign Missionary Service in the Reformed Church in America in the Late Nineteenth Century," in House and Coakley, *Patterns and Portraits*, 119-40. See also Jennifer Mary Reece, "They Publish Glad Tidings: American Women in Mission and the Evangelical Sisterhood of Letters in the United States and Japan, 1861-1911," Diss., Princeton Theological Seminary, 2002, UMI Microform 3061058; and Ratmeyer, *Hands, Hearts, and Voices*, 22-24.

Bread of Life, and the inability of our depleted missionary band to supply the need.[77]

And for the same year, the report from China read:

> More serious even than the interruption of the work by the ubiquitous Spanish influenza has been the effect of the Civil War in South China. Against their will our Sio-khe and Chiang-chiu missionaries were detained in Amoy and Toa-bo until it was considered safe for them to return to their stations. Schools were late in opening and depleted in numbers and up-country visiting was prohibited. At last account, however, the mission was running normally.[78]

Catastrophic events occurred, and sharing the sorrow of these events with empathetic women on the home front helped to make the pain bearable. The tragic loss of life on the British passenger ship *Lusitania*, which was sunk by the German navy without warning May 7, 1915, was one such event. Among the passengers were Margaret and The Reverend James A. Beattie, RCA missionaries to India. James Beattie was among the 1,198 passengers whose lives were lost. Margaret Beattie survived the tragedy, and, in the fall of 1915, she bravely returned to the mission field, thus inspiring the admiration and prayers of all church women. In *Fifty Years in Foreign Fields*, Mary Chamberlain writes:

> Mrs. Beattie's courage in returning to India was beyond praise. In the autumn of 1915 she sailed for India with the ever present memory of that last voyage on the *Lusitania*. It could not have been easy to face again the perils of the sea, but love for the work in Chittoor where she and her husband had spent twenty-one happy and useful years gave her strength for the ordeal. Even on that voyage the passengers were told to be ready for whatever might happen and more than once life belts were put on and men, women and little children waited not knowing at what moment they might be plunged into the sea. With all lights out, with people talking in whispers, they waited, watching the smooth waters and quieting as best they could their fears. Port Said was reached in safety, however, hearts were lifted in thankfulness to God for deliverance and Mrs. Beattie arrived at last in Chittoor.[79]

A tragic fire and earthquake in Yokohama, Japan, September 1, 1923, claimed the life of Jennie M. Kuyper. Kuyper was a teacher and the principal at Ferris Seminary. Amid the fire, which totally consumed the seminary and almost everything in the surrounding area, Jennie Kuyper died. Her young and dedicated life served as a model of Christian heroism, faith, and sacrifice, and the mourning for her life was felt as

---

77. *ARWBFM*, 1919, 53-54.

78. *ARWBFM*, 1919, 54.

79. Chamberlain, *Fifty Years*, 224. Margaret Beattie continued to serve as a missionary to India for five additional years.

Jennie Kuyper

much in Japan as it was throughout the church on the home front.[80] Ferris Seminary named its new chapel in her memory.

The adverse times noted in the annual report included not only problems of illness and war and catastrophic occurrences. News of the special times in the lives of missionary women, notably the births and deaths of children, was also reported. Giving birth in a foreign land, away from family and medical care, must have been a frightening experience for any woman. Yet, for missionary women, that's just the way it was. Even more difficult was the separation from loved ones when a baby or a young child died.

In 1897, the WBFM initiated a program called the Baby Roll. Anyone or any organization was free to enroll a child in the Baby Roll. By enrolling a child, that child was prayerfully dedicated to continue throughout his/her life the work of mission. Each annual report contained a report from the Baby Roll secretary that stated the number of new enrollees for the year. The program itself was described this way:

> By the payment of twenty-five cents, a child's name is entered and the same amount pledged for four succeeding years, although the entire amount for the

---

80. For a dramatic account of events surrounding the death of Jennie Kuyper, see Chamberlain, *Fifty Years*, 253-54. See also *ARWBFM*, 1924, 36-38. In addition to the death of Jennie Kuyper, the *Annual Report* of 1924 notes that "two very valuable teachers succumbed to illness due to lack of facilities for proper care because of the earthquake, and thirteen girls lost their lives."

Zwemer
family

five years may be paid at the time of enrollment. The card tells its own story—having a picture of Our Blessed Saviour with a group of little ones about Him and His hands resting in tenderness and love upon them. It is our earnest desire that all the baptized children of our Church should become members of this precious circle, that from it a missionary influence may surround the cradle of babyhood and, through a mother's prayers, early taught to send to the Christless ones God's precious truth.[81]

The income produced by the Baby Roll was earmarked for the Children's Home in Amoy, China, and when the program began, the first child enrolled was Amy Katharina Zwemer, who had been dedicated by her parents to the work of the WBFM in Arabia. Little Amy Katharina Zwemer became "the Board's own baby"[82] and held a special place in the hearts and minds of WBFM women.[83]

It was with extreme sorrow that word was received of Amy Katharina's death at seven years of age, and this was compounded by the tragic death of her younger sister Ruth at about the same time. The secretary of the Baby Roll wrote:

Katharina, though only seven years old, was a beautiful little Christian character, the true missionary spirit having been instilled into her from her birth. She was filled with love for her Heavenly Father and His work.

And so the chain is broken; from time to time letters most touching and full of pathos come to me telling of the sorrow that has come to hearts and homes in the loss of a dear little, and mingled with the pleasure I find in this work, comes

---

81. *ARWBFM*, 1898, 10.

82. *ARWBFM*, 1905, 25.

83. In 1945, the last full year of WBFM existence, it was reported that "With Amy Zwemer as its first member more than 21,000 other names have been added to our roll. These names have meant that many dollars have been converted into food, shelter, clothing in consecrated lives. Who can really measure the scope of influence of these dollars throughout the year." *ARWBFM*, 1945, 7.

Left to right: Bessie Zwemer, Francis Marion Thoms, Fred S. Barny, Ruth Zwemer, Katharina Zwemer

many a feeling of sadness, for my heart goes out in loving sympathy to those afflicted ones.[84]

Amy Katharina Zwemer and her younger sister Ruth were only two of the many children of missionaries whose lives were unduly short and whose families were comforted by sympathetic church friends—especially by empathetic women on the home front—after news of their deaths was conveyed by the annual report. The annual report also told about the times when women missionaries experienced loneliness and fatigue, hoping that prayers and letters from the home front would encourage the missionaries to press on. In the *Annual Report* of 1893, it is noted:

> Our dear Mrs. Chamberlain, who has labored so untiringly for many years, has been left alone with the whole burden of the girls' boarding school at Madanapalle resting upon her already over-taxed strength. The money to equip and send out a teacher is now being gathered, and we trust the whole amount will soon be secured.[85]

Two years later, in 1895, we read:

> In Vellore we find Mrs. W. I. Chamberlain, and we hardly know which predominates, our sympathy for her natural homesickness for Chittoor and the heavy burden she takes up alone, with her husband, or our amusement at the cheery, clever descriptions of her attempts to fill the places of "Mrs. Jared and Mrs. John." We feel sure that, as far as one woman can do the work of two, or rather, four, she will do it.[86]

---

84. *ARWBFM*, 1905, 25-26.
85. *ARWBFM*, 1893, 23.
86. *ARWBFM*, 1895, 19. "Mrs. Jared" is Julia Goodwin Scudder (1832-1913), who served in India from 1855 until her death in 1913. "Mrs. John" is Sophia Weld Scudder (1838-1925), who served in India from 1861 until her death in 1925.

Such lives of dedicated service couldn't help but inspire and raise to extreme heights the admiration of the folks on the home front. Missionaries became heroes and heroines. Everyone at home waited to meet the missionaries who were home on furlough and to learn the latest news of the work in the field. Furloughs for missionaries, which were intended for rest and renewal, often became traveling and speaking marathons. Conferences, mission festivals, classical union meetings, church services, Sunday school gatherings—church members waited to greet their heroes and heroines. The *Annual Report* in 1900 noted:

> ...We would also very gratefully acknowledge the loving services of our Missionaries who are now with us, and who are going about constantly, for there are earnest pleadings from our Societies that they may have a real live Missionary visit them. There is an inspiration from the real face, and living voice that is very helpful, but there is a limit to the endurance of these willing Missionaries, whose strength must not be over-taxed, for the home coming must be a time of rest, that they may return to their stations with renewed health and vigor for the years of service before them.[87]

And in the 1902 *Annual Report* it was noted:

> The question often arises how much can be expected from our missionaries on their return home. It is a very natural desire for those who have been following them through their letters to meet them personally.
>
> In a pastor's home where a missionary was visiting for the first time, and where our workers are remembered in the morning and evening prayer, a little four-year old boy asked "Mamma, is he a real live missionary?" We of older years are not far in advance of the child for there is nothing that tells in its influence so much as looking into the faces and hearing the voices of those fresh from the battle-fields.[88]

Annual reports shared news of the good times as well as the hard times. With publication of a missionary birthday calendar, the lives of the missionaries were remembered and celebrated. Anniversary celebrations of faithfulness in service to the cause of missions were recognized and celebrated. For example:

> Miss Moulton has celebrated the 30th anniversary of her arrival in Japan and Miss Lansing and Miss Couch have passed their 25th year. "Enlisted for the period of the war" should be the honor chevron of these veteran missionary soldiers. We congratulate them, ourselves, and the Mission upon their long and valiant service.[89]

---

87. *ARWBFM*, 1900, 15.
88. *ARWBFM*, 1902, 15.
89. *ARWBFM*, 1919, 54-55.

Anniversaries of organizations were times of celebration and remembrance. These celebrations often called for special gatherings of the WBFM family and the whole church and for undertaking special projects or a new work in thanksgiving for the years of God's blessing and care. Reflections and histories were often written for such occasions, as these special times served to mark the stages or chapters in their organizational lives. Jubilee celebrations were particularly celebrated, such as the WBFM Jubilee year in 1925. The Jubilee Planning Committee identified four objectives that the celebration sought to achieve. These included:

> the enlargement of our missionary forces in the field, the improvement of our equipment through gifts to the Jubilee fund, the augmenting of our working forces at the home base by addition of new members and new societies, the increase of power through increase of prayer.[90]

The purpose of the celebration was clearly defined:

> In this lies our hope of achieving our high purpose that, through the observance of this hallowed year, "there may come to our whole Reformed Church a mighty spiritual uplift, which shall be felt in every congregation and in every home."[91]

To gain a sense of the magnitude of the board's Jubilee celebration in 1925, the *Annual Report* of 1924[92] noted:

> The first public offering for our Golden Jubilee was the Birthday Gift of $4,615.58 in memory of Miss Kuyper, to be applied to a residence for unmarried women missionaries in Japan. The total amount received for the Jubilee offering to May 1, 1924, is $25,816.66, more than half of which was contributed by the Members and Life Members of the Board before the public announcement of the financial goal. A detailed report of the Jubilee Fund will be published at the close of the campaign.
>
> ...And what more shall we say of the Jubilee? We cannot reduce the spirit of a movement to numerical figures; yet numbers are not without significance. Five hundred churches are co-operating through 527 Women's Societies, 112 Young Women's Societies, 50 Children's Societies and 196 Bible Schools. By the middle of May, 28 Jubilee Rallies will have been held in 26 Eastern Classes and 21 in the West under the direction of Mrs. Wayer and Mrs. Pietenpol, Vice-Presidents for

---

90. *ARWBFM*, 1923, 60.
91. *ARWBFM*, 1924, 57.
92. There is no confusion in these dates. As the *Annual Report* of 1924 explained, "We remind ourselves that the first Annual Meeting of the Board was held in the month of May following its organization in January, 1875, so that our Fiftieth Annual Meeting and our Fiftieth Anniversary antedate by several months our actual uncompleted fifty years, but of a part of the 49th and a part of the 50th year, we dismiss the temptation to reminiscence and 'invite your attention' to the story of the year now closing. For convenience we shall call it our Fiftieth Year." *ARWBFM*, 1924, 57.

the Synods of Chicago and Iowa.
We have distributed:
26,500 Intercession Folders
16,500 Children's Prayer Cards
10,000 Why you Should Belong to the Missionary Society
15,000 What Your Jubilee Dollars will Do
3,500 Historical Sketches
900 Programs
4,500 Pledge Slips
3,600 Coupon Books
12,000 Children's Dime Cards
10,000 Mite Boxes, with orders on hand for 2,000 more.
The Golden Jubilee posters and the "Pity Little Children" posters have been sent to all known Societies.[93]

Retirements and departures from the mission field and from staff positions, like anniversaries, were times of celebration and remembrance. Most often these occasions celebrated long years of service.[94] Whether the retirement was from the position of honorary vice-president, from the Board of Managers, from a classical committee, or from the field, these changes in individual lives were noted in the annual report with expressions of affection and thanksgiving.

Reporting the celebrations of birthdays, anniversaries, and retirements in the annual report was also accompanied by reporting the celebrations of life at the time of death. The loss of WBFM family members and friends brought a special sense of sorrow among church women. Over many years of working together, the proverb that "many hands make light work"[95] generally proved to be true among WBFM women. By working and praying together, these women together experienced times of weeping and times of laughter. WBFM women grew to develop exceedingly strong bonds of friendship that weathered times of adversity as well as times of celebration. Because the women worked at what was perceived to be a "sacred cause," it's not surprising that friendships among all church women became known as "holy bonds of

---

93. *ARWBFM*, 1924, 62-63.

94. Such was the suggestion in this notice: "Peculiarly tragic circumstances surrounded the death of Miss Dora Eringa of the Japan Mission. After *only* thirteen years of faithful, effective work, with the promise of many years of faithful service before her, she was forced by ill health to return to America in October, 1935, and died of pneumonia on February 11th, 1936." *ARWBFM*, 1936, 4. Author's emphasis.

95. A variant of this proverb is, "By the hands of many a great work is made light." According to Wolfgang Mieder, Stewart A. Kingsbury, and Kelsie B. Harder, eds., in *A Dictionary of American Proverbs* (New York: Oxford Univ. Press, 1992), 276, this proverb was first cited ca. 1330 in *Sir Beyes*, Early English Text Society (1885). Twentieth-century citations include *The Concise Oxford Dictionary of Proverbs*, 146; *Early American Proverbs and Proverbial Phrases*, 169; *The Oxford Dictionary of English Proverbs*, 509; *The Macmillan (Home Book of Proverbs, Maxims and Familiar Phrases)*, 1060:11; *A Dictionary of American Proverbs and Proverbial Phrases*, 169; and *Modern Proverbs and Proverbial Sayings*, 283.

Helen (Mrs. Leonard) Kip and Charlotte (Mrs. Jacob) Chamberlain

friendship."[96] Nothing could restrain the affection and feelings of loss reported in the notices of dear friends who died. Endearing insight into a departed friend's life was often provided, such as, "She carried the world upon her heart and burned out in service."[97] In another instance, a long farewell remembrance ended:

> Later we learned that she had been occupied in the work of her Master literally until He came, for though suffering acutely and knowing that the time of her departure was at hand, she spent her last hours preparing a program for use in the Missionary Meeting to be held that afternoon. Hers was an unpretentious but effective life.[98]

Friends whose names had become familiar over the years were mourned throughout the church, but especially by church women. Among the recurring themes in annual reports were references to the past, suggesting that WBFM members needed to

---

96. In her presentation at the Columbian Exposition in 1893, Ellen C. Parsons spoke about the sacred bonds of friendship. In an address, "History of Woman's Organized Missionary Work as Promoted by American Women," she said:

The history of this woman's missionary movement is a history of holy fellowship that was impossible in the ancient world. It overlooks denominational boundaries; the active missionary spirits in different branches of the church are those who are closest together in Christian sympathy. No ocean can affect this tie. A British sister has but to step into one of our Mission Rooms and inquire for a leaflet, or bring a message into our meetings, and we recognize at once the bond of fellowship in a sacred cause.

In Wherry, *Women in Missions*, 85.

97. This particular description was given to Mrs. Isaac W. Gowen, who served "as a member of the Board for twenty-five years—a quarter-century of signal devotion to the work of Missions in the Board, in the Classes that she has served as Classical Committee, in her own church and in the Church at large."*ARWBFM*, 1922, 53.

98. This particular remembrance referred to Mrs. Philip Van Alstine, who for twenty-four years served on the Board of Managers, five years as vice-president, and for twenty-five years on the classical committee for the Classis of Paramus.

remember their own history. Their indebtedness to the founders of the WBFM was a continuing refrain. In the 1886 *Annual Report*, it was noted:

> As, in the retrospect we linger for a moment and recall that cold dreary, stormy morning in Jan. 1875, when a little company of twelve "entered earnestly upon the work," new, and all untried before them; when the Woman's Board of Foreign Missions of the Reformed Church was fully organized, and prepared for the cultivation of the wide field, that only waited for the hand of the sower; and contrast this, with the harvest the "great husbandman" has permitted us to gather, our own hearts are led to rejoice in the blessings and success attending the work undertaken for love of Him, whose we are and whom we serve.[99]

And again, in the *Annual Report* of 1902:

> More keenly than we are aware are we indebted to those "elect women," who, in the early years of the Board, were blessed with a prescience to know "when to take occasion by the hand," and to quickly fall in line with the Divine timeliness as to the next thing to be done. The increase of the years is due to the wealth of prayer and gifts; gifts of time and thought, the labor of head, heart and hand; and the record of the treasury proves that a noble army of givers have "their treasured store," found "no offering too costly or sweet to lay at the Master's feet."
>
> This beautiful mosaic of thirty years is made up of the devotedness of every Christian woman "who hath done what she could" to make it "the perfect plan that the Master meant."
>
> Whenever we make a grateful review it should mean instant commitment to a better future.[100]

WBFM women were very aware of themselves in time. They took great care to remember and to leave written records of what was important to them. By keeping careful records, by systematic communication, and by using the occasions of anniversary celebrations, the women of the WBFM used the work of their lives to inspire future generations of women.

---

99. *ARWBFM*, 1886, 19.
100. *ARWBFM*, 1904, 9-10.

Chapter 6

Beyond the Foundational Documents

> We believe there have been holy-hearted Hannahs who have dedicated their children to God as they have given their names to be enrolled with the prayer, "As long as he liveth he shall be lent to the Lord." The Lord never breaks His covenant with those who fulfill their covenant with Him.
>
> Report of Mrs. Hamilton V. Meeks
> Secretary of the Baby Roll
> *ARWBFM*, 1901, 11

The preceding chapters make clear that the Woman's Board of Foreign Missions was no ordinary church board. The commitment and passion of its members on behalf of women and children in foreign lands created a new kind of energy. Contributing to the generation of this energy were forces not explicitly defined in the foundational documents. These forces include communication, education, ecumenism, and volunteering. How these four forces contributed to the energy of the board will be the subject of this chapter.

Communication

For the first eighteen years of its existence, the business and work of the WBFM took place in rooms provided by the Marble Collegiate Church consistory.[1] Since

---

1. *ARWBFM*, 1892, 26-27. Although the Collegiate churches are yoked by a single collegiate consistory, each collegiate church has a local consistory as well.

almost all the work of communication at that time was done by hand, these rooms must have been a beehive of activity, with many women volunteers present to provide the necessary manual labor for accomplishing the tasks presented. Enjoying the company of one another as they worked, gathering as a group to make important decisions, and coming together to pray and to study, these rooms became especially significant to WBFM women. Here "the chosen"[2] pioneer women began their work. Here historic beginnings took place, and over time, these rooms—this physical space—assumed a sense of the sacred.[3]

In 1882, when the denomination purchased its own "Reformed Church Building," located at 25 East 22nd Street, the Board of Direction allotted space in that facility for the operations of the WBFM. While the women were excited to occupy their own space for the first time, the event was bittersweet with the pang of leaving their rooms at Marble Collegiate Church. The *Annual Report* of 1892 recorded:

> It was through the kindness and courtesy of the Consistory of that Church that we remained there so long, and we are deeply sensible of the favor conferred upon us. In that dear Church our Board first had its beginning, and precious memories come echoing to us from out the past. There earnest women prayed and consulted together as to the best interests of the sacred work committed to their care. There too, have been vacant seats, and bitter tears shed for the faces that we still miss from the chosen thirty. From those hallowed associations we cannot part without feelings of sincere regret.[4]

What became known simply as "Room 10" became "home center"[5] to the WBFM. It would remain so until May 10, 1939, when a fire of unknown origin destroyed the building and forced all church offices to move to 156 Fifth Avenue.[6]

---

2. *ARWBFM*, 1892, 26.

3. As students at New Brunswick Seminary, James Cantine (NBTS 1890), Samuel Zwemer (NBTS 1890), Philip T. Phelps (NBTS 1889), and others would be joined by Professor John G. Lansing (NBTS 1884-1898) on the fourth floor of Hertzog Hall to study, to pray, and to scheme about establishing a mission to the Arab world. The small apartment under the cupola where they met was affectionately referred to as "Abraham's Bosom," and this apartment came to be understood as sacred space. When Hertzog Hall was demolished in 1968, the loss of this sacred space was felt keenly among the alumni/ae of the seminary, and it is remembered by many yet today. See Robert L. Gram, "An Original Play: in celebration of the Bicentennial of New Brunswick Theological Seminary," [1984] New Brunswick Theological Seminary Archives, Gardner A. Sage Library, New Brunswick, New Jersey.

4. *ARWBFM*, 1892, 26-27.

5. *ARWBRM*, 1892, 26.

6. The building located at 156 Fifth Avenue was owned by the Presbyterian Church, USA. Immediately after the fire, the Presbyterian boards of foreign and national missions "very generously offered space sufficient for temporary quarters for this Board [all boards and offices], without rental charge, until a new headquarters could be found." Report of the Board of Education, *MGS*, 1939, 24. See also pp. 14-15. Arrangements were made to remain permanently in this location until after the Interchurch Center at 475 Riverside Drive was built (1957-1959), where all church offices were subsequently moved and denominational offices remain today.

About ten years after the fire, the Reformed Church Building at 25 East 22nd Street was remembered as "an old-fashioned mansion with three or four floors connected by a rather antiquated

The women were quick to turn Room 10 into their own distinctive space. In keeping with their commitment as trustees "that every penny dropped into the missionary box"[7] should be spent only in the cause of missions, decorating their new quarters became a matter of "family liberality."[8] According to the 1893 treasurer's report, board members and friends contributed $275 toward room furnishings. The treasurer's report also noted that the paid expenses for Room 10 furnishings totaled $276.07. Carpeting, shades, a desk, chairs, a lounge, a clock, and other sundry items were purchased.[9] Curios, costumes, and items of educational interest that were brought back from the mission field were displayed, thus giving the space a distinctive Victorian look.[10]

Moving into space of their own suggested permanence.[11] This was underscored by announcing that "the rooms are always open from 10 a.m. to 3 p.m., except Saturday, and a cordial welcome is extended to all."[12] A commitment to regular business hours implied permanence. It also meant that someone had always to be present during these hours. At the time of the move, Mary Cushing served as home corresponding secretary, a position she held for eighteen years (1888-1902). Mary Cushing oversaw the room with quiet grace. At the time of her death in 1902, the board remembered her this way:

> From the time that Room 10 was opened in the Reformed Church Building, it became the centre [sic] of the Board's activities and influence, and a rallying point for its friends. It witnessed alike the tireless energy born of love, with which she pursued her work, as well as the gracious manner, kindly welcome, thoughtful sympathy, and Christian courtesy which made it attractive to members of the Board, to all our missionaries, and to multitudes of friends throughout the church.[13]

---

elevator and difficult stairways." RCA Archives, "Report of the Special Committee for Church Headquarters and the Federal Council of Churches General Synod 1948 in RCA Archives," in folder 1 of 3 titled "RCA—History of Controversies—Relationship of RCA with the Federal Council of Churches, National and World Councils."

7. *ARWBFM*, 1875, 6.

8. *ARWBFM*, 1893, 26.

9. *ARWBFM*, 1893, 26.

10. One could surmise that eventually the room would become congested with objects, and that is exactly what happened. In the 1914 *ARWBFM* it was noted, "To relieve the congested state of Room Ten a friend provided a capacious rack for our leaflets. The rack is a great convenience, but the congestion, alas! Remains. Our defective housekeeping, however, has not prevented our exercising the grace of hospitality." *ARWBFM*, 1914, 18.

11. Articles of Incorporation, which were signed January 30, 1892, also contributed to this sense of permanence. As noted in the 1892 *Annual Report*, "Among the changes that have come to us as a Board, not the least in importance is the adoption of a Constitution, whereby we are enabled to receive and hold all money bequeathed to us for the advancement of the Redeemer's Kingdom in heathen lands." *ARWBFM*, 1892, 26.

12. *ARWBFM*, 1893, 26.

13. *ARWBFM*, 1903, 17-18. Nothing yet has been written on the life of Mary Cushing (Mrs. A. Loring Cushing). Her service as home corresponding secretary extended from 1888 to 1902, and her tireless work on behalf of the WBFM is revealed in the annual reports she penned.

Room 10

Following the death of Mary Cushing, Olivia Lawrence[14] became home secretary, and in 1903 the board installed Anna Fosdick Bacon[15] as "Room 10 assistant," a position she held for three years. In 1907, the board established the position of room

---

14. Nothing has yet been written on the life of Olivia Lawrence. At the time of her death, the following obituary appeared in the BFM Report to General Synod:

With the death of Miss Olivia H. Lawrence on November 21, 1942, another old friend long identified with the missionary work of our Church was lost from our circle.

Miss Lawrence became a member of the Woman's Board of Foreign Missions in 1895. She served as Chairman of various Field Committees of that Board and in 1903 became the Corresponding Secretary. She continued in that capacity until 1917 and then became Editorial And Educational Secretary, serving the Woman's Board actively until 1933. At that time she retired and was elected as an Honorary Secretary, a title which she held up to the time of her death.

Miss Lawrence had one deep, absorbing passion, the work of the Church in foreign lands, and she devoted all her rich talents to the development of that work. She visited all the fields of the Board in 1906-7 and so became an able interpreter of the enterprise to the church constituency at home. Her pungent, inspiring speeches and articles will not soon be forgotten. *ARWBFM*, 1943, 8.

15. Anna Fosdick Bacon, her brother, her sister, and her parents, Mr. and Mrs. Francis Bacon, were involved members at the Bronxville, New York, Reformed Church. Mrs. Bacon was among the charter members of the Bronxville Auxiliary and served as secretary. Francis Bacon served the congregation for twenty-nine years as deacon and elder and died October 9, 1873. Mrs. Harry Leslie Walker and LaMont A. Warner, eds., *A History of the Reformed Church of Bronxville in Commemoration of its Centenary November 5, 1950* (Bronxville, N.Y.: Published by the Consistory, 1951), 34, 80-92.

Among the essays in the WBFM's *The Story of the Seventh Decade 1935-1945* (New York: Woman's Board of Foreign Missions, 1945), appears Ella Dutcher Romig's essay, "The Seventh Decade in the Home Base." In it she has this to say about Anna Fosdick Bacon:

A financial report of the Board cannot be given without reference to the late Miss Anna F. Bacon, who served the work so unselfishly in three capacities, first as Secretary, 1903-06, then as Assistant Treasurer, 1916-26, and finally as Treasurer, 1926-38. The record of gifts since her death reflects the faithfulness with which she carried on through the 35 years of her membership on the Board. In a beautiful memorial tribute to Miss Bacon, Miss Eliza P. Cobb said, "Statistics were not mere figures on a balance sheet to Miss Bacon, but living people and the institutions where they learned to walk in the steps of the Master. She was faithful in the tasks He assigned to her as her share in God's universal plan." Many will remember the expression of joy on her face when she could report that the annual budget had been met. She took no credit to herself, but always rejoiced in "What God hath wrought" (72-73).

Mary Cushing

secretary, and Eliza Polhamus Cobb assumed that position and remained the room secretary until 1916.[16]

By May 1, 1892, the WBFM included 364 auxiliaries. Acknowledging the need for local auxiliaries to meet and receive encouragement from someone representing the "home front," the Board of Managers in 1892 invited Olivia Lawrence to be its representative to travel and visit local auxiliaries and classes. At the end of her first year, the 1893 *Annual Report* noted:

> The year's experience has shown the wisdom of personal contact with our auxiliary societies. Miss Lawrence has visited many of our churches, attended 69 meetings,

---

16. Although the editor of the *Mission Gleaner* was the first WBFM woman to receive a salary ($100 annually), the move to Room 10 in 1892 brought about the employment of the home secretary. From 1893 through 1902, the year of her death, home secretary Mary Cushing received an annual salary of $600 (inflated to $12,000 in 2002 dollars). This salary jumped to $1,600 (inflated to $32,000 in 2002 dollars) in 1904, when Olivia Lawrence became home secretary and Anna F. Bacon became Room 10 assistant. Following Anna Bacon's resignation from this position in 1906, the position of room secretary was created in 1907, and by 1909 all WBFM salaries were accounted in the total amount of $2,000.02. (Yes, that is the exact amount appearing in the treasurer's report! -or inflated to $40,000.40 in 2002 dollars.)

The question of WBFM salaries and expenses was discussed in the *Mission Gleaner*:

There is a question so frequently asked, that it seems best to answer it here.

"What are the expenses of the Woman's Boards, and does it pay to print literature, to send out speakers and to carry on organizations distinct from Synod's Board?

We can of course, answer only for The Woman's Board of Foreign Missions. As to the expense of home administration. Any one can satisfy herself by looking at the annual report, where every dollar received, and every dollar spent, with every separate item, is plainly given.

We think that few business enterprises, involving such wide extent of territory to be looked after, such numerous branches and collection of littles [sic], can make as economical showing. Every expense in carrying on office work is carefully considered. Salaried work is extremely small, and much of the labor given is entirely gratuitous. Our speakers and representatives, in journeyings [sic] many, through heat and cold, sunshine or storm, receive naught for service save the joy of serving, and are cheerfully ready to meet all requests. Some refuse even their traveling expenses. *Mission Gleaner*, XIV, no. 2 (March-April 1897), 11.

and traveled 4,510 miles. Often the distances have been long and tedious, but, "In His Name," she has gladly gone forth to tell of the work and its pressing needs. Several other young ladies have also rendered this loving service, and all have been warmly welcomed by our societies. To these dear Home Missionaries we would record our grateful acknowledgements.[17]

Olivia Lawrence continued to travel on behalf of the WBFM. In 1903 she replaced Mary Cushing as home secretary and held the position for fourteen years.

Room 10 seemed to serve as an elixir to those who volunteered[18] and those who visited Room 10. This sense of excitement resonated in the report of the home secretary, which appeared in the *Annual Report* of 1910:

> To the casual visitor Room Ten is the mere workshop of the Woman's Board where the drudge-work of missions is done, but to those who share its secrets Room Ten is "full of a number of (pleasant) things." Here
> "Every day brings a ship,
>   Every ship brings a word,"
> a message of progress and encouragement from some auxiliary, a call for sympathy and help, an opportunity for service. And daily the ships go out again with their message of response in letters of suggestion or helpful literature.[19]

To the delight of all, Room 10 was a welcoming place—a place where hospitality was practiced. As Eliza Cobb, the room secretary, wrote in the *Annual Report* of 1912:

> While intent on distributing to the necessity of the saints, we are not unmindful of St. Paul's further injunction to be "given to hospitality." Room Ten is the Social Center of our Board life and its doors are wide open to all on missionary interest intent.[20]

Room 10 became "the common meeting ground for missionaries,"[21] both returning and departing missionaries and for the workers at home as well. When missionaries returned, "home-coming ones have been joyfully welcomed and given the freedom of our room. Old friends and new acquaintances have alike entered its open door,

---

17. *ARWBFM*, 1893, 24.

18. According to the third edition of *America's History,* "Contemporary beliefs about womanhood largely determined which women entered the work force and how they were treated when they became wage earners.... Wives were not supposed to hold jobs. In 1890 fewer than 5 percent of married white women worked outside the home. Black married women had a much higher labor participation rate of over 30 percent. Except in affluent families, young women generally worked until they married." James A. Henreeta, W. Elliot Brownlee, David Brody, Susan Ware, and Marilynn S. Johnson, *America's History,* 3rd ed. (New York: Worth, 1997), 568.

19. *ARWBFM*, 1910, 18.

20. *ARWBFM*, 1912, 18.

21. *ARWBFM*, 1917, 12.

and we trust none sent empty away."[22] When it came time for missionaries to depart and to face the unknowns of overseas travel and begin or resume their lives in a foreign land, a last visit to Room 10 meant a farewell embrace from women on the home front and farewell prayers for safe travel. One such farewell was recorded in the 1893 *Annual Report*:

> Miss Thompson from Yokohama, Miss Harris, returning with three managers of the "Woman's Foreign Board," met in Room 10 of our "Church Building" for a few words before parting. As the time came to separate, they knelt, a little company—six women and the Lord—while the travelers were tenderly committed to His keeping.[23]

This kind of affirmation and sense of closeness caused the home secretary in 1901 to exclaim:

> Room 10 has been more than usual the meeting place between our home workers and our missionaries who are in this country on furlough. The greetings have been warm and tender as these tired servants return after an absence of five or seven years. Here, too, we bid God-speed to those who go forth to their distant stations. Each year makes the home of our Board more real and precious, and the friends who frequent it often exclaim, "How did we ever get along without it!"[24]

Room 10 became used as a "house of prayer." Beginning in 1893, members of the executive committees of both WBFM and WBDM gathered for prayer on the second Tuesday of each month. "The numbers gathered have ranged from twenty to fifty or more, while the personnel has varied greatly, as one or another from distant Churches or Auxiliaries have dropped in to meet, 'around one common mercy seat.'"[25] Weekly Thursday noon prayer meetings were also held to which all in the office and in the area were invited.[26] Busy schedules aside, taking one-half hour[27] to pray each Thursday noon was recognized to be both essential and vital.

In order to share the prayer life of Room 10 with members near and far, the women began publication in 1895 of a missionary prayer calendar. The calendar contained "the names of all our missionaries, where stationed, and an appropriate Scripture selection for every week. As we reverently turn the leaves each month and the names of our devoted workers come before us, we seem to hear their oft-repeated words,

---

22. *ARWBFM*, 1905, 14.
23. *ARWBFM*, 1983, 24.
24. *ARWBFM*, 1901, 10.
25. *ARWBFM*, 1894, 21.
26. These represent the regularly scheduled prayer times in the early years of the WBFM in Room 10. They would not always remain the same.
27. *ARWBFM*, 1908, 11.

'Oh, pray for us.'" Because of the impulse to add to the mission coffers, prayer calendars were routinely sold. In the first year of publication, it was reported:

> The Missionary Prayer Calendar that was prepared for the New Year found a ready sale. Out of the one thousand copies published but few remain. Not only has the expense been met, but Fifty dollars in excess has already been paid into the Treasury.[28]

At the time the WBFM moved into Room 10 in 1892, its work continued to focus on increasing the number of auxiliaries and bands, nurturing existing organizations and building relationships, both human and financial, with women missionaries. In a day and age of radical changes in technology, the WBFM in 1892 was about to be affected by two communication technologies in particular—the invention and availability of the typewriter and the telephone.

It is doubtful that typewriters were in use at the time of the move to Room 10. Originally invented by Franz X. Wagner and purchased and manufactured by John T. Underwood, the Underwood No. 1 typewriter was the first typewriter to use a front-strike mechanism. This mechanism made writing fully visible, and, using this technology, the Underwood No. 1 typewriter began to be manufactured in 1897.[29]

With this in mind, it is interesting to note in the 1898 *Annual Report*:

> It has been a busy year, too, at our office; hundreds of calls have been received from our workers desiring information in regard to some special work in which they were interested, or seeking counsel as to the best methods of conducting the meetings of their Societies, and no week has passed without some member of the Board being sent to speak to our Auxiliaries. Over two thousand letters have been received, and many more sent out, four thousand eight hundred circular letters scattered among our Churches, four thousand five hundred Catechisms given and nineteen thousand copies of "The Mission Gleaner" mailed; besides this our leaflets have been distributed with a liberal hand. These are but a few of the details that come into the daily round of our work.[30]

The arrival of the telephone marked a similar kind of paradigm change in communication. Although Alexander Graham Bell received a patent for the telephone in 1876, his Bell Company controlled only 240,000 telephones in 1892. It took time to install telephone poles across the country, and it was January 25, 1915, before the first transcontinental telephone line opened between New York City and San Francisco.[31]

---

28. *ARWBFM*, 1895, 10.

29. Information on the Underwood No. 1 typewriter was obtained from http://www.sciencemuseum.org.uk/online/typewriters/page2.asp.

30. *ARWBFM*, 1898, 7-8.

31. This information comes from Tom Farley at http://www.privateline.com/TehephoneHistory2A/Telehistory2A.htm and http://www.privateline.com/TelephoneHistory2/History2.html.

For the women of the WBFM, it appears that telephones were installed in Room 10, and presumably the entire Reformed Church Building at 22nd Street, in 1910.[32] In the 1910 *Annual Report,* reference is made to Room 10 this way:

> From Room Ten the *Mission Gleaner* is distributed to its 3500 subscribers. This involves much clerical work and the expenditure of much time in ways that seem at sight unprofitable; but when the details of the work seem petty we think of the infinite issues with which they are fraught and Room Ten becomes to our vision a great distributing center, a sort of central switch-board by which the essential connections are made for local and long-distance wires and communication established between the workers at home and the workers abroad.[33]

And then:

> It was good to hear a voice through the telephone recently: "This is Mrs._____ of Milwaukee. I am sailing for Europe to-morrow and I promised our ladies that I would stop in at the Church House and see you at your work."[34]

As technology expanded, the needs and demands for information from Room 10 continued to grow. By 1908, ten years after the move to Room 10, WBFM women referred to Room 10 as a "bureau of information." The 1908 *Annual Report* notes:

> Room Ten is becoming more and more a bureau of information and suggestion, its manifold activities, mentioned in full would give the gamut of the year's missionary story. There have been more calls, and a larger number of requests for helps, and more literature sent out than in any previous year. The "seemingly trivial details are fraught with infinite issues" in the growth of the work with a proportionately wider and more diversified influence. Three hundred packages of literature, exclusive of the bundles for each conference, have been sent out; two hundred and twenty-seven library books have been in circulation, and the Corresponding Secretary has written two thousand letters.[35]

---

32. This is one year after Pennsylvania Station was built in New York City (1910). Grand Central Station in New York City was completed in 1913.

33. *ARWBFM*, 1910, 19.

34. Ibid. In addition to the typewriter and telephone, the proliferation in new technology made possible photographic advances including the use of moving pictures. Adapting this technology to its own purposes, it is interesting to note in the 1908 *Annual Report*:

> Three unusually pleasant events mark the year. An enjoyable evening at the home of Mr. And Mrs. E. E. Olcott, when we had the pleasure of seeing the moving pictures illustrating missionary work. *ARWBFM*, 1908, 12.

> Kate Olcott (Mrs. Eben E.) served in many WBFM capacities and in 1908 was serving as foreign corresponding secretary for Arabia.

35. *ARWBFM*, 1908, 11.

Two additional WBFM services that were made possible by the move to Room 10 included the availability of a circulating library and a costume department. The circulating library contained books on missions—books that probably were unavailable in public libraries—if indeed there was a public library available in your locale at that time. These books on missions were borrowed by local auxiliaries and often used to provide missionary intelligence for programs and meetings. The number of books must have been sufficiently large to warrant a card catalogue, which was made in 1918,[36] although in 1917 the *Annual Report* notes:

> Probably owing to the increasing number of public libraries all through the country, there are fewer calls for the books in the Circulating Library.[37]

Communicating a sense of what missionary life was like often occurred through the use of pageants and plays, which were used in auxiliary programs and classical meetings. In the early years of the twentieth century, pageants and plays were often used in anniversary celebrations to communicate the story of an organization's history. Sometimes the plays were large with many actors and actresses, as in the denomination's tercentenary anniversary celebration in 1928.[38]

---

36. *ARWBFM*, 1918, 18.

37. *ARWBFM*, 1917, 12.

38. The following was noted in Edgar Franklin Romig, *The Tercentenary Year: A Record of the Celebration of the Three Hundredth Anniversary of the Founding of the First Church in New Netherland, Now New York, and the Beginning of Organized Religious Life Under the Reformed (Dutch) Church in America Held under the Auspices of the General Synod, R.C.A., A.D. 1928* (New York: Published by the RCA, 1929), 96:

> The producing of a pageant was regarded as an essential of a successful Tercentenary from the beginning. Indeed, there were some, in those early months when all plans were more or less nebulous, who thought of the Tercentenary quite in terms of drama. But the first efforts to make this enthusiasm fruitful were not encouraging. Requests in the *Intelligencer* for "pageants, masques, tableaux, etc.," glorifying the history of the Church, brought no result. It became clear that whatever was to originate in the way of pageantry must be "made to order."

> Observation of the 300th anniversary of the RCA consisted of a number of events and undertakings spearheaded by the women. A Women's Tercentenary Committee of two hundred women, chaired by Louise Chambers Knox (Mr. De Witt), president of the WBFM, oversaw the pageant which dramatized three centuries of RCA history. Ella Dutcher Romig (Rev. Edgar F.) served as pageant chairman and took charge of the approximately 650 RCA actors and actresses who took part in the one-time presentation of the pageant on Friday, May 4, 1928, at the Mecca Temple on West 55th Street in New York City. The Mecca Temple was a new building, and the only building available to seat an audience as large as 3,900. The pageant took approximately three hours to present. It is interesting to note that "the cost of the production was great" (121). [Later figures have proved that it was entirely self-financing, and indeed netted a small profit, which was given to the Ministerial Pension Fund.]. Once again the women came through with a profit!

> Also contributing to the celebration was a unique project undertaken by the Women's Tercentenary Committee. Sensing and celebrating a tremendous connection to their seventeenth-century Dutch past, the committee researched and prepared a book of the Dutch lineal descendants for all committee members and used this genealogical information as the basis for honoring "The Goede Vrouw of Manahata" [the Good Wives of Manhattan] at a women's tercentenary luncheon April 14, 1928. Nearly seven hundred guests attended the luncheon, which took place

In support of this use of the arts, the 1912 *Annual Report* noted:

> One interesting development of the Jubilee is the popularity of impersonations and representations in costumes to give novelty to the missionary program. Room Ten's wardrobe has been largely drawn upon not only by our own constituents but by other denominations, resulting in a considerable addition to our costume fund. We would recommend to the Costume Committee a thorough over hauling of the supply before fall and the purchase of new costumes to replace those rendered unpresentable by constant use.[39]

Communication and the volume of business emanating from Room 10 continued to grow over the years. In the *Annual Report* of 1939, the last year a separate *WBFM Annual Report* was published, this review of the work was recorded:

> Every morning's mail brings in a multitude of letters; each letter is a strand joining us with loyal women carrying the burden of eight hundred missionary societies, east and west. By ten o'clock Miss Martha Andersen has them all sorted out, – checks to the Treasurer's Office, where Miss Edwina Paige, our new Assistant Treasurer, toils over the books with Miss Alice Bratt; appeals for costumes and literature and programs, sometimes enclosing dimes and nickels, to Miss Dorothy Burt, who runs a parcel port-office of her own; affairs of the Sewing Guild to Miss Mina Hennink, who has aroused such interest wherever she has gone with

---

at the Hotel Roosevelt in New York City. It was a lavish affair with the names of those attending and the seating arrangement carefully preserved in Rev. Romig's text (65-87).

The book of seventeenth-century Dutch lineal descendants suggests that there was some basis for viewing anniversary celebrations as family reunions.

For interesting insight into the role of women and how that role was understood and celebrated in the tercentenary celebration, see Abigail Norton-Levering, "Women Writing History: The Tercentenary Celebration of 1928," Independent Study Project for Prof. John Coakley, December, 2002, New Brunswick Theological Seminary. Paper available in NBTS Archive Collection at Sage Library.

The centenary celebration of the Board of Foreign Missions in 1932 included a centenary pageant titled, "The Highway of the Lord," written by Charlotte Wyckoff. Lamenting their financial condition due to the economic depression, the WBFM reported:

We have great sympathy for the Board in the coincidence of its Centenary Year with this time of financial depression. Unfortunately we have not been able to express our interest by any financial gift, but we have given as far as possible our practical support—accepting responsibility for the Centenary Reading Competition, and co-operating with the Pageant Committee. We are proud to recognize as author of the Centenary pageant, "The Highway of the Lord," our own gifted missionary, Miss Charlotte Wyckoff. *ARWBFM*, 1932, 68.

According to Sarella Te Winkel, the pageant was used throughout the church. See Sarella Te Winkel, *The Sixth Decade of the Woman's Board of Foreign Mission, Reformed Church in America 1926-1935* (New York: Woman's Board of Foreign Missions, 1935), 12.

For an interesting analysis of the appeal of historical pageantry and the pageantry craze of the early twentieth century in particular, see David Glassberg, *American Historical Pageantry: The Uses of Tradition in the Early Twentieth Century* (Chapel Hill: Univ. of North Carolina Press, 1990).

39. *ARWBFM*, 1912, 18.

her kit of samples; requests for speakers Miss Andersen attends to herself, each involving telephone calls and many adjustments; everything else goes to the General Secretary who, with Miss Andersen's aid, struggles to keep up with a rising tide of correspondence. You who receive Board letters and perhaps cast them aside half read with a sigh of impatience, do you know what labor lies behind that mimeographed sheet that strives to jog your memory? First a Joint Committee meeting with officers of the two Women's Boards, or a Board meeting of our own, where the plan for the letter is hatched. Then its composition by one of the General Secretaries, with numerous trips back and forth between the offices for approval; then the mimeographing; then the addressing by hand of eight hundred or more envelopes; and finally "the mailing" when we all join together to fold the letters, seal the envelopes and carry them to the post office.[40]

Over the years, the work undertaken in Room 10 continuously carried the same refrain:

There is a poignant sweetness and infinite pathos in common things. Sympathy for the disheartened, cheer for the discouraged, suggestion for timid workers, advice to new ones, the heart story of possible candidates—these, and yet more of which time doth not permit the mention, books from the library, costumes to make the meetings an attraction, are some of the links of influence that are globe encircling and heart enshrining.[41]

Education and Publication

In their quest to generate a knowledgeable understanding of the critical needs and important advances of world mission, WBFM women relied on the most powerful resource at their disposal—the printing press. Over the years, the printing press poured out information to educate and inspire. "The printed page should stimulate, instruct and interest. Let everybody read," enjoined the education secretary Olivia Lawrence in 1932.[42] "Every one knows the importance of *intelligent* interest in anything"[43] was the mantra. And the opposite of *intelligent* interest was clearly spelled out in the *Mission Gleaner*:

Zeal not "according to knowledge" works confusion sometimes, but the pages of our magazine keep us in touch, and in line with the working out of God's plan in our mission fields.[44]

40. *ARWBFM*, 1939, 59.
41. *ARWBFM*, 1909, 12.
42. *ARWBFM*, 1932, 69.
43. *ARWBFM*, 1898, 37.
44. *ARWBFM*, 1907, 11.

Within the first year of its existence, the Board of Managers recognized the need for a resource that pooled all of the relevant data known about each of the three RCA missions. It was a struggle to locate the needed data, but with the help of missionaries, and the drive and efficiency of the Board of Managers, an attractive, hardcover textbook, *The Manual of Missions*, was published by the end of December 1877. It was the hope of the board that:

> ...it may come into the possession of every family in the Church, so that mothers, with better knowledge themselves, may be enabled to interest children and imbue them with a Missionary spirit caught from their own enthusiasm.[45]

The measure to which this hope was realized is unknown. One thing, however, can be documented. President Mary Sturges was convinced of the need for the data to be disseminated,[46] and she single-handedly underwrote the cost of publication and distribution of one copy of *The Manual of Missions* to every newly formed auxiliary of the WBFM.[47] Fifteen years after its publication, *The Manual of Missions* was still being sent to newly formed auxiliaries, and letters of appreciation continued to be received attesting to its usefulness.

In 1893, the WBFM published a second book. Titled *Far Hence*,[48] this book contained observations and reflections by the Reverend Henry N. Cobb, secretary of the BFM, who had visited Reformed church missionaries and mission stations the year before. It served as an informed and reliable update of the mission work and was sold to the churches. In this same year, a special gift in support of the WBFM circulating library was received. Given by an unknown donor, the gift allowed the addition of ten volumes on missionary subjects to be added to the circulating library each year through 1902. This gift provides further evidence of how books and information on missions were valued by WBFM women.[49]

It was clear to the pioneer leaders that personal letters from missionaries and travelers provided the most immediate information available. Yet, missionaries could not possibly keep up or be expected to write individual letters responding to each auxiliary's request for updated information.[50] Equally clear was the need to keep church women informed. As Mary Chamberlain pointed out:

---

45. *ARWBFM*, 1876, 7.

46. *ARWBFM*, 1889, 22. See also *ARWBFM*, 1891, 25.

47. Mary Sturges was both generous and astute. She paid $100 for the publication of the book and hoped the sale price of the book would offset the cost of giving a copy to each new WBFM auxiliary, after which time all profit would revert to the WBFM treasury. As the *Annual Report* is careful to point out, "We mention this, that our friends everywhere may be stimulated to make its circulation as large as possible." *ARWBFM*, 1877, 6.

48. Henry N. Cobb, *Far Hence* (New York: Woman's Board of Foreign Missions, RCA, 1893).

49. *ARWBFM*, 1893, 25.

50. In 1877, the auxiliary of the Second Reformed Church in Jersey City, New Jersey, reported: The quarterly meetings have been well attended. The interest of these meetings is very much promoted by letters from our missionary ladies, and if they could know with what power these communications react upon the cause to which they have devoted themselves, they would make an extra effort and take up the cross of letter-writing to those societies particularly interested in their schools or charge. *ARWBFM*, 1877, 15.

No permanent interest could be maintained in the auxiliaries upon which the Board depended for its funds, if the women who composed them were in ignorance as to what was actually being accomplished with their money.[51]

At first, the WBFM used the denomination's periodical, the *Sower and Gospel Field* (which in 1881 became the *Sower and Mission Monthly*), to disseminate this information.[52] One-quarter of the space in the *Sower* was to be made available to the women.[53] But as reported by Mary Chamberlain, "It was felt that these [this] did not, for various reasons, wholly meet the need."[54]

In May, 1877, the board decided to publish "in tract form"[55] letters from missionaries and "interesting missionary matter."[56] By the fall, one thousand leaflets were printed and distributed to the auxiliaries. At this point, board members came to recognize both the necessity and opportunities represented by the publication of a periodical entirely their own. Neither columns in the *Sower and Mission Monthly* nor the publication of leaflets could adequately convey to women the information that the WBFM sensed was so critical to understanding the work.

In November-December, 1883, the WBFM began publication of a bimonthly periodical called the *Mission Gleaner.*[57] It would continue to be published through December 1917, when it merged with the denomination's mission periodical the *Mission Field*, "for reasons of greater efficiency and broader readership."[58] A one-year subscription to the *Mission Gleaner* cost twenty-five cents, a price believed to be within the financial reach of all households. The editor and manager of the publication was Matilda Van Zandt Cobb, whose husband, Henry N. Cobb, served as secretary of the BFM 1883-1910. Matilda Cobb served in this position for twenty-three years.[59] She

---

51. Mary Chamberlain, *Fifty Years in Foreign Fields, China, Japan, India, Arabia: A History of Five Decades of the Woman's Board of Foreign Mission, Reformed Church in America* (New York: Abbott Press, 1925), 34.

52. For a history of denominational periodicals, see "The Missionary Periodicals of the Reformed Church," by A. De W. Mason, editor of the *Mission Field*, in Edward Tanjore Corwin, *A Manual of the Reformed Church in America (Formerly Ref. Prot. Dutch Church)* (New York: Board of Publication of the Reformed Church in America, 1902), 228.

53. This figure is reported in House, "Women Raising Women," in Coakley and House, *Patterns and Portraits*, 106.

54. Chamberlain, *Fifty Years*, 35.

55. It is interesting that in the 1902 *Annual Report*, the home secretary notes, "The time has long passed by when the name "Tract" was spoken almost in derision; perhaps there was some reason for it, but surely not in these days, for some of the richest gems of thought are enfolded in these little leaves." ARWBFM, 1902, 12. WBFM records indicate that the word "leaflets" was routinely used.

56. Chamberlain, *Fifty Years*, 35.

57. In 1855 the Board of Publication began publishing a monthly paper called the *Sower*, which became the *Sower and Missionary Recorder*, and in 1870 the *Sower and the Gospel Field*. By choosing the *Mission Gleaner* as the name for their periodical, WBFM women signaled their awareness of their place in the gender culture of that day. Edward Tanjore Corwin, *A Digest of the Constitutional Legislation of the Reformed Church in America* (New York: Board of Publication of the RCA, 1906), 685-86.

58. ARWBFM, 1918, 15-16.

59. The death of Matilda Cobb May 11, 1911, occurred within one month of her husband's death. Her funeral tribute was given by the Reverend John G. Fagg and is recorded in Chamberlain, *Fifty Years*, 189. See also Una Ratmeyer, *Hands, Hearts, and Voices, Women Who Followed God's Call* (New York: Reformed Church Press, 1995), 4-5.

was succeeded as editor by Elizabeth Lindsley Conklin (Rev. John W.). Of these two women Mary Chamberlain, in her Jubilee history, notes:

> It is not too much to say that, but for their labors and for the faithful letters of the missionaries about their work, no adequate record of the work of the Woman's Board during the first four decades of its existence would have been available. These letters, published month by month and year by year in the *Mission Gleaner* have contained in large part the real history of the Woman's Board of Foreign Missions.[60]

Reneé House describes the content of the *Mission Gleaner* this way:

> The magazine was written entirely for women, by women, and, mostly about women. For the most part, the *Gleaner* is composed of excerpts from letters written by female missionaries to the women's board, to close friends in the States, and to women's auxiliaries and children's mission bands; endless stories about girls, boys, and women who are exemplars of the appropriate response to Christian missions; numerous detailed reports on the activities and meetings of women's auxiliaries and classical unions—the scriptures they read, the hymns they sang, the titles of the papers that were read, and the names of the women and men who read them; and practical tips on how to organize and energize women, girls, and boys for mission work.[61]

Additionally, exhortations to "Little Self-Denials" and chilling reminders of the need for Christian education in their desperately evil times[62] routinely found a place in the *Mission Gleaner*, as well as the more specific listings of prayer needs, individual and group contributions, lists of available leaflets, and new books added to the circulating library.

Conceived of as a periodical for women, the *Mission Gleaner*, like the women's periodicals of other denominations, fostered a sense of intimacy among church women. It created a feeling much like the intimate conversations women shared between mothers and daughters and among sisters. The magazine contributed "something from their lives that cannot be supplied through any other source."[63] The 1900 *Annual Report* noted:

> Every woman needs the inspiration that is given through the letters fresh from our missionaries. They are the love messages from them to the women in our churches. They are often written under stress of care and labor, that those at home may rejoice with them over the blessed results of their efforts.[64]

---

60. Chamberlain, *Fifty Years*, 276.
61. House, "Women Raising Women," in House and Coakley, *Patterns and Portraits*, 105.
62. *Mission Gleaner* 14, no. 2 (March-April, 1897), 14-15.
63. *ARWBFM*, 1900, 13.
64. Ibid.

In the early years of publishing the *Mission Gleaner*, subscription sales often failed to cover expenses. The need for the periodical, however, was clear to the members of the Board of Managers. In 1890, the home secretary reported:

> The "Gleaner" is in every sense the Board's paper, and through it more intimate relations are established and maintained with our auxiliaries. This is very important. We are to a great extent trustees of these Societies, receiving their money, to expend it for the objects so dear to us all. Through its columns we should consult and advise together; and in its pages, containing nearly all the letters received from the Foreign Field, the christian [sic] givers can learn of the blessing of their gifts.[65]

This awareness of need, coupled with a belief that the periodical could become profitable and make an annual contribution to the WBFM treasury,[66] led the managers to take the *Mission Gleaner* "under their control"[67] in 1892. At this time subscriptions totaled 1,500. The managers immediately established a committee that in turn recommended that each local auxiliary appoint a special committee to canvass and solicit a subscription from each household in the congregation.[68] This was done, and, in 1893, the annual report noted that subscriptions had increased from 1,500 to 2,500. This number continued to increase, and in 1912 subscriptions totaled 4,500, but the targeted number of potential subscriptions, 10,000, was never reached.[69]

During the early years of the *Mission Gleaner*, letters from missionaries, which formed the basis for programs used by local auxiliaries, were printed in the periodical and not published in separate "leaflet"[70] form. However, this began to change in 1893 when the WBFM published its first leaflet, *What the Chinese Woman Told the Missionary*, by Gertrude L. Vanderbilt. Supplementing this with "a large number [of leaflets] purchased from other Boards," there followed in 1895 the publication of three leaflets: *A Day in India, The Top of One Little Green Tree*, and *How the Auxiliary at Myrtle Grove was*

---

65. *ARWBFM*, 1890, 24-25.

66. *ARWBFM*, 1892, 26.

67. Originally an independent publication, the *Mission Gleaner* was intended to be financially self-sustaining. This plan did not work out, leading the Board of Managers to assume financial control of the publication in 1892. *ARWBFM*, 1893, 25.

68. *ARWBFM*, 1892, 26.

69. The 1894 *Annual Report* noted, "This may seem a large number, yet, when we consider that there are over 25,000 Christian women in our communion, and the homes into which this little magazine never enters, the proportion is indeed small. While the number of subscribers has increased, we must still urge our Societies to have a special committee appointed to look after its interests" (20). For an entertaining account of promotional tactics used to increase the circulation of the *Mission Gleaner*, see *ARWBFM*, 1902, 11-12.

In 1896, *The Mission Gleaner* was reported to be self-supporting, and credit for this was given to "the persevering efforts of efficient Committees in our Auxiliary Societies, and we wish to extend to them our grateful appreciation of their ready assistance." *ARWBFM*, 1896, 8, and *ARWBFM*, 1912, 17.

70. In a technical sense, a "leaflet" is four pages in length. WBFM women used the term to include brochures, play scripts, etc., of varying lengths, and they often exceeded four pages.

Formed. This act initiated a large and effective publishing program, with Room 10 serving as the distribution center. As noted in the 1910 *Annual Report*:

> Room Ten is not only a Bureau of Information, but in a modest way a publishing office as well. When the Publication Committee has determined what leaflets shall be issued by the Board, the form in which they shall appear and all the details of the press-work are left to the superintendence of Room Ten.[71]

While WBFM women believed that "Mission Study is the prime factor for generating an intelligent interest in Missions,"[72] the writing and publication of educational leaflets made contributions to the mission program in other ways. Differences in language tended to separate the English-speaking women in the East from the Dutch-speaking women in the West and the German-speaking women throughout the denomination. By 1894 there were thirty-eight auxiliaries in the western church, where Christine Van Raalte Gilmore (Rev. William B.)[73] worked to organize auxiliaries and classical unions and to provide active leadership. A pivotal event was noted in the 1900 *Annual Report*:

> What led us to feel the necessity of providing the means by which our Western sisters could become partakers in these letters, was that when our annual reports were sent out, one dear woman, on receiving a copy, laid it down, and, with tears in her eyes, said: "I cannot read one word of it." And, upon inquiring, we found there were many such. And this is also true of many of our Societies where only the German language is spoken.[74]

To counteract this separation by language, the following actions were taken. The first was described as follows:

> Through the courtesy of the editors of the "Heidenwereld" space has been set apart in this Holland paper for the Woman's Board of Foreign Missions. For each issue, Mrs. L. B. Halsey, our representative, sends communications from our missionaries to Rev. James F. Zwemer, who has kindly offered to translate them into the Dutch language for printing.[75]

The second action involved the publication of leaflets in Dutch and German.

With the formation in 1902 of a "Leaflet Committee" as a standing committee of the board, sensitivity to the need for leaflets in Dutch and German was carefully

---

71. *ARWBFM*, 1910, 18.
72. *ARWBFM*, 1909, 13.
73. Christine (actually Christina) Van Raalte Gilmore was the daughter of Albertus and Christina Van Raalte, the founding family of Holland, Michigan. For biographical data on Christine Van Raalte Gilmore, see Elton J. Bruins, Karen G. Schakel, Sara Fredrickson Simmons, and Marie N. Zingle, *Albertus and Christina: The Van Raalte Family, Home and Roots* (Grand Rapids: Eerdmans, 2004), 147-58.
74. *ARWBFM*, 1900, 14.
75. *ARWBFM*, 1900, 13.

Christine Van Raalte Gilmore

monitored, and leaflets in Dutch and German were routinely published. As reported in the 1900 *Annual Report*:

> Four thousand copies of "Our Work," "How Hindu Christians Give," and "What the Chinese Woman Told the Missionary," have been translated into Dutch, and two thousand into German. These have been sent to our Western Churches, where they have been freely distributed.[76]

In 1903 the *Annual Report* notes:

> The series of leaflets, one for each of our four fields, published a year ago, has had a second edition in the Holland language and now through the kindness of Rev. Mr. Barny, the set has been translated into German. That this work of translation has been appreciated let the many kind words testify. One good brother wrote, "Keep on translating such leaflets, they will do good work for the cause.[77]

The writing and publication of leaflets also provided an opportunity for WBFM women to use their individual journalistic skills and to experience having written

---

76. *ARWBFM*, 1900, 14.

77. *ARWBFM*, 1900, 12-13. It is interesting to note that Mary Chamberlain's *Fifty Years in Foreign Fields*, published in 1925, was translated into Dutch by Dr. W. J. Van Kersen, and "it was the last attempt of the Board to publish missionary information in their own tongue for the diminishing generation of Holland women who do not understand English—those staunch supporters of the Mission cause, whose homes have sent many sons and daughters to the Mission Field and exerted an inestimable influence on future generations." Te Winkel, *The Sixth Decade*, 9.

pieces of their own published. As the number of female college graduates grew, the WBFM championed their writing skills and provided needed opportunities for using them. While missionaries wrote a steady stream of leaflets that were used for women's programs, individual women and auxiliary groups[78] on the home front also wrote leaflets, and when any woman from the home front traveled to visit the mission stations, one could be almost sure that a mission program and/or leaflet would result. The number of leaflets grew steadily, so that by the 1920s the leaflet publication list included thirty-two leaflets on India, sixteen leaflets on China, seventeen leaflets on Japan, twelve leaflets on Arabia, and eleven leaflets of a general nature for a total of eighty-eight leaflets available in 1922.[79] As noted in the 1909 *Annual Report*, "Missionary literature fairly glows and almost explodes with the dynamic urgency of the Church's opportunity."[80]

"Where are the missionary workers of the coming years to be found, if the children of this generation be not trained to a missionary spirit, missionary intelligence, and missionary giving?"[81] Education for children and young people was paramount to WBFM women, and in 1896 the women experienced rising concern, especially for children. The 1896 *Annual Report* notes:

> The importance of bringing the children of our different organizations into closer sympathy with our Mission work was a thought that had rested upon the hearts of our Managers for many months, and it was finally decided to give them a Missionary of their own. Miss Lelia [sic Leila] Winn was set apart to be the Children's Missionary, as her work is largely that of gathering the Japanese children into Sunday-schools. A circular letter was prepared and a copy, with a leaflet describing her work, and also a "Star Card," sent to each Junior Christian Endeavor Society and Mission Band. Nearly 4,000 cards have been given to the children in these societies. As these cards are returned, with the light shining through each tiny star and the name of the giver inscribed upon them, they are sent to Miss Winn to be distributed among her Japanese children. The letters that have accompanied these cards as they have been returned to your Secretary have told in pathetic words of the love of Jesus shining in many a young heart. A mother writes: "Every night since my little children had their 'Star Cards' they never have forgotten to pray for Miss Winn."[82]

This action was coupled with the decision to publish a children's paper, called the *Day Star*, that Mary Chamberlain describes this way:

> The children's missionary paper, the Day Star, was first sent out as a sample number in October 1896, and the reception it received was a surprise to all. In

---

78. *ARWBFM*, 1914, 16.
79. *ARWBFM*, 1922, 147-148.
80. *ARWBFM*, 1909, 12.
81. *ARWBFM*, 1898, 36.
82. *ARWBFM*, 1886, 7-8.

four months it had become self-supporting, showing that the children in the Sunday Schools were waiting for some such messenger. The subscription list numbered almost at once 12,600 copies. Miss R.V.Z. Cobb was the editor as her mother was of The Gleaner, and in her hands the little paper exercised a great influence among the children of the Church and Sunday Schools, as shown by the interest they evinced in their own missionary, Miss M. Leila Winn. The Day Star contained many letters from missionaries written especially for children and throughout the decade it gave to the children of the Church a knowledge of missions and an interest in them which could hardly have been inspired in any other way.[83]

Stimulating a missionary spirit and fostering missionary intelligence were further encouraged in 1896 by WBFM publication of a mission catechism. The catechism, the major teaching tool and mainstay of RCA curriculum, was thought "to supply a need long felt by many of the leaders of our different organizations. It will be published in booklet form with questions and answers relating to our Missionaries and their work, beside general Missionary information."[84]

In 1897, the published catechisms, which were provided at no cost, were available and described this way:

> They are invaluable for reference, and some of our Sunday-school Superintendents are using them as text-books, giving out several questions each Sabbath, to be answered by the children on the following Sabbath, thus bringing our Mission work into each Sabbath's teaching.[85]

Teaching self-denial to children by training them in the habit of giving their own money systematically to the cause of missions was also valued and felt to be the responsibility of WBFM women. For years children had been encouraged to save their pennies by using missionary boxes.[86] These boxes, later called "mite boxes," were little paper boxes into which pennies were collected in support of the mission cause. In 1901, the *Annual Report* noted:

> The question has been asked, "Does God need our mites?" Yes, He needs them for our own sake. Many a box has been brought to our rooms filled with the love tokens from little hands where the mother in her quiet home has taught her children to save for Christ's sake. But this quiet reminder gathers in the littles [sic] too from those who are older. One batchelor [sic] friend sends regularly every year the contents of a mite box with which we are careful to keep him always supplied.[87]

---

83. Chamberlain, *Fifty Years*, 111. The *Day Star* was not the only children's missionary paper to be published. In 1910 a children's paper called *Everyland* was published and paralleled the rise of the Children's Department. *ARWBFM*, 1910, 19.

84. *ARWBFM*, 1896, 9.

85. *ARWBFM*, 1897, 8.

86. See *ARWBFM*, 1885, 22.

87. *ARWBFM*, 1901, 13.

Ecumenism

When Sarah Doremus founded the Woman's Union Missionary Society in 1861, the organization represented a "union" of women from several denominations. In time, this "union" came to be understood as "ecumenical," meaning an inclusive, worldwide partnership comprised of denominations of various Christian traditions. It is not possible, therefore, to discuss the history of the WBFM or the educational program of WBFM women without understanding the great ecumenical involvement of Christian women that began in the last years of the nineteenth century and the earliest years of the twentieth. We can best sense the energy generated by ecumenism through the words of Mary Chamberlain, who was active in the WBFM during those years:

> The Woman's National Foreign Missionary Jubilee swept across the Continent from the Pacific to the Atlantic in the spring of 1911, culminating in a final celebration in New York City in March of that year. A writer in the *Presbyterian* asked: "Did this marvellous [sic] movement begin the other day in Oakland, Cal., or ten years ago at the Ecumenical Conference in New York, when the Central Committee on United Study was formed, or fifty years ago when Mrs. T. C. Doremus started what might be called the first Woman's Club, the Union Missionary Society? Launched on the eve of the Civil War by persons inexperienced in public affairs, opposed by the clergy, without financial backing, [the Union Missionary Society] is now one of forty Boards with more than 57,000 foreign missionary societies and auxiliaries in the United States and Canada and which in 1910 raised more than $3,000,000.[88] In this interdenominational school of missions our mothers and grandmothers learned their first lessons before it occurred to them to form Boards within the limits of their own Christian communions.

Mary Chamberlain further appraised the educational impetus of such ecumenical relationships. She observed:

> In 1900, as a result of the Ecumenical Conference, an interdenominational committee of women was formed to promote the study of foreign missions. The first text-book, *Via Christi*, was published and a movement was started which was destined to create a wider and more intelligent interest in foreign mission than had ever before been known. To the Chairman of the Central Committee for United Study, Mrs. Henry Peabody, came the vision of a nation-wide Jubilee celebration of the founding of the Woman's Union Missionary Society in 1861, a movement which was to ignore denominational lines and which was to draw all Christian women together....The call was sounded and the response was immediate. Jubilee meetings were held all the way from California to New York.

---

88. Restated for inflation, three million dollars in 1910 would equate to approximately sixty million dollars in 2002.

The largest churches were filled and from five to fifteen hundred women gathered at the luncheons to hear addresses on foreign missions....Meetings were held in many smaller towns and cities where the emphasis was laid upon *united*, undenominational effort. Programmes for study, for addresses, for ten minute talks, for the story of the Jubilee, for prayer, for denominational rallies, were carried out in many small centres which were too distant from the main Jubilee meetings for the women to conveniently attend.

The great aims of the Jubilee were to revive an interest in foreign missions where it had flagged, to awaken an interest in them where it had not before existed, to increase the number of volunteers for the work of the foreign mission fields and to raise the sum of $1,000,000[89] for advance work in foreign lands.

The message of this Foreign Missionary Jubilee made an especial appeal to the women of the Reformed Church. It was David Abeel, a missionary of the Reformed Church, who had first stressed the need of the co-operation of women in the work of converting the Eastern world. It was he who had been the means of the organization in 1834 of the first Woman's Foreign Missionary Society in the world. It was Mrs. T. C. Doremus of the Reformed Church who was the founder and first President of the Woman's Union Missionary Society, the first definitely organized and incorporated body of its kind in America. Every denomination of any size now had its own Woman's Board of Foreign Missions, but the women of the Reformed Church felt a deeply rooted interest in the society of which their own Mrs. Doremus had been the founder and the head. They took a deep interest in the Jubilee and did all in their power to further its purposes and achievements. Mrs. De Witt Knox, then the Recording Secretary of the Woman's Board of the Reformed Church, became the Secretary of the Jubilee Committee. Of the Federation of Women's Boards of Foreign Missions which grew out of the Jubilee, she became the first Chairman. The churches of the denomination in New York City were thrown open for the Jubilee meetings and the President of the Board, Mrs. David James Burrell, took an active part in the programmes for the various meetings.[90]

When Christian women from different church traditions gathered at the Columbian Exposition in Chicago in 1893 for the Woman's Congress of Missions, there was generated both enormous energy and a new sense of united strength. This energy and united strength, at the turn of the twentieth century, enabled new ecumenical efforts to create a systematic study of missions and to explore new frontiers for mission involvement.

Formed in 1900 as a committee of the New York Ecumenical Missionary Conference, the Central Committee on the United Study of Foreign Missions:

---

89. Figured for inflation, one million dollars in 1910 would equate to approximately twenty million dollars in 2002.

90. Chamberlain, *Fifty Years*, 191-92.

...commencing with $25.00 capital, and Lucy [Peabody] and Helen [Barrett Montgomery] in its membership, produced a steady flow of two study books per year for twenty-seven years (publishing a total of four million volumes), earning it Pierce Beaver's assessment as the most successful publisher of mission books.[91]

The first textbook, *Via Christi: An Introduction to the Study of Missions*, was written by Louise Manning Hodgkins and published in 1901. Although it was a challenging textbook,[92] it and those that followed "proved to be best-sellers, and cumulative sales figures indicate that by 1905 nearly fifty thousand copies of each text had been distributed."[93]

The WBFM heartily recommended that its auxiliaries use *Via Christi* and successive United Study texts.[94] In 1903 the home secretary reported:

> Growth in work is due to growth in knowledge. If the women in our churches and auxiliaries would fall in line with the United Study of Missions, which is the greatest movement yet organized for missionary study, their interest would be vastly intensified. The second book in the series, *Lux Christi*, being upon India, should incite our perusal. We urge the societies where possible to undertake a systematic course of study like the one just indicated, or in the exceedingly helpful one as arranged by Miss Cobb's leaflet, "The Monthly Topics."[95]

At the WBFM annual meeting held at Marble Collegiate Church in 1904, Louise Manning Hodgkins spoke to RCA women, using the occasion to point out the advantages of the United Study of Missions.[96] In the same year, the home secretary noted in the annual report:

> United Study is no longer an experiment, rather it is a remarkable and increasing success, with its hosts of readers, East and West, using the third text-book of the

---

91. William H. Brackney, "The Legacy of Helen B. Montgomery and Lucy W. Peabody," *International Bulletin of Missionary Research* 15, no. 1 (January, 1991), 175.

92. In *The World Their Household: The American Woman's Foreign Mission Movement and Cultural Transformation, 1870-1920,* (Ann Arbor: Univ. of Michigan, 1985), Patricia R. Hill describes Louise Manning Hodgkins' text this way:

Hodgkins's text is a comprehensive overview of the history of missions from St. Paul to Adoniram Judson. Hodgkins managed to compress an enormous wealth of detail into 250 pages, heading each chapter with chronological tables listing great events, great names, and great productions. Suggestions for discussion and further research follow each chapter. The volume, in the context of the proposed course of mission study, is remedial in intent; it sketches general background for subsequent volumes treating the history of missions in particular countries through the nineteenth century to the present. The content of Hodgkins's text is, however, not elementary; she presents the complexities of Christian history with remarkable deftness—and a fair-mindedness unusual in rabidly anti-Catholic evangelical circles (144).

93. Hill, *The World Their Household*, 144.

94. *ARWBFM*, 1902, 14.

95. *ARWBFM*, 1903, 13.

96. *ARWBFM*, 1904, 8.

series, *Rex Christus*. One should not lose the inspiration of keeping in step with the great movement of the missionary world, it is a grand company of thousands of women.[97]

By 1906 the home secretary reported, "Contagion of study classes is spreading. Not to be intelligent concerning Missions will soon be, to be behind the times."[98]

Twenty-five auxiliaries in 1908 were reported to be using "wholly or in part, the United Study Course; and in forty societies there are Mission Study Classes."[99] This was a beginning, and within a few years, a more systematic course of mission study materials became available for all ages.[100]

The shift to the use of textbooks and the orderly sustained study of textbook facts served as signs of changing times. Patricia Hill points out:

> Science was in the ascendancy in America at the turn of the century; "scientific" methods were recommended for solving every conceivable problem. In an age of increasing specialization, laymen and women turned to experts for answers—and leadership. This was so within the foreign mission movement at large as well as among the women's societies. For women, however, the adaptation of scientific pedagogical principles to mission study created special difficulties since—or so the leadership believed—women were not in the habit of study.[101]

Increasingly the question became, "Where would the new, educated leadership for mission be found?" Higher education was increasingly open to women, although college educations were limited, for the most part, to those whose families could afford to send their daughters away to school. The question of training nonordained leaders for mission, both those with college educations and those without, became the issue.

In 1904, leaders attending the Sixth Interdenominational Conference of Woman's Boards decided to establish a summer school for missions at Dwight L. Moody's school for girls in Northfield, Massachusetts.[102] This became the first of numerous mission summer schools.

---

97. *ARWBFM*, 1904, 12.

98. *ARWBFM*, 1906, 12.

99. *ARWBFM*, 1908, 11.

100. Report of Mr. H. A. Kinports, for the RCA Department of Young People's Work, *ARWBFM*, 1916, 30-31. For evidence of this concern, see *ARWBFM*, 1900, *13*.

101. Hill, *The World Their Household*, 148-49.

102. Dorothy Jealous Scudder, in *A Thousand Years in Thy Sight: The Story of the Scudder Missionaries of India* (New York: Vantage Press, 1984), has chronicled the life of the young Ida S. Scudder. Born in India, the spirited daughter of Dr. and Mrs. John Scudder (John Scudder, RCA medical missionary to India, 1861-1900, and his wife, Sophia Weld Scudder, missionary to India, 1861-1925), Ida had returned to America with her mother and brothers. In 1884 Mrs. Scudder returned to India, leaving fourteen-year-old Ida and her brothers in the care of various relatives. Ida was left in Chicago with her Aunt Fanny and Uncle Henry Martyn Scudder, who was a pastor. Given Ida's rebellious temperament, this family arrangement didn't work out, and "the way opened for a solution when Dwight Moody asked to have her at his Northfield Seminary; the Scudders gladly complied with the request, especially as

Left to right: Ida S. Scudder, Sophia Scudder, and Julia C. Scudder

Uncle Henry was considering Japan as a new field for his missionary labors."

Dorothy Scudder provides delightful insight into Ida S. Scudder's educational experience at Northfield Seminary. She wrote of the future Dr. Ida S. Scudder:

At Northfield, Ida's high spirits had free rein. She was a leader in whatever took place, studies, athletics or pranks—especially pranks. These were never premeditated. It was usually thoughtlessness that led her into scrapes. When she thought of something that would be fun to do, she acted immediately: Once she and her roommate found the German teacher's horse and carriage tied to a hitching post in front of their dormitory. Ida had not spent four years on a farm without learning to drive. They unfastened the horse, climbed into the carriage and drove gaily out into the countryside and had a glorious time. Since Ida was always suspect in such matters, she was the first one summoned for questioning. She took her punishment in good part, for she knew she had been wrong. On another occasion, Thanksgiving Day, she and some friends got permission to go to Brattleboro for dinner. They ran into some Mr. Hermon boys who had a similar idea. What more natural than for the boys and girls to have dinner together! But it was

Summer schools for missions were not entirely new. In 1874 John Heyl Vincent (1832-1920) and Lewis Miller established Chautauqua in upstate New York.[103] Patricia Hill wrote:

> Such conferences were already well-established features of the millennialist, evangelical subculture in England and America. In Britain, the Keswick conventions were an influential force. The Student Volunteer Movement, born at Dwight L. Moody's first summer school for college students at Mount Hermon in 1886, relied heavily on such models—the camp meeting, Chautauqua, and summer county institutes for schoolteachers—the leaders of the woman's mission movement set about training a corps of "professional" teachers to take charge of mission study in local churches. The decision to institute summer schools of missions in scattered locations around the country was made by a handful of women who considered themselves mission experts.[104]

According to Patricia Hill, the first summer school for missions at Northfield attracted 235 delegates.[105]

> Helen Montgomery and Louise Manning Hodgkins taught women how to conduct mission classes in their home churches. Dr. T.H.P. Sailer was imported to discuss pedagogical techniques. He condemned three methods: the lecture, the paper—which he criticized as "the weakness of women"—and recitation. In place of these outdated methods he recommended roundtable discussion.[106]

---

against the rules and, unfortunately, there was a Northfield teacher dining at the same hotel. Here Ida displayed her dominant characteristic—the ability to meet a situation full face and more than half way. When the teacher returned to her room she found a big box of flowers with a card from Ida and her friends thanking her for *allowing* them to have such a nice Thanksgiving Day! Fortunately for them, this teacher was exceedingly fond of flowers.

Soon, Ida began growing up. She was learning to control her temper, although it was manifest on occasions then and continued throughout her life. Those lovely blue eyes could snap when she heard of any injustice, whether to herself, to her loved ones, or to her Indian "children" (188-89).

Ida S. Scudder returned to India in 1890. Following a tragic experience of three Indian women dying in childbirth, which convinced Ida of God's call to become a medical missionary, she returned to the United States and attended medical school, which was a major feat for a woman in those days. Ida S. Scudder attended the Women's Medical School in Philadelphia 1895-1898 and received her M.D. degree from Cornell Medical School in New York City in 1899. Cornell Medical School in New York City became open to women in 1898 (188-89).

See also Ratmeyer, *Hands, Hearts, and Voices*, 71.

103. For an interesting study of John Heyl Vincent, see Sonja Marie Stewart, "John Heyl Vincent: His Theory and Practice of Protestant Religious Education from 1855-1920," (PhD diss., University of Notre Dame, 1977). See also Norman J. Kansfield, "Christian Education and the Ten-Year Goal," *Reformed Review*, 57, no. 1 (Autumn, 2003), 53-62.

104. Hill, *The World Their Household*, 145.

105. Ibid. Hill goes on to note that in 1915 there were 916 delegates registered for Northfield.

106. Hill, *The World Their Household*, 146.

Other summer mission schools throughout the country rapidly became established.[107] For RCA women, the summer mission schools at Northfield, Massachusetts, and at Silver Bay, New York, became the major centers for mission study in the East. RCA women and families in the Midwest used Bible and mission schools at Northern Baptist conference center (now ABC) at Lake Geneva, Wisconsin, and at the Billy Sunday center at Winona Lake, Indiana.[108] After the Sixth Interdenominational Conference of Woman's Boards in 1904, a standing committee oversaw summer conferences for mission workers, and WBFM women regularly participated on the Northfield and Silver Bay conference boards.

The Young Woman's Branch of the WBFM was established November 20, 1900, an event which Mary Chamberlain described as "one of the most important and far-reaching movements inaugurated by the Woman's Board."[109] What led to the formation of the Young Woman's Branch of the WBFM was described this way in the 1901 *Annual Report*:

> There had been in the hearts of some of the members of our Board for several years a great longing to bring the young women of our Church into close union with the work of the Woman's Board. This need is all the greater as year by year the demands for assistance from our Societies increase and our lines of helpfulness must be extended. A committee was chosen from the Board to prepare a plan for such an organization, and on November 20th twelve young ladies were invited to meet the committee and the "Young Woman's Branch" came into being, and the hope of years realized. Already its influence is being felt and the bright young members are devising ways and means by which their organization may be a true helpmeet to the mother Board.[110]

---

107. Hill notes that in 1915, "The Ninth Minnesota Summer School drew 1,300; the School of Missions for Oklahoma and the Southwest enrolled 404 in its fourth year of operation. California boasted both the Mount Hermon Federate School of Missions and a Woman's Congress of Missions at San Francisco in the summer of 1915." *The World Their Household*, 147.

108. In the 1933 *Annual Report*, the following is noted:

The Home and Foreign Missionary Conferences at Northfield, Mass., in which our Boards have cooperated from the beginning, underwent a significant change. By popular vote at both Conferences decision was made to combine the two in a joint conference, the direction of which is now in the hands of the "Women's Interdenominational Committee of the Northfield Missionary Conference" with membership from both Home and Foreign Boards. The Silver Bay Conference of the Missionary Education Movement, after celebrating its 30th Anniversary, ended its career as a separate conference, but continues as a Summer Training School in Missionary Education in connection with the New Jersey School of Methods in Christian Education at Blairstown, New Jersey. At the close of the Northfield Conference the Secretary of the Board was summoned by telegram to conduct a study class for the wives of ministers attending the School of Theology at Pine Lodge, Michigan, which has resulted in the organization of a more formal School of Missions at that conference center for this coming summer. *ARWBFM*, 1933, 53.

In 1937, the WBFM broadened its leadership involvement at the summer mission camps at Lake Geneva, Wisconsin, and Winona Lake, Indiana by establishing committees of RCA representatives to each of these conference boards. *ARWBFM*, 1937, 7.

109. Chamberlain, *Fifty Years*, 114.

110. *ARWBFM*, 1901, 11.

The charter members[111] immediately assumed financial support of Miss Mary Deyo, missionary to Japan 1888-1905, and set to work contacting each church urging the formation of a young woman's circle. The next year they reported:

> This involved quite an amount of writing, as each Circle in the Church was written to. In the eastern classes there are 97 circles, while in the west they seem unknown. Twenty-three circles responded, and we trust more will do so.[112]

Within two years, membership increased.[113] In 1903 they noted:

> During the year the interests and influence of this organization has enlarged its scope by forming Branches in the Particular Synods of Chicago and Albany. The initial meeting of the former was fittingly called while Mrs. Burrell was in Michigan. For weeks prior to her expected visit, Mrs. C.V.R. Gilmore, our highly prized honorary Vice-President, had been selecting from the various churches the young women, who on the evening designated met at her home in Holland, when the Branch of the Particular Synod of Chicago was organized. One month later the one in the Particular Synod of Albany was formed, in which valuable aid was rendered by Mrs. William B. Jones, an honorary Vice-President.[114]

In addition to expanding their membership, members of the Young Woman's Branch "helped with the clerical work at Room 10, the Summer Sewing Guild, the *Gleaner* and *Daystar,* and to make ourselves useful at the various conferences during the year."[115]

The formation of the WBFM Young Woman's Branch in 1900 and the rise of summer mission schools beginning in 1904 grew in parallel. Northfield and other summer mission camps often played a pivotal role in the lives of Reformed Church women of high school and college age. Furloughing missionaries frequently participated in "camp life" by teaching, worshiping, and taking part in the daily round of social activities. Dr. Ida S. Scudder usually participated at Northfield when

---

111. According to Mary Chamberlain (*Fifty Years*, 113), the charter members included:
Miss Anna F. Bacon – President
Miss Matilda S. Janeway – Secretary
Miss Maud Clark   Miss Margaret Coe
Miss Elizabeth Andrews   Miss C. Ditmars
Miss Alice Castree   Miss R.V.Z. Cobb [Rita Van Zandt]
Miss A. Van Cleef   Miss C. Duryee
Miss Katharine Wood   Miss S.A. Bussing
Miss Jennie Whitehead   Miss Edith Raven
Miss S.P. Du Bois   Miss Annie Wyckoff
112. *ARWBFM,* 1901, 24-25.
113. By 1902, they reported, "We have thus far enrolled 104 Circles, but only 36 have pledged their support." *ARWBFM,* 1902, 23.
114. *ARWBFM,* 1903, 11-12.
115. *ARWBFM,* 1901, 25.

she was in the country, and that was always special for everyone—especially young women. Dr. Ida loved to play tennis. WBFM leaders and women denominational leaders also participated routinely at Northfield and Silver Bay, serving as counselors and models for Christian living, teaching, and coming to know the "campers" personally.

Among these counselors, Louise Decker (Rev. Irving) participated at Northfield from 1939 to 1941. In 2000, in the latter years of her retirement, Louise Decker continued to remember her Northfield days with clarity and fondness:

> I remember that Julia Heines [WBFM secretary for young women's work] was in charge of the high-school aged girls at Northfield. She asked me to serve as a counselor and to be in charge of the girls living in tents. I had never slept in a tent before. One year Dr. Ida Scudder was there, along with her lady companion [Miss Gertrude Dodd]. Dr. Ida had just come from being honored by the Queen of England, and her friend was along to help her write her book, *Dr. Ida*. Dr. Ida was involved in everything. She was so much fun to be around, and she was such a regular person. She and I played tennis together, which is something I'll never forget.[116]

The excitement of attending Northfield in the early years was pitched even higher, after Lucy Waterbury Peabody[117] proposed to the Central Committee a Jubilee celebration to mark the founding in 1861 of the Woman's Union Missionary Society. Helen Barrett Montgomery had just finished writing the manuscript for her sixth textbook for the Committee on United Study. After reading the manuscript of Helen Montgomery's book, Lucy Waterbury Peabody, her dear friend and Baptist colleague, persuaded her "to rewrite the last chapter of the book to include notice of this golden

---

116. Author's telephone interview with Louise Decker, February 22, 2000.

117. Lucy Waterbury Peabody and Helen Barrett Montgomery were pivotal leaders in the women's missionary movement at this time. In 1914, Lucy Peabody, having returned from a world tour with her good friend Helen Montgomery, spoke at the WBFM annual meeting held at the First Reformed Church in Passaic, New Jersey. Her presentation was described this way:

As soon as the next speaker was announced the loud applause told the advent of a universal friend of Foreign Missions, one who heard the call, years ago, to active service, and has only changed the sphere of her activities until to-day Mrs. Henry W. Peabody represents the Foreign Mission Women of the States on the Continuation Committee of the Edinburgh Conference.

We listened with joy to the message she brought from the land we love, by inheritance—Holland, the land of dykes, and canals, and windmills, the land of Rembrandt, of William the Silent, and the Prince of Orange, and of the Queen we love, because she looks not only on her own people and her own responsibilities, but her heart goes out to every sad and lonely heart of womanhood. All hail, Wilhelmina, Queen of The Netherlands!

How inspiring to hear of her great appreciation of our Mission stations, of Dr. Zwemer and his standing in Egypt, of Dr. Ida Scudder and her associates in the Mary Taber Schell Hospital at Vellore, India; Mr. And Mrs. Booth in Yokohama, Japan. The best singing in any girls' school, Mrs. Peabody said, she heard in Ferris Seminary. Shimonoseki welcomed her with cherry blossoms, and on the fourth of April she went out with all the world of Japan to see and admire the famous flowers. *ARWBFM*, 1914, 9-10.

Helen Barrett Montgomery

anniversary. Perhaps this book would spark interest in a national celebration of the occasion."[118]

The textbook by Helen Barrett Montgomery, *Western Women in Eastern Lands*,[119] was described this way:

> In *Western Women in Eastern Lands,* Mrs. Montgomery reviewed the history of the woman's missionary movement, and showed the social and religious forces that produced it. The major thrust of the book was to trace the conditions of women in Oriental lands so that women at home could understand the need to minister to them.
>
> Her appeal was emotional, but tempered by her scholarship. She explained that the situation she described and the emphasis of her book would not be "upon exceptional cases of horror, but upon standards of conduct and upon national custom." It was an appeal that touched the hearts of women in America. Most of them did not appreciate the traditions and complications of Oriental religions. But they could immediately understand the specific wrongs to women as Mrs. Montgomery presented them.[120]

---

118. Louise Armstrong Cattan, *Lamps Are for Lighting: The Story of Helen Barrett Montgomery and Lucy Waterbury Peabody* (Grand Rapids: Eerdmans, 1972), 51.

119. Helen Barrett Montgomery, *Western Women in Eastern Lands* (New York: The Central Committee for United Study of Missions, 1910).

120. Cattan, *Lamps Are for Lighting*, 52. In the 1911 *Annual Report*, the secretary of the Department of Young People's Work reported, "There were probably more books of 'Western Women in Eastern Lands' used in our church than any other single textbook in this or previous years." *ARWBFM*, 1911, 24.

The Jubilee celebration in 1911 that Mary Chamberlain described in her history, *Fifty Years in Foreign Fields*, was charged with energy and a sense of united strength as the women rededicated themselves to the work of missions. In addition to the publication of the systematic study of missions and the rise of mission summer schools, there were other new frontiers of ecumenical cooperation and involvement. Little would WBFM women in 1911 have guessed what cooperative efforts the years ahead would bring. To gain a sense of what these ecumenical involvements included, the 1937 *Annual Report* reported:

> There is often too little known about the interdenominational activity of our Board, that part of our work which we do in cooperation with others. Not only support of Union Institutions in which we have a large part, but hours of active work in Boards and Committees and on Conference platforms are contributed by many of our members. The list of agencies is a long one and indicates not only the wide extent of our interests, but our strong and growing belief in a united Christian Advance. The Foreign Missions Conference, Committee on Christian Education in India and in Japan, Central Committee on the United study of Foreign Missions, Committee on Christian Literature for Women and Children in Mission Lands, Women's Christian Colleges in India, Madras, Vellore, St. Christopher's, Women's Christian Colleges in Japan, Women's Medical School, Shanghai, Northfield, Winona and Geneva Summer Conferences, and the Missionary Education Movement.[121]

By 1937, dark clouds filled the sky. Almost everyone felt the impact of the worldwide economic depression that began with the stock market crash in October 1929. War clouds portending World War II loomed. These and other changes could not help but be felt on the mission field and among the ecumenical sisterhood of Christian women everywhere. WBFM women pressed on. With or without the full awareness of the denomination, the circumstances of these times and other changes contributed to the downward trend of mission engagement and mission support. Major WBFM organizational changes followed the end of World War II. At that time the WBFM merged with the BFM to assume oversight of the denomination's foreign mission program.

Volunteering

> Our ladies were all very eager to help and
> it seemed as if they thought that every little
> stitch taken was an advancement for God's Kingdom.[122]

---

121. *ARWBFM*, 1937, 58. It is interesting to note that the first listing of WBFM interdenominational committees and the names of representatives serving on those committees appeared in the *ARWBFM*, 1924, 7.

122. *ARWBFM*, 1907, 15.

Although nothing was specifically mentioned in the WBFM foundational documents, the work and actualization of the WBFM rested almost totally upon women volunteers or unpaid laborers. Nurtured by the culture of separate spheres, the nature of volunteering did not remain static throughout the years of this study, but it evolved along with the changing times and the changing roles of women. For WBFM women, however, the most grassroots, far-reaching, and inclusive undertaking of women in mission work began with the creation of the Hindu Petticoat Guild in 1895. It seemed like such a logical undertaking at the time—using ordinary skills and ordinary resources to meet the needs of missionaries.[123] Although the sewing machine was patented by Elias Howe in 1846, and over 110,000 sewing machines were produced by Isaac M. Singer by 1860,[124] sewing and handwork by women, with or without a sewing machine, was a necessary feature of everyday living and the hallmark of home life.

In 1895, the mission work in India became especially worrisome.[125] In the summer of 1894, Dr. and Mrs. Jacob Chamberlain, the Reverend William W. Scudder, Miss Kitty Scudder, and Dr. and Mrs. John Scudder and young daughter Ida all had returned to the States for rest, leaving the fifteen remaining missionaries[126] overworked, and the work understaffed. Then, on March 4, 1895, William Scudder died. The remaining missionaries were exhausted and in dire need of furloughs. How to help them became the question.[127] The Board of Managers met and the foreign secretary for India, Clara DeF. (DeForest) Burrell, called for help:

We must have *men, women, money* for India, *now*. I beseech you therefore, that you

---

123. This reference was made by the Sewing Guild secretary in 1906, when she said:

One aspect of the work of the Summer Sewing Guild is the coming together of a need and its supply. Our busy missionaries in foreign lands have only to send word of the need in their work, for anything within the bounds of the Sewing Guild, to find a host of waiting, loving, eager-to-help women, girls and boys in the homeland ready to lift the care and thought of it all from them in their own willing fingers. *ARWBFM*, 1906, 17.

It is unlikely that in 1906 the Sewing Guild secretary could have foreseen the request of a missionary in 1917 "for a set of tires for a Ford car!" *ARWBFM*, 1917, 18.

124. *New Encyclopedia Britannica Micropaedia* (Chicago: Helen Hemingway Benton, 1974), 91.

125. *ARWBFM*, 1895, 17-21.

126. This is the author's count using the *MGS*, 1895, 15. Also used was *ARWBFM*, 1895, 17-21.

127. In its report to the General Synod in 1897, the BFM referred to the Women's Board and "its generous pledge, also, to provide for the Hindu Girls' Schools in India, threatened with discontinuance by reason of retrenchment ordered by the Board." *MGS*, 1897, xx-xxi.

In the 1897 *Annual Report*, the WBFM response for additional funding for India is noted this way:

Nothing has cheered the hearts of your Board of Managers so much as the prompt and ready response to the appeal for help to save our Hindu Girls' School. When the promise was made to "Synod's Board," and the pledge given that the means would be provided, it was with fear and trembling—not on account of any want of faithfulness or loyalty on the part of our Societies, but knowing the depressed financial condition of the country—we feared it might be impossible for the needed amount to be raised. With overflowing hearts we can recount that God has been better to us than our fears, for the entire sum has been paid into our treasury. *ARWBFM*, 1897, 9.

present your bodies, not those of workers already over-burdened, but *your* bodies a living sacrifice—your reasonable service.[128]

With this call for help came the creation in 1895 of the Hindu Petticoat Guild. The culture of separate spheres in the 1890s continued to mandate that women wear floor-length skirts, under which they wore garments commonly referred to as petticoats.[129] Made of large amounts of cotton material, ordinary petticoats could be transformed from clothes into bandages and blankets, and their usefulness extended long after their suitability as petticoats had passed. At the mission's girls' schools in India, Hindu girls from families in poverty often arrived at the beginning of the school year wearing rags. This situation required missionaries to expend valuable time and energy instructing young Hindu girls in sewing appropriate clothing.[130]

With the creation of the committee and a request to WBFM women for sewn petticoats, 1,238 garments were received for India. They were sorted and packed over the summer months of 1895, "thus saving $500 to the Mission."[131] In 1896, the number of garments increased to 2,526, and throughout the following years the number continued to increase. Katharine Van Nest, a remarkably ordered and efficient woman, served as chief organizer and packer, and she would continue doing this work for the next twelve years.[132] Other women worked with Katharine Van Nest in the job of sorting and packing, a task that grew larger with each succeeding year.

Several observations about the early years of the guild reveal facets of this evolving program. After the first year, the name was changed. The Hindu Petticoat Guild became the Summer Sewing Guild, a name which was again changed in 1909 to reflect the request of missionaries to receive the boxes earlier in the school year and

---

128. *ARWBFM*, 1895, 21.

129. In a one and one-half page, single-spaced, typewritten history of the Sewing Guild, believed to be written in 1948, petticoats were identified as "really full percale skirts." "Sewing Guild History 1900-1957 Clippings and Typewritten Resume" File, RCA Archives.

130. In 1898 a thank-you letter arrived from India and noted that Mrs. Lewis Scudder had supervision of more than seventy girls. Once the boxes arrived, there was "No need to select and buy materials, no need to call up girls and measure them for clothes, no need to tear off each length of sleeve, waist and skirt, no need to oversee days and weeks of sewing in order to have the girls properly clothed. All this has been saved Mrs. Scudder, and you would have realized it, had you seen her beaming face, as she looked over her stores of wealth." *ARWBFM*, 1898, 38.

131. *MGS*, 1896, xxi.

132. According to Mary Chamberlain:

Miss Katharine Van Nest was the efficient, resourceful, indefatigable Secretary of the Sewing Guild in its early years and to her wise judgment and careful administration its great success was chiefly due. The sorting and packing of the thousands of articles which were sent in to the Board rooms became, in her hands, a task reduced to the minimum of labor and the maximum of efficiency. Chamberlain, *Fifty Years*, 110.

Katharine Van Nest served as secretary of the Sewing Guild from its organization in 1895 through 1907. She also served as a member of the Board of Managers 1896-1930. Te Winkel, *The Sixth Decade*, 108.

Hindu girls wearing jackets and "ravekas" made by the Sewing Guild (*Mission Gleaner*, Aug. 1899).

before the holiday season. The work of sewing then shifted from summer to the winter months, which benefited most women, especially those living on farms.

From the beginning, the organizers wanted to make clear that contributions to the Sewing Guild were not to subtract from those gifts that would normally find their way into the WBFM treasury. "We want always to emphasize that the work of the Sewing Guild is a special and extra gift; it is not an obligation, but rather a cup of cold water given for love's sake."[133] And auxiliaries were quick to respond, "Everything has been donated as you requested and not one cent taken from the treasury."[134] The names of individuals and groups contributing to the Sewing Guild were listed each year in the *Annual Report*.

After the success of the first year, the work was broadened, so in subsequent years, boxes were sent not only to India, but also to China[135] and Japan and, beginning 1899, to Arabia. In 1899, missionaries began to be asked what they needed and wanted. This information proved extremely helpful. Knowing that missionaries needed dolls and Christmas gifts, prizes to be given as rewards, basted patchwork, prepared sewing patches, hospital supplies, and simple clothing such as jackets, mittens, and socks all helped women at home provide what was specifically needed. Contributions of money were welcomed to cover transportation costs. The system became streamlined and more efficient. As the secretary characteristically emphasized, "We shall be able to send to each missionary just the size and sort of article she can use, *with no waste*."[136]

From its earliest beginnings, WBFM women recognized the multiple values of each gift, and how the act of giving itself affected human lives. In the work of the Sewing Guild, everyone benefited. There was a kind of hidden magic at work between those who did the sewing and those to whom petticoats and socks were given, and WBFM women understood this. Mary Baldwin, who would succeed Katharine Van Nest as secretary of the Sewing Guild and serve as president of the WBFM from 1918-1921, identified this hidden magic this way:

---

133. *ARWBFM*, 1900, 40.

134. *ARWBFM*, 1904, 16.

135. In 1903, shipments to China ceased. In that year the *Annual Report* stated, "It was with deep regret that we crossed China off our list, but because of the high duties the missionaries have to pay on goods from America it was deemed right." *ARWBFM*, 1903, 20.

136. *ARWBFM*, 1899, 36.

Our work is like Shakespeare's conception of mercy, "It blesseth him that gives and him that takes." In the making of these garments we are enabled to express our sympathy in a very definite form, and thereby our interest in the whole cause is stimulated, and the good that comes to us in the doing of this work may even outweigh the benefit it brings to the recipient.[137]

Beginning in 1898, separate reports on the sewing project began to appear in the WBFM *Annual Reports*. These Sewing Guild reports almost always contained testimonials or words of appreciation from those who received and from those who gave. These letters of appreciation communicated much about the nature of giving and the nature of the WBFM. A sampling from these letters allows a sense of the impact of this program.

From India:

One needs to have the care of a Girls' Boarding School to know the true value of these boxes and the joy they bring to our hearts.... Besides the clothes, the pads, pencils and other things save us much when we have prize-givings, and the dolls! What would we do without the dolls? One of the Zenana workers told me that they, almost as much as anything incline the hearts of the Hindus to listen to us and to the old story that is so ever new.[138]

From China:

Last night had you been with us you would have had another proof of the good work done by the Sewing Guild. We closed our school after weeks of hard study. Each pupil received a bag, a pair of wristlets, a book and a card. I wish all who had helped make the bags and wristlets could have seen the happy faces, and could have heard how the gay cretonne of the bags and the pretty colors of the wristlets were admired. When we told the women and girls kind friends at home had made these gifts for them, several spoke up at once saying, "Thank them very much for us."[139]

The Sewing Guild Secretary reported this word from Japan:

In Japan we hear of two Sunday Schools where no Christmas gifts could have been given had it not been for the Sewing Guild boxes. At one there were just

---

137. *ARWBFM*, 1908, 16.

138. *ARWBFM*, 1906, 18.

An additional letter from India noted:

The girls are making quilts for Dr. Hart's Hospital beds of the patch work sent so abundantly last year. They work in Kensington stitch, on a wide border at top and bottom or on large squares in the center [with] such words as "Ask and it shall be given." "Seek and ye shall find." We mean to have every spread speak to the onlookers one verse at least from the "Word of Life." *ARWBFM*, 1901, 20.

139. *ARWBFM*, 1902, 20.

enough, only one card left. From the other a native worker writes: 'I was surprised to see so many dolls. They seem to want to say something to me when I opened the box. One hundred and fifty children each had a gift.'[140]

From Arabia:

I have given away a very large number of garments this winter to the school children, and they have been the means of keeping some desirable pupils in our school. The people are *so* poor. I wish you could get a glimpse of an old woman who comes to have her foot dressed each morning; she is blind and a young girl guides her to the hospital. For absolute raggedness and dirt I have never seen anything like them. The foot was in a condition beyond description; now it is sweet and healing, and to [sic] morrow she and her niece will be dressed in brand new garments from the new boxes, and I wish you might hear and understand the blessings she will call down upon you, something like this: "God bless you, God prolong your life, God give health to your children, God protect and guard you," etc. etc. These two have not had a new garment for many a long day, and, as I told the old lady this morning, she will feel like a new woman.[141]

Women on the home front wrote letters to the secretary of the Sewing Guild, and these messages were often noted in the annual reports. A sampling of these letters follows:

Into the making of the baby socks, how many prayers have been woven that the little feet might walk the "narrow way"; and with the quilts for the hospitals, has there not been the intercession that the Great Physician would be with them, with His healing touch for body and soul?"[142]

It has been interesting to watch the work at home. Many of our members have given the time for this hand service from the days of the summer resting time; busy farmers' wives have given the spare moments; groups of young girls have gathered sometimes for an hour a day to help us; to be sure they were learning to sew, but they were learning other lessons as well, as the gift of $2.37 from one group of seven proved.[143]

Sad hearts have been helped by working for others through the Guild, and the whole is summed up by one Society: "Our gift is small, for we are a band of busy mothers and wives, but we trust this little may do some good, for we all feel that we were working for the 'Master.'"[144]

---

140. *ARWBFM*, 1906, 18.
141. *ARWBFM*, 1904, 17-18.
An additional letter from Arabia noted:
I know the garments have been the means of opening doors and hearts where we trust the name of Christ will yet become precious and having received earthly good at our hands may they become willing to listen to heavenly things. *ARWBFM*, 1901, 20.
142. *ARWBFM*, 1898, 39.
143. *ARWBFM*, 1898, 37.
144. *ARWBFM*, 1900, 40.

Loading sewing guild boxes
at 25 E. 22nd St., 1924

An ever increasing number of auxiliaries is at work during the summer months. Word comes of a little group of five farmers' wives who went through winter snow to lend their aid in the sewing, because in the summer they were too busy in the fields and they *must* have their share in the work.[145]

One secretary tells thus of the pleasure side of the work: "The young ladies *did not* dress the dolls, only the *old* ladies, some with very white hair at that, and we had a very pleasant time doing them.[146]

Twenty-six dolls were dressed by a dear friend of our Church, whom God has laid on a bed of sickness for eighteen years, and who writes, "I am so thankful I can use my hands for Him who has done so much for me."[147]

Each year a greater variety of gifts is sent, perhaps by those who do not love the needle. One box seems to have given special pleasure and the missionary writes: – "I want to send my hearty thanks for the variety of things in my box this year."[148]

One president of an auxiliary writes: "We are only few in number, and all have many home cares, so our work will not amount to much, but little as it may be, I feel sure it will be a blessing to us to do it, and a little help to our missionaries."[149]

The Sewing Guild continued to grow and evolve with the passing years. During occupancy years at the RCA Church House at 25 East 22nd Street, the sorting and packing process took place in the basement. Following the fire in 1939 and the move to 156 Fifth Avenue, the sorting and packing took place once more in the basement.

---

145. *ARWBFM*, 1903, 19.
146. Ibid.
147. *ARWBFM*, 1904, 16.
An additional comment by the Sewing Guild secretary noted:
It is a comfort to know that after other forms of service must be relinquished, many are still able to continue their activities in this department of church work, and by so doing are saved from that sad experience of feeling they are outliving their usefulness. *ARWBFM*, 1909, 16.
148. *ARWBFM*, 1907, 17.
149. *ARWBFM*, 1908, 16.

By the end of 1948, the fiftieth anniversary of the Sewing Guild, the 2,155 articles sent in 1898 had grown to approximately 50,000 articles weighing nearly fourteen tons.[150] The size of the project required renting warehouse space in Jersey City, New Jersey, to accomplish the task. In a 1952 letter to all auxiliaries, the executive secretary, Ruth Ransom, reported:

> In all, 138 large wooden cases were packed and shipped as follows: 1 to Africa, 63 to Arabia, 14 to Iraq and 60 to India. In addition $1,500 is being sent to those missionaries who reported they could purchase their needs more advantageously on the field. The total value of these supplies was over $21,000. We can honestly admit we were over whelmed by the response to the requests of the missionaries. However, even this amount did not completely fill all the needs. The upward trend in prices which is still with us made that impossible. This, together with the shortages in some of the assignments sent to us, made it very difficult....
>
> You may not know just how Sewing Guild functions after you have done your part. On the lst of May, Mrs. G.R. Gnade, member of the Department of Women's Work, Mrs. P.T. Wagner, chairman of the Sewing Guild committee and Mrs. A.W. Schwager, secretary in charge of Sewing Guild, went to the warehouse in Jersey City, New Jersey, to do the preliminary sorting of the cartons. They are classified according to the Unions so now you can understand how important that number given to you for your Union is in this process. It saves a great deal of time and much of the sorting can be done by the men at the warehouse when the number is clearly indicated on the carton. From there on the women of the local churches come in groups of from six to ten each to do the actual packing. There are many problems involved in this. We owe a great deal to these women who give of their time and strength to save on the labor charges.[151]

The story of women volunteers and the emergence of women as professional volunteers is a story that awaits further research and scholarship.[152] It is a story in which WBFM and WBDM women were powerfully involved.

---

150. *Minutes of the Department of Women's Work*, December 14, 1948, 6.

151. Letter dated September 2, 1952, to all auxiliaries from Ruth Ransom, executive secretary, BFM. "Sewing Guild History, 1900-1957, Clippings and Typewritten Resume" file, RCA Archives.

152. In an article titled, "Women in the Professions: A Research Agenda for American Historians," published in 1982, historians Joan Jacobs Brumberg and Nancy Tomes posed the question of the professional volunteer. They say:

> Within the nineteenth-century woman's sphere, unpaid work outside the home became a route to self-respect and power oftentimes involving a lifetime commitment to a single organization or cause. As volunteers, women participated in a broad range of activities: religious schools and missions, military nursing, social work, and institutional management. Patterns of female persistence in volunteer groups suggest that we consider seriously the notion of a volunteer "career" which embodies some important professional qualities. Joan Jacobs Brumberg and Nancy Tomes, "Women in the Professions: A Research Agenda for American Historians," *Reviews in American History* 10 (June, 1982), 275.

Historian Patricia R. Hill pursues this question in *The World Their Household.* See especially the chapters, "The Science of Missions," and "Changing Worlds."

Hospitality

For WBFM women and other church women, showing hospitality reflected who the women were and how they understood themselves as members of Christ's church. No mention was made in the foundational documents about hospitality. Yet, Sarah Doremus herself stood at the docks waiting for departing and returning missionaries, and she welcomed people into her home. She was joined by a host of women who did what she did. They welcomed people with Christ-like attitudes. This attitude was not formalized through the establishment of a separate specialized group. It simply pervaded.

From the time that the WBFM moved into Room 10 and could claim its own space, hospitality came to reflect that place as well as an attitude. Room 10 was furnished to be an intentionally welcoming place, where visitors were invited and expected. It was a place for social interaction, for working together, for praying and studying together. Out of town visitors to New York City of course stopped in at the Church House to say hello. They were expected.

As the number and needs of missionaries increased along with the expense of staying in New York City, the WBFM in 1938 established a Hospitality Committee. Members of this Hospitality Committee included Mrs. J. Preston Searle, chair, Miss E. Van Brunt, Mrs. Claude J. Fingar, Mrs. Charles E. Tuxill, Margaret G. Fagg (Rev. John G.), and Mrs. J. M. Montgomery. The following year, Margaret G. Fagg, who herself had served as a missionary to China 1887-1894 and who was a veteran WBFM leader and volunteer, took the chair, a position she held through 1945. Hazel Gnade followed Margaret Fagg as chair of the Hospitality Committee, and Hazel Gnade remained in this position until the formation of the National Department of Women's Work in 1960, at which time the Hospitality Committee came to an end.

This story of the role and nature of WBFM hospitality cannot be told without mentioning two women, whose love for showing hospitality and whose contributions to mission work might not be otherwise noted—Kate Olcott (Mrs. Eben E.) and Margaret Gillespie Fagg.

Before the Hospitality Committee became formalized in 1938, Kate Olcott functioned as the unofficial head of hospitality. She served on the Board of Managers 1901-1934, and for twenty-nine of those years served as the Secretary for Arabia.

As a woman of means, Kate Olcott loved to travel. She served on deputation teams visiting foreign mission stations[153] and participated in international gatherings representing the WBFM.[154] In *The Sixth Decade* anniversary history, the following tribute is paid to Kate Olcott:

"Neglected Arabia"[155] paid the following tribute to Mrs. E.E. Olcott who served from 1901 to 1930 as Secretary for Arabia of the Woman's Board, and who passed to her reward on Thanksgiving Day, 1934. "Hers was never a formal interest in

153. See *ARWBFM*, 1905, 7 and *ARWBFM*, 1908, 12.
154. *ARWBFM*, 1916, 13.
155. This was a missionary periodical on the work in Arabia, that was published 1902-1949.

Mission work. Generous as were her gifts for the support of missionaries and their work in many lands, she will be remembered best for her rich gifts of time and personal service. Her home was shared with every missionary who came to New York City. She was at the docks to meet them when they landed and to wave them farewell as they departed. In the hot months of summer many a missionary enjoyed her hospitality in the Catskill Mountains, and her letters, written always in her own hand, went constantly to the missionaries in Arabia. Another in her position might have been content to make gifts of money only or to maintain through a secretary her wide contacts with friends the world around. Mrs. Olcott gave always of herself and so became enshrined in the hearts of all who knew her.

'One does not analyze the character of a mother and pay measured tribute to her virtues, and to our missionary family Mrs. Olcott was just that. We mourn the loss of one very near and dear to us and we thank God for the sweet inspiration of her life.'[156]

Margaret Gillespie Fagg served as a "missionary assistant" in China 1889-1894, along with her husband, the Reverend John G. Fagg.[157] Upon their return,[158] Margaret joined in the work of the WBFM. Until her death on July 2, 1955, Margaret Fagg worked tirelessly on behalf of the WBFM board.

From 1898 through 1910, Margaret Fagg served as the corresponding foreign secretary for China. After twelve years at this position, she took up the work in 1910 as chair of the Missionary Candidate Committee. This standing committee, which had been created in 1903, was charged with the task of receiving all applications from women who wished to be considered for missionary candidacy by the WBFM board, corresponding and conducting interviews with the candidates, and recommending candidates to be taken under appointment by the WBFM and approved by the BFM. As the number of missionaries increased, so did the demands of the missionary candidate secretary position. These demands required not only time, but also the ability to discern the character and commitment of each candidate.[159] Following her service of seven years as missionary candidate secretary, Margaret Fagg served on the Nominating Committee and Publication Committee.

---

156. Te Winkel, *The Sixth Decade*, 104.

157. For comments about Margaret Fagg during her missionary days in China, see Gerald F. De Jong, *The Reformed Church in China 1842-1951*, Historical Series of the Reformed Church in America, no. 22 (Grand Rapids: Eerdmans, 1992), 114-17.

158. When they returned from China, John Fagg became pastor of the Reformed Church in New Paltz, New York, where he served for one year. In 1895, he became pastor of the Middle Collegiate Church, New York City, replacing the Reverend Talbot W. Chambers. Here he remained until his death May 3, 1917, at fifty-seven years of age. In 1898 he was elected to the BFM, and in 1910 served as president. He also served as president of the trustees of the Arabian Mission, and in 1914 became president of the General Synod. *MGS*, 1917, 258-259.

159. The following women have served as chairman of the Missionary Candidate Committee:

1903-1909	Olivia Lawrence, home corresponding secretary
1910-1916	Margaret Fagg
1917	Olivia Lawrence
1918	Katharine Van Nest

In 1938, when the new Missionary Hospitality Committee was formed, Margaret Fagg was a member. For the years 1939-1945, Margaret Fagg served as chair of the Missionary Hospitality Committee. In her report, which appeared in the *Annual Report* for 1945, she noted:

> After a long lull in the movements of our missionaries, now that the war is over and peace—tho' slowly—is beginning to brood over the earth, there has been a great stirring among our missionaries.... And—after a long delay—many have sailed away to take up their beloved work on the mission field....
>
> This year over 125 furloughed missionaries and children of missionaries and newly appointed missionaries, singly and in groups, have been guests in the homes of the Hospitality Committee at luncheons, dinners, shopping, and sightseeing expeditions....
>
> Acknowledgment must be given to the western members of the committee who have had many opportunities to follow the injunction of the Apostle Paul to be "given to hospitality" to our missionaries not only but also to the sons and daughters of missionaries, now students at Hope College and Central College.[160]

On March 6, 1945, the WBFM Board of Directors met and clarified its understanding of "Hospitality For Missionaries on Furlough or New Candidates."[161] It established that the WBFM and its future incarnations would continue to do what Sarah Doremus and her friends did years ago. Much would depend on the leadership of the person heading the Hospitality Committee. Who that person was, her availability, skills, and her dedication to the mission cause would determine the effectiveness of what was meant by hospitality. Sarah Doremus understood this. So did Kate Olcott, Margaret Fagg, and Hazel Gnade.

1919-1920	Margaret B. Scudder (Mrs. Henry J.)
1921-1925	Ella Dutcher Romig (Mrs. Edgar)
1926-1931	Elizabeth Van Brunt
1932-1942	Frances Beardslee (Mrs. John W. Jr.)
1943	transition year
1944-1946	Marjorie James (Mrs. M. Stephen)

Following the 1946 merger of the WBFM and the BFM, the Reverend Abraham Rynbrant became chairman of the Missionary Candidate Committee in 1947.

160. "Annual Report of the WBFM" Box 712, folder 22, RCA Archives.

161. "Woman's Board of Foreign Missions October 1944-April, 1946" file, Box 710.1, RCA Archives.

Chapter 7

Post WBFM Years

We have been workers together for Christ, and rich have been the blessings granted to us. Our efforts have been crowned with a good measure of success, but we have not yet reached the limit of our possibility or our responsibility.

Mary A. Loring Cushing
Home Corresponding Secretary
ARWBFM, 1895, 11

On May 1, 1946, the organization known as the WBFM came to an end. In the postwar years, there was a strong movement to address the issue of greater corporate efficiency.[1] When considering the tremendous grassroots involvement of church

---

1. According to Patricia R. Hill, "Helen Montgomery had argued eloquently against the proposed merger of women's societies with denominational mission boards at the Ecumenical Conference of 1900, with apparent success. But pressure for such mergers mounted as the women's societies wielded ever greater financial and administrative influence. At the World Missionary Conference in Edinburgh in 1910 several denominational board leaders announced that the time had come for merger; the issue was thereafter contested, denomination by denomination. The Methodist Episcopal Church (South) merged its societies in 1910. In 1922, the Presbyterian General Assembly, without prior consultation of the bodies involved, merged the woman's board with the general board. In 1924, the National Council of Congregational Churches ordered a similar merger of its women's boards with the American Board. Baptist women resisted merger successfully until 1955, but then their society had never enjoyed the same degree of autonomy that several other major women's boards exercised. Methodist women maintained a separate Woman's Division within their denomination after the union

130

women and their amazing success in raising and administering "their own" money for missions, there was no doubt that "woman's work for woman"[2] had placed the WBFM in a position of power.[3] In recognition of this success, the General Synod encouraged a merger of the WBFM with the denominational BFM largely in the name of corporate efficiency. By a majority vote of their WBFM Board members, the women agreed.[4] They came to the belief that overall efficiency and greater church unity would be gained by merging the two boards, and no loss of individual involvement would result. In a letter to the presidents of local missionary societies dated July 13, 1945, Lilian Van Strien (Rev. David), president of the WBFM wrote:

of the Methodist Episcopal Church (North) with the Methodist Protestant Church and the Methodist Episcopal Church (South) in 1939, but this division was not concerned solely—or even primarily—with foreign missions. Such mergers inevitably diluted the power formerly wielded by women in foreign missions. Women members were usually in a minority on merged boards and rarely held the top executive posts. When they retired, they were generally replaced by men." Patricia R. Hill, *The World Their Household: The American Woman's Foreign Mission Movement and Cultural Transformation, 1870-1920,* (Ann Arbor: Univ. of Michigan, 1985), 167.

2. See Leslie A. Flemming's essay, "Introduction: Studying Women Missionaries in Asia," in Leslie A. Flemming, ed. *Women's Work for Women: Missionaries and Social Change in Asia,* papers growing out of a panel on women missionaries given at the 1986 meeting of the National Association for Women's Studies (Boulder: Westview Press, 1989), 1. See also Dana L. Robert, *American Women in Mission: A Social History of Their Thought and Practice,* 130. Dana Robert notes,

As Women's groups founded their own journals to disseminate missionary intelligence to their constituencies, a common missiology emerged, known as "Woman's Work for Woman." The basic goal of "Woman's Work for Woman" remained the same as in the mission theory of early nineteenth century wives—to evangelize women and to bring them to salvation. But the end of evangelization was not the establishment of three-self churches: for "heathen" women, evangelization was intertwined with "civilization," with being elevated by Christianity into social equality with western women and into positions of respect in their own societies. The proponents of "Woman's Work for Woman" assumed that non-Christian religions led to the degradation of women, while Christianity provided not only salvation but "civilization," the nineteenth-century term for social liberation, albeit in western dress. The early stages of the woman's missionary movement kept "evangelization" and "civilization" in tension, believing that each led to the other—that the Christian gospel was one piece with western-style social progress.

3. This was true for the Women's Board of Domestic Missions as well. Ten years earlier, in 1936, a Special Committee on Denominational Organization made a report to the General Synod. The special committee took care to note that the BFM and the WBFM "seem to be working out together their mutual problems harmoniously and effectively." But regarding the BDM and the WBDM, "It is the belief of your Committee that there is harmony in the operations of those Boards but we would call to the attention of the Synod that the Women's Board has entire control of the work which is being done by it among the Indians and in Kentucky and that the title to the valuable real estate holdings is held in the name of the Women's Board which distributes and applies the large amount of donations and contributions which it collects through its own Treasury and not through the Synod's Board or with its authority." *MGS,* June, 1936, 403.

4. After agreeing among themselves that the vote must be a majority vote, thirty-eight written ballots were received and counted. Of that number three ballots were discarded for lack of signature, seven votes favored additional study, and twenty-eight votes were cast in favor of the merger. *Minutes of the Special WBFM Meeting,* May 15, 1945.

As you will see, this means that <u>beginning on May 1st, 1946,</u> we will have a United Board of Foreign Missions where there will be men and women working together in policy making and administration of our foreign work.

At Synod, different people asked if it would change the purpose of our Woman's Board of Foreign Missions. <u>It will not in any way change this purpose</u> because we have said repeatedly as we have worked out this plan that it is defined to develop the strength of joint activity while at the same time preserving the value of existing organizations of women. We do not feel that there will be any great change in the local organization in your church. As far as we can see, the only change will be that after <u>May 1, 1946</u> the money will all be sent to one Treasurer.... In our change of organization we see no reason why women's work shall feel the change. The only great change there will be is in the work at headquarters. It has been felt that much work has been duplicated. Therefore, we are trying to make our Board more efficient, but, of course, we do not want to loose [sic] any interest of the individual woman.[5]

Yet, it was an agonizing and painful time for RCA church women and the women's boards. In agreeing to the merger, the women agreed also to a representation of fifteen women on a new Board of Foreign Missions composed of forty-two members, or a 37 percent share of the leadership on the new board, thereby losing majority control over their organizational structure and their considerable finances.

In regard to their organizational structure, Marjorie H. Stauffer (Rev. Milton T.) was among the seven board members who voted in favor of an additional year of study. On her ballot she wrote:

If and when the two Foreign Boards unite and I hope <u>eventually this will be,</u> I trust that it may mean a fifty-fifty representation of the two Boards on the Executive Comm. The fact that the Woman's Board contributes only one third of the money toward the Foreign Board budget, does not seem to me to be a <u>sufficient</u> reason for having the Women's Board represented by a minority number.[6]

In the minutes of the newly merged Board of Foreign Missions dated May 21, 1946, the treasurer's report states that as of April 30, 1946, the WBFM showed cash, excess assets, and legacies totaling $219,688.66. The denominational BFM on the same date recorded a cash statement of cash, excess assets, and legacies totaling $287,680.63. It is easy to see why the women were hopeful for a good result, yet were experiencing such distress. Perhaps the pathos is nowhere more evident than in the comments of an unnamed at-large Woman's Foreign Mission Board member, whose

---

5. Underlining in the original. Letter from Lilian Van Strien (Rev. David), president of the WBFM, to all WBFM auxiliary presidents, July 13, 1945. WBFM Correspondence Box 712.1, folder 1, RCA Archives.

6. Underlining in the original. Ballot and note from Marjorie H. Stauffer to Ruth Ransom dated May 11, 1945, WBFM Correspondence Box. RCA Archives.

response to the idea of a unified board was solicited in a WBFM letter sent to all board members, members-at-large, and honorary vice-presidents for that purpose:

> The first reaction to the disbanding of the Woman's Board of Foreign Missions is a sense of great loss, but on going into it more fully one realizes the many advantages in unification with the Men's Board so we would give whole-hearted approval. However, for the sake of our local women's groups (missionary societies) we hope the Department of Woman's Work will have definite projects, peculiarly their own, big enough to challenge interest and giving.... Just as in a family each child should have definite tasks and responsibilities so we wish for our Church women, something which is their responsibility, in addition to sharing in the whole Foreign Missions program. (I hope there will not be the "missing" we fearfully anticipate even though being convinced its all for the best interest of the work—to many who have loved the WBFM, sharing its work with prayer and interest.[7]

A newly created Women's Executive Committee of the BFM was organized to help with the process of merging the two foreign boards. The process was complex in many ways. Hard decisions had to be made regarding representation on the new BFM, and who among the many committed WBFM women would serve in the board positions made available to women. With the approval of the 1946 General Synod, however, the new board's membership was established.

Almost immediately the new BFM was faced with controversy. In late November 1946, the Reverend Henry Bast, a member of the new BFM board and pastor of the Bethany Reformed Church in Grand Rapids, Michigan, abruptly resigned from the board. The reasons for his resignation were spelled out in a publication he wrote titled, "An Appeal to the Ministers and Laymen of the Chicago and Iowa Synods," and circulated only to the ministers and laymen in all the RCA churches in the regional synods of Chicago and Iowa.[8] In addition, Bast wrote a letter to the editor of the *Church Herald* dated November 29, 1946, which further distilled and publicized his points of objection. Bast's arguments were many, although taken collectively they all seemed to hinge on matters of power, money, democratic representation, and ecumenism.[9] RCA churches in the Midwest had grown to maturity, he claimed, and now leaders of these Midwest churches wanted to share the power that, according to Bast, had heretofore been disproportionately entrusted to pastors and laymen in the RCA churches on the East Coast. Bast called for a more equal representation of Eastern and Midwestern representatives on all denominational boards and agencies.

---

7. Comments on the Proposed Plan for Unification Received from Board Members, Members-at-large, and Honorary Vice-Presidents of the WBFM" found in RCA Archives, WBFM Correspondence Box 712.1, folder 1.

8. Henry Bast folder, RCA Archives.

9. For a description of how Bast's objections involved ecumenism, and our mission in India in particular, see Heideman, *From Mission to Church*, 5-8.

Bast's scathing indictment of the new BFM and denominational leadership in general erupted after years of frustration. In retrospect, it may certainly be perceived as a high point of denominational tension.[10] This tension can be traced back to two distinct Dutch immigration patterns—immigration to the East Coast in the seventeenth century and to the Midwest in the nineteenth century—and the RCA has struggled with this tension for many years.[11]

For the women on the newly formed BFM, Bast's appeal had special impact. Research sources reveal how the women of the old WBFM collaborated. They worked together unstintingly and developed immense loyalty to one another in support of their desire to aid the women and children of foreign lands.[12] They had become accustomed to expecting the very best from one another, and they delighted in one another's company. They enjoyed facing challenges together, and they enjoyed mutual respect in the process of learning about and supporting foreign missions. The fifteen women on the new BFM were dealt a blow by Bast, and several of their faithful number were singled out in his *Appeal*.[13] What was an attack upon one woman felt like an attack on all women.

In 1947, the General Synod appointed committees to review Bast's accusations, and, subsequently, corrective actions were taken.[14] Reformed Church women soldiered on.

---

10. For an insightful study of conflicts within the RCA, and the Henry Bast conflict specifically, see Lynn Japinga, "Differences in Theory, Friends at Sight: Conflict in the RCA," unpublished paper presented at the conference, "The Reformed Church in America: Searching the Past, Anticipating the Future," Hope College, March 27-29, 1998.

11. See Mary Kansfield, "Dutch Immigration," unpublished paper presented to the Raritan Millstone Heritage Alliance, New Brunswick, N.J., April 27, 2003, in possession of the author.

12. John W. Beardslee, III, pointed out that the WBFM was made up of volunteers, who did a lot by proxy and were extremely loyal to one another. Denominational boards were made up of representatives, who were appointed or elected and often were representative of various geographical parts of the church. The difference between volunteers and representatives is significant. Interview by the author with Edith and John Beardslee, March 14, 2001, New Brunswick, N.J.

13. Frances Beardslee (Rev. John Jr.), Marjorie James (Rev. M. Stephen) and Christine Van Raalte Van Westenberg (Rev. Anthony) received Bast's condemnation because their husbands were also elected to the new BFM, thus making three husband-wife teams, and all lived on the East coast. Two wives of New Brunswick Seminary Professors were singled out. As candidate secretary for the WBFM for ten years (1932-1942), Frances Beardslee and her successor Marjorie James were charged by Bast with favoring New Brunswick Seminary graduates for missionary appointments over graduates from Western Seminary. The appointments of board secretaries, who were hired from outside the RCA, also troubled Bast. This had to be directed at the hiring of Ruth Ransom, who in 1943 was hired by the WBFM and became the first woman to serve as an executive of an official RCA board. Ruth Ransom was of Methodist background, non-Dutch parentage, and, of course, she was a woman. After the merger, Ruth Ransom served from 1946 to 1960 as one of three executive secretaries of the BFM.

Christine Van Raalte Van Westenberg was the great-granddaughter of Albertus and Christina Van Raalte, the founding family of Holland, Michigan. For information on her life, see Elton J. Bruins, Karen G. Schakel, Sara Fredrickson Simmons, and Marie N. Zingle, *Albertus and Christina: The Van Raalte Family, Home and Roots* (Grand Rapids: Eerdmans, 2004), 76-77.

14. Among the actions taken by the 1948 General Synod was the establishment of a permanent Committee on Nominations that was charged to make all boards and agencies of the church "as

Ruth Ransom

In 1950 plans were made for the Women's Board of Domestic Missions (WBDM) to follow the same merger pattern that the WBFM had taken. On January 1, 1951, the merger of the WBDM and the denomination's Board of Domestic Missions was effected. On the newly merged Domestic Board of forty-eight members, women held twenty-one positions or 44 percent of the voting membership on the new board, thus losing control of their organization and funds as well. It was an agonizing and painful time for the women of the WBDM, as it had been for the WBFM women.

In May 1952, following the merger of the WBDM and the Board of Domestic Missions, all women of the denomination were joined into the Department of Women's Work of the Mission Boards. Once again this organization functioned as an auxiliary to the two mission boards. But this arrangement lasted only five years, for it was realized that women in the Midwest and the West needed to be more directly involved in the national work of women.[15] The high cost of travel and the expense of

---

nearly evenly balanced in representing the whole Church as is possible" (*MGS*, 1948, 151-52). Boards and agencies were also urged "to reframe their By-laws or Constitutions so that the Executive Committees of the several Boards and Agencies of the Church shall always be representative of all the Particular Synods of the Church and to keep this balance as nearly as practicable remembering the requirement to have quorums in order that business may be legally transacted" (*MGS*, 1948, 164). The General Synod also accepted the recommendations of the committees to keep the location of the church headquarters at 156 Fifth Avenue, New York City, for not less than five years and to continue RCA membership in the Federal Council of Churches (*MGS*, 141-78).

15. At the annual meeting of the Department of Women's Work of the Mission Boards on January 14, 1958, Alma G. Resch (Arthur E.), who had served as executive director of the Department of Women's

travel accommodations had traditionally entered the consideration of women when they scheduled their meetings and business.[16] But expensive as travel was, women increasingly recognized that a different kind of women's organization was needed to meet the needs of women so geographically distant from one another. The General Synod agreed.

In 1956 the General Synod voted:

> In view of the lack of an over-all organization of the women of our churches, we recommend to the Department of Women's Work that a thorough study be made by them of the women's work in the Presbyterian Church in the United States and similar denominations; that they present a complete program for the women of our churches to the General Synod of 1957 for their approval; and that the General Synod of 1957 recommend to each church in the Reformed Church in America the adoption of this program by the women of the local churches.[17]

A committee was composed of nineteen women members, representing the BFM, the BDM, all RCA educational institutions, and ex officio persons.[18] Gladys L. Pabrey

---

Work and would soon be replaced by Anita Welwood (Rev. J. Foster), reminisced about her involvement with the Department of Women's Work of the Mission Boards. She said:

> In 1952, the Department of Women's Work of the Board of Foreign Missions and the Department of Women's Work of the Board of Domestic Missions, were united to become the Department of Women's Work of the Reformed Church in America. In order to get this Department under way, a temporary plan of organization was outlined by a Committee under the direction of Mrs. Alvin J. Neevel. Mrs. Resch served as Director of this new Department under Mrs. John M. Scutt who was the first President and under Mrs. William J. Pabrey who succeeded her, and since 1957, under Mrs. Robert G. Dickson, the present President.

Minutes, Department of Women's Work of the Mission Boards, January 14, 1958. Box 1, RCA Archives.

16. In her essay, "The Decline, Fall, and Rise of Women in the Reformed Church in America, 1947-1997," Carol Hageman remembers,

> The executive committee met monthly and all members at large were invited and received minutes of all meetings. However, the women's board was not about to use any more money on itself than was absolutely necessary, so there was no budget item for board travel. That precluded many who lived at a distance from attending, since all the executive committee meetings were held in New York City. However, the membership generally wanted it that way, in order that as much money as possible could go directly into field work. Distance did not seem to diminish interest and commitment. I remember well women coming to New York City by train from the Midwest, sitting up, traveling coach all the way and sharing with us the bag lunches we brought for the meeting day!

In Reneé House and John Coakley, eds., *Patterns and Portraits, Women in the History of the Reformed Church in America*, The Historical Series of the Reformed Church in America, no. 31 (Grand Rapids: Eerdmans, 1999), 151.

17. *MGS*, 1957, 324.

18. Committee members included Gladys L. Pabrey (William J.), chairman; Ruth Dickson (Rev. Robert), Ruth Ransom, Beth Marcus (ex-officio), Alma G. Resch (Arthur E.), Molly Dykstra (Rev. Adelphos A.), Dorothy Scutt (John), Jean Koster (Rev. Gerard), Mary Blair Bennett (Rev. William), Frances Gideon (M. Howard), Elizabeth Shade (Rev. Howard), Ann Hoek, (Herman J.), Mrs. Henry Johnson, Dee de Ruyter (George), Martha Lautenbach, (Robert), Jantina Holleman, Marjorie James (Rev. M. Stephen), Iola M. Hoffman (Rev. Harvey B.), and Mrs. George Sluyter. *MGS*, 1957, 324.

(Mrs. William J.) served as chair. Over the year, this committee investigated the organizational structures of fourteen denominations.[19] In June 1957, the committee reported to the General Synod, and the synod passed the following recommendations:

1. That a National Department of Women's Work be established to promote the work of the Program Boards of General Synod.
2. That the purpose of this National Department be:

> The Purpose of the National Department of Women's Work shall be to unite all the women of the Reformed Church in America in Christian fellowship; to make Christ known throughout the world; to deepen the spiritual life of each of its members and to develop a sense of personal responsibility for the whole mission of the Church, through a program of Education, Service, Prayer and Giving.

3. That the year 1958 be used as a year of Education, and that the year 1959 be used as a year of Preparation and Promotion, and the organization begin to function January 1, 1960.[20]

The new National Department of Women's Work ushered in a new vocabulary for Reformed Church women. Guilds and Circles became familiar words. Although not all local missionary societies and ladies aid societies adopted the new terminology, the new guild structure was exciting and forward looking. The structure of the new organization was based on four areas of involvement: spiritual life, education, service, and organization. There was a place for everyone who wanted to participate, and a representative Board of Managers oversaw the entire organization. An annual Bible study book for use by all women was published, often written by someone within the denomination, and, due to the relatively small size of the denomination, the author of the Bible study was or soon became personally known to many women. The women were excited that"for the first time, in 1961, we will have a Bible Study

---

19. These denominations included American Baptist, Christian Methodist Episcopal Church, Church of the Brethren, Congregational Christian, Evangelical and Reformed Church, Evangelical United Brethren Church, Methodist Church, National Baptist Convention, U.S.A. Inc., Presbyterian Church U.S., Presbyterian Church U.S.A., Protestant Episcopal Church, United Church of Canada, United Lutheran Church, and United Presbyterian Church. *MGS*, 1957, 324-25.

20. *MGS*, 1957, 328.

The substance and wording of this purpose statement differs significantly from the stated purpose of the WBFM ("to aid the BFM of the RCA by promoting its work among the women and children of heathen lands.") Missing is the mission vocabulary and a focus on the world "out there." The new statement of purpose seems to suggest a turning away from "the world" and a shift inward, "to unite in fellowship in order to make Christ known throughout the world," which is the wording of the statement of purpose in *The Handbook for Women's Organization, RCA* (n.p. 1960). For an insightful study into the decline of the Board of Foreign Missions, later the Board of World Mission, see Donald A. Luidens, "National Engagement with Localism: The Last Gasp of the Corporate Denomination?" unpublished paper delivered at New Brunswick Theological Seminary, April, 2002, p. 12. Soon to appear in David Roozen, ed., *Denominational Identities in Unsettled Times: Theology, Structure, and Change* (Grand Rapids: Eerdmans, n.d.).

book written and published expressly for use in our Guilds. Dr. Vernon J. Kooy of New Brunswick Seminary has graciously consented to write this study for us on the Gospel of John."[21]

The new structure of the National Department of Women's Work united RCA women by tying them together across the country. Strengthening the relationships among Reformed Church women was further enhanced by holding national gatherings of women. The First National Women's Assembly was held in 1957 in Buck Hill Falls, Pennsylvania. Beginning in 1962, RCA Triennials have been held in various cities throughout the country every three years.[22] Multiple skills, honed over years of practice within the women's boards, have enabled women so carefully to organize and administer these events that hundreds of women from across the country and around the world gather for worship, Bible studies, and presentations by gifted speakers. Meeting new friends and greeting old friends at Triennial gatherings have given the occasions the feeling of a family reunion. This is true currently as much as it has been true in the past.

---

21. *MGS*, 1960, 305.
22. See Appendix B for a complete list of the Women's Triennials.

Chapter 8

Hazel Gnade's Life and Ministry

Hospitality as it evolved for the Christian is an expression of love. It involves giving a piece of one's life to another with no thought of return. But hospitality is not limited to people as such. We must be hospitable to new ideas, to the leading of the Holy Spirit into new forms of service.

Ruth Dickson
1966 Guild Study Book
Glory Be . . .

Hazel Blanche Brown was born about dinner time May 30, 1902, in Ridgewood, New Jersey, the youngest of three children born to Blanche Stockton and James Lewis Brown, II. Both parents were of English descent. Hazel, along with her brother James and sister Gertrude, grew up in an upper-middle-class environment in Ridgewood. The Browns were religious people. They lived their lives in the context of a local Methodist church. Both Hazel's mother and father were generous, warm, and loving parents, although they were strict with their children, especially regarding Sunday observance. As was customary for the time, Hazel's mother was a housewife and church worker. Her father was a successful contractor and owned his own contracting business.

As a child, Hazel was happy and displayed amazing energy, as she would her whole life.[1] She loved outdoor games and playing with other children. She played and fought

---

1. In reflecting on Hazel Gnade's life and ministry, the Reverend Ted Zandstra, a close friend of the Gnades and successor to the Reverend Garry Gnade as secretary of the board of pensions, remembers

139

with her siblings, especially her older sister Gertrude. As adults Hazel and Gertrude would come to enjoy a close life-long friendship. Generally speaking, Hazel was an obedient child, although not always successful at controlling her childish impulse to throw stones at passing trains. She learned to play the piano, which became one of many activities she enjoyed throughout her life. As an elementary student at Union Street School in Ridgewood, Hazel was a good student, and she loved school. Early on she knew she wanted to become a missionary. Above all else, Hazel Blanche Brown grew up filled with the sure knowledge that she was loved—loved by her parents and family, loved by her church, and loved by God.

In time, the Brown family moved to Ho-Ho-Kus, where their upscale home and new Buick sedan mirrored the growth and success of James Brown's construction business. But dark days lay ahead for the family. James Brown became the victim of tuberculosis. In spite of good medical care, which at that time included a prescribed diet, bed rest, and time spent breathing fresh air, James Brown's health declined. With no money coming in, and with the protection of Social Security not yet available, the family's savings began to dwindle. The family sold the Ho-Ho-Kus house and bought a small house in nearby Midland Park, which had a large outdoor porch on which Hazel's father could sit and breathe fresh outdoor air. The family's Christian faith in the resurrection and assurance in God's future only increased. At one point, when James Brown seemed very near death, young Hazel penned a birthday letter to her father that gave expression to her belief in miracles and healing. Shortly thereafter, Hazel was told her father was out of immediate danger.

Hazel graduated from Ridgewood High School and was offered a college scholarship, but the condition of the family's finances would not allow her to attend college. So Hazel took business courses and lived at home to help her mother with her father's care. As Hazel's mother was a good cook, Hazel too learned to prepare and to serve outstanding meals. Cooking delighted Hazel, and her ability to cook and to entertain would one day become legendary.

One evening at a Methodist church service, the special music was presented by a quartet, and Hazel was introduced to the baritone singer. Garry Gnade had a lovely voice. On their first date Garry invited Hazel to accompany him to a worship service at a mission for alcoholics in Paterson, where Garry sang a solo. At first this twenty-year-old Dutch immigrant didn't seem particularly romantic to eighteen-year-old Hazel, but he did seem friendly, and he was an engaging conversationalist. Garry's strong Christian faith impressed Hazel, as did his passion to evangelize. As their relationship deepened, Hazel's family wasn't so sure about their daughter marrying a Dutchman. A lot of stereotypes circulated about those stubborn Dutch.

Garry's large family had come to this country from the Netherlands when Garry was seven, and they were members of the Midland Park Christian Reformed Church. After graduation from Ridgewood High School, Garry worked as a secretary to the president of Standard Oil and subsequently became the private secretary to the

---

Hazel's amazing energy level. "She was short, stocky, talked fast, walked fast, and always appeared to be going somewhere." Oral interview with Theodore F. and June Zandstra, Holland, Michigan, June 30, 2002.

Hazel Brown Gnade, at age 21, shortly after her marriage to Gerard Rudolph Gnade on December 26, 1922

treasurer of their domestic coke operations. At the deathbed of one of his brothers, Garry felt a call to ministry and soon began working with the Evangelical Ministers Association in Brooklyn and was ordained a minister of the gospel at the Greene Avenue Baptist Church in Brooklyn. In spite of their reservations about his being Dutch, the Browns approved of the marriage, and Hazel and Gerard Rudolph Gnade were married in the Ridgewood Methodist Church December 26, 1922.

Following their marriage, Hazel and Garry were hired jointly by the Clinton Avenue Reformed Church for one year, to work with young people and to conduct evangelistic efforts. As a result of this experience, they realized that Garry needed a seminary education. They moved to New Brunswick, New Jersey, where Garry spent four years at Rutgers College, and then three years at New Brunswick Theological Seminary. As part of Garry's education, and as a means of income, Garry was employed as the student pastor of the Clover Hill Reformed Church in Flemington, New Jersey. While living in the parsonage there, Hazel gave birth to twin boys—Gerard Jr. and Ronald—on July 26, 1926. Within a short time, Ronald died. Gerard Jr. was a healthy child, and Jerry, as he was called, grew, went to college and medical school, continues to practice medicine, and served as the inspiration for the publication of the letters to his mother.

In 1930 Garry graduated from seminary. He was called to become pastor of the First Reformed Church in Walden, New York, and was ordained by the Classis of Orange. Life was good in this rural upstate area, and the Gnades fit in well. Hazel blossomed as a minister's wife. She participated in the women's organizations of the church, often serving as leader. Every church event and every church breakfast, lunch, or supper, Hazel was there organizing and working. Often she awakened Garry early to play tennis before breakfast, and in their spare time the family loved to go camping. By this time both Hazel's widowed grandmother and mother had joined the family in the parsonage at Walden, and on June 13, 1934, another son, Kenneth, was born. Those were good days.

In 1937 the Gnades moved to Schenectady, New York, where Garry was called to lead the Second Reformed Church. From 1937 to 1945, Hazel and Garry came to know and to love their parishioners. Hazel was a gifted speaker and gave addresses with increasing frequency to women's church groups in the area.[2] Hazel also headed the local chapter of the Women's Christian Temperance Union. Throughout her life, Hazel was vehemently against the use of alcohol.

In 1945, Garry was offered a position in New York City heading the RCA Ministers' Fund, which in 1954 would become known as the Board of Pensions. With Hazel's full concurrence and support, Garry accepted the job, and the family moved back to the little house of Hazel's parents in Midland Park—the one with the large outdoor porch. It was a tight squeeze for a family of their size.

Once back in New Jersey, the family joined the First Reformed Church in Ridgewood, where once again Hazel plunged in with all of her usual energy. Hazel particularly enjoyed the young adults. One of them, Katharine (Kitty) Bosch Crandall,[3] who with her husband Lee served as RCA missionaries 1949-1959, remembers Hazel from these church days. Kitty remembered:

> I was a young adult in the First Reformed Church of Ridgewood, N.J. when Hazel Gnade's qualities were imbedded in my heart and mind. Hazel was a model of Christian joy. She was joy personified. The love and happiness that was in her heart was clearly reflected in her countenance and spilled out into her speech. Because of this quality, Mrs. Gnade, some twenty years my senior, was someone I wanted to be with for she was pure delight…. Reflecting on those years we had together as members of the First Reformed Church in Ridgewood, I am certain God had a reason for placing her in my life. She was the example of Christ-like living I needed. I praise and thank God for the impact she had on my life.[4]

From earlier days living in Upstate New York to the present, Hazel and Garry enjoyed camping, and frequently they would pack up the family and head to the Adirondacks to enjoy a time away. Sometimes Hazel and the boys would remain at the campsite

2. News clipping, n.p., n.p., n.d., "Mrs. Gnade Gives Address At Bellevue."
3. See Una Ratmeyer, *Hands, Hearts, and Voices, Women Who Followed God's Call* (New York: Reformed Church Press, 1995), 81-83.
4. Letter from Kitty Crandall to the author, October 26, 2002.

The house in Midland Park, New Jersey, where the Brown family lived following Hazel's father's illness. In 1945, Hazel and Garry, their two young sons, and Hazel's mother and grandmother returned to live in this house

while Garry returned to the City to work. One night during a family camping trip to the Adirondacks, the family waited for Garry's return from several days' work back at the office. The time passed his scheduled return. No Garry. The family became frightened, and finally—just before midnight—in drove Garry. He had returned late because he had bought a house. His brother-in-law, a Ridgewood contractor, had remarked to Garry that he had taken in a house "on trade" and could sell the house to them at a favorable price. Garry quickly visited the three-story Tudor stucco and brick house in Ridgewood and immediately agreed to buy the house before his brother-in-law could change his mind about the price. Hazel loved the house. There were bedrooms for everyone and then some—not to mention large front rooms for entertaining and ample space for the piano.

In 1941, while they were still living in Schenectady, Hazel had been elected to a three-year term as a member-at-large of the Women's Board of Foreign Missions. Attending board meetings meant that Hazel had to journey by train to New York City five times a year at her own expense. Probably because of distance, Hazel was not put on a committee during this three-year period. During these years, Margaret Gillespie Fagg chaired the Hospitality Committee of the WBFM. Margaret Fagg, who lived in New York City, had for many years provided hospitality to missionaries and guests of the denomination on behalf of the Woman's Board. But these were war years, and returning missionaries, if they could get home, arrived at secret times and at secret destinations, which precluded anyone meeting them at the docks or airports.[5] When this happened, Margaret Fagg and members of her committee wrote

5. *WBFM Minutes,* October 10, 1944, 4. RCA Archives, Box 710.1.

In 1948, the Gnade family moved into "the big house" at 148 North Maple Avenue in Ridgewood, New Jersey. With three floors of living space, there was room for family and guests.

letters of welcome and communicated their availability to help the missionaries after they arrived.[6]

Following the Gnades's return to New Jersey in 1945 and their move into "the big house in 1948," Hazel was again elected to the WBFM board. At this point, Hazel's life changed significantly. With their son Jerry in military service and Grandma Brown at home to cook and to run the house in Hazel's absence and to be at home for Ken, Hazel increasingly became available to join in the work of the WBFM. She lived close enough to take the train or bus into New York City, a trip that took about forty-five minutes.

From her election to the WBFM board in 1941 to January 1960, when the National Department of Women's Work ceased to maintain a hospitality committee, Hazel Gnade worked tirelessly on behalf of the WBFM and its successor organizations.[7]

---

6. Although national security during the war years precluded meeting returning missionaries at the docks, Margaret Fagg and her committee continued to meet and to care for missionaries once their arrivals were known. Margaret Fagg and her committee members entertained missionaries in their homes, such as in January, 1944, when Margaret had a dinner for all the active and inactive China missionaries. "This year over 125 furloughed missionaries and children of missionaries and newly appointed missionaries, singly and in groups, have been guests in the home of the Hospitality Committee at luncheons, dinners, shopping and sightseeing expeditions." *WBFM Minutes*, January 2, 1945. RCA Archives, Box 710.1.

7. It is important to remember that Hazel Gnade's ministry took place on the East Coast, and missionaries and denominational guests arrived and departed from the West Coast also. From 1942-1949, Inez (Van Ins) Dumville and her husband, the Reverend Charles Dumville, lived in California's San Francisco Bay area. As part of their pastoral ministry, they provided hospitality to missionaries and denominational guests on the West Coast in ways similar to Hazel Gnade's ministry of hospitality on the East Coast. See *MGS*, 1947, 18.

Hazel and Garry host a dinner party for the members and spouses of Garry's 1930 class at New Brunswick Theological Seminary. Seated from the left: Garry Gnade, John Dirksen, Mary Luidens, Nelson Doak, Esther Soeter, Fred Bosch, Adeline ten Hoeve, Hazel Gnade, Thomas ten Hoeve, Alice Bosch, John J. Soeter, Alida Doak, Theodore Luidens, Lydia Dirksen

She became part of the WBFM Sewing Guild, working routinely at the warehouse sorting and packing boxes of clothes and gifts from RCA church women for shipment to mission stations. WBFM participation in administering the Northfield Massachusetts Summer School for Missions found Hazel often serving on the Northfield board, attending summer sessions for her own edification, as well as serving as a youth counselor at summer conferences.[8] It was, however, in her ministry of hospitality that memories of Hazel Gnade have been committed to paper and saved to remind us of who she was, how she represented the work and spirit of many WBFM women, and what legacy she left for others to follow.

In 1946, just as the WBFM and the BFM organizations were merging, Hazel Gnade became the chair of the WBFM Hospitality Committee, a post she held until 1960.

---

8. *Department of Women's Work Executive Committee Minutes*, December 3, 1957, 1. RCA Archives, Box 1.

Hazel's dock pass

In this, the new Department of Women's Work of the Board of Foreign Missions (DWW), fifteen members composed the Hospitality Committee,[9] with at least two members appointed from each of the five particular synods.[10] During all of those years, Hazel's task and the task of her committee remained about the same. The clearest definition of their task, which appeared in 1950, stated:

> The Missionary Hospitality Committee assists the missionaries and their families in every possible way. This means meeting boats, arranging for stays in New York, keeping in touch with missionaries, round robin letters, seeing off the missionaries, visiting Board members who are ill, etc.[11]

The "etc." at the end of the statement never seemed to bother Hazel. She understood the missionary hospitality task this way:

> In these days we hear and read a great deal concerning activities along the waterfront. These activities often have to do with unrest, hatred, and sometimes even violence. The Missionary Hospitality Committee is active along the waterfront, but our activities are quite the opposite. They have to do with love and peace, the love of families towards their departing or returning members, the love of friend towards friend whom he will not see again for a long time, or whom he is greeting after years of separation, and most of all love towards Christ on the part of our missionaries who are willing to leave all to take the message of

---

9. Temporary Rules of Organization Department of Women's Work of the Board of Foreign Missions, March 25, 1946. RCA Archives Box 710.1. Prior to this the WBFM Hospitality Committee had included nine members, including the chair.

10. The particular synods at that time included New York, Albany, New Jersey, Chicago, and Iowa.

11. DWW Statement of Purpose, April 48, 1950. RCA Archives, Box 712, Folder 2.

Hazel with group
meeting M. J. John

Jesus to the uttermost parts of the world—the message of Him who said, "My peace I leave with you. My peace I give unto you."[12]

As the newly appointed chair of the Hospitality Committee, Hazel began her routine trips into the city. She fetched missionary families staying at the modest Prince George Hotel and guided them to the right dock. She waited with them, standing on the dock until the ship was pushed away and pulled out into the ocean—all the while waving her handkerchief as if each departing missionary were her own child. Or sometimes Hazel would wait at the docks for arriving missionaries—regardless when a ship was scheduled to come in. More often than not, ships did not arrive on schedule. Hazel waited because she knew how frightening it could be. She would help them with their odd assortment of parcels and bags and usher them through the maze known as customs. As if by magic, a cab large enough to hold all the luggage would appear—or perhaps Garry would assist his wife by making the family car available, and, before you knew it, Hazel had directed them to the Prince George Hotel or wherever else the missionaries had to go.

Hazel Gnade knew New York City. Unable to drive but on a first name basis with local bus drivers, Hazel understood the public transportation system as well as she understood how to cook. She knew the bus system, the train system, the subway system, and how to hail a cab night or day. Her arrival and departure haunts in 1954 were noted in the *Minutes* this way:

The comings and goings of our missionaries have taken our committee members to Idlewild Airport, to La Guardia Field, to the various piers in Manhattan, to

---

12. Annual Report of the Standing Committee on Hospitality, *DWW Minutes*, 1954. RCA Archives, Box 1.

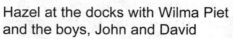
Hazel at the docks with Wilma Piet
and the boys, John and David

the Grand Central and Pennsylvania Stations, to the Bush docks in Brooklyn, to
the waterfront in Hoboken and Jersey City and last (and also <u>least</u>) to the Erie
Basin in Brooklyn. According to all available maps the Erie Basin is situated in
the United States, but we feel sure that Port Said or Singapore couldn't seem
more inaccessible or desolate.[13]

All of this, coupled with her tremendous energy, is reflected in the following story:

> Although the latest trip we took was not specifically to meet a missionary, we
> were asked to do it because the people involved, Mr. and Mrs. Miyake, had a
> connection with our Japanese Mission. We had the pleasure of meeting these
> folks in December when they arrived in Hoboken on a Holland-American liner.
> Mrs. Miyake was scheduled to do the soprano solo work in the Hope College
> Annual rendition of Handel's *Messiah*. The ship was scheduled to arrive on a
> Monday and the concert was to be on Tuesday evening. The ship, however, was
> delayed a day and did not dock until 8 o'clock on Tuesday morning. Through
> the courtesy of the Holland-American Line agent, the Immigration officers, and
> the Customs officers—all of whom co-operated wonderfully, and through the
> efforts of Dr. Shafer and his secretary, Mrs. Heckle, and also with the help of my
> husband who drove his car, we were finally able to get the Miyakes on a plane
> which left La Guardia at 11 A.M. At 5 o'clock in the afternoon the Miyakes arrived
> by plane, via Chicago, in Muskegon, Mich. By 6 o'clock Mrs. Miyake was rehearsing
> in Holland, and at 8 P.M. she was singing in the *Messiah* at Hope. All reports from
> the students there indicated that she did great justice to that most beautiful of
> all Oratorios.[14]

Hazel Gnade had great capacity to empathize with the missionaries. Of all the
anxieties shared by the missionaries, fear of the city seemed to stand at the top of the

---

13. Ibid.
14. Ibid.

list. Fear of getting lost, fear of not being in the right place at the right time, fear of having to find one's way alone, all of these fears outweighed for many missionaries and guests the happy experience of exploring and enjoying New York City. Hazel also understood their anxieties about leaving and returning home to America. It wasn't as though e-mail or the inexpensive use of the telephone were available to keep families in immediate touch with one another. Hazel was there physically and emotionally for them. She would reassure them that she and members of her committee would help get them to the right place at the right time. Hazel knew all kinds of things—how to obtain immediate medical or dental care, where to shop within one's budget, where to post last-minute packages that had to be put in the mail. Hazel had the answers, and Hazel made accomplishing the tasks manageable. To reduce anxiety regarding the children, Hazel would often baby-sit. Hazel loved children, and children loved Hazel. It was Hazel's considered opinion that every married couple ought to have a night alone without children before heading out to the foreign field where they might not have that luxury for six or seven years. In such cases, the children often returned with Hazel to "the big house" in Ridgewood, and in the morning Hazel would return them to their parents.

Until 1948, it is doubtful that, beyond the essential expenses, the WBFM and DWW provided any additional funds for meeting and entertaining missionaries. This changed in April 1948, when an amount of $200 was voted to be included in the budget to meet some of these costs.[15] This is the only indication that individual largesse sufficed to meet missionary needs of the hour up to this time. However, Hazel was careful to point out in her annual reports that the work of the Hospitality Committee was given a loving and special kind of support from Margaret C. Warnshuis (Rev. Abbe L.)[16] In her annual report for January 1957, Hazel says:

> We are grateful to Dr. and Mrs. A.L. Warnshuis who pay the expenses of any extra entertainment we need to do. Of course, the Board pays for all the necessary expenses such as meals and hotel bills, but naturally they could not pay for such things as a visit to Chinatown or a trip to the Statue of Liberty. So, Mrs. Warnshuis, calling herself C.L.E.M. (Committee for Little Expenses for Missionaries) has graciously offered to help our Committee by paying for this extra entertainment and by paying for a farewell gift of fruit or candy. We are deeply appreciative to

---

15. DWW *Minutes*, April 13, 1948. RCA Archives, Box 712, Folder 1.

16. Margaret C. Warnshuis was the former Mrs. Charles W. Halsey, and upon the death of her husband married Abbe Livingston Warnshuis, which was his second marriage as well. Both were involved members at the Reformed Church in Bronxville, New York. Mrs. Harry Leslie Walker and LaMont A. Warner, eds., *The History of the Reformed Church of Bronxville* (New York: Published by the Consistory, 1951), 45.

It is unknown exactly how long this form of kindness had been practiced by Margaret Warnshuis and her husband. In her annual report for 1954 Hazel notes, "Our committee has been grateful to Mrs. A. L. Warnshuis, who as in previous years, has graciously made funds available to enable us to give a farewell gift to our missionaries or to entertain them in some special way if they are detained in New York City." DWW *Minutes*, 1954. RCA Archives, Box 1.

Dr. and Mrs. Warnshuis for this service which they render with love because the Missionary Enterprise is so dear to their hearts.[17]

In the June 24, 1955, issue of the *Church Herald* an article, "A Family Parting," by Florence Gordon, read in part:

> In the course of the same evening, the Board honored another of its members,[18] Mrs. Gerard R. Gnade, who has for years served as hospitality chairman, seeing the missionaries off to their fields of services, welcoming them as they have come home on furlough, doing countless personal services for their cheer and comfort. In recognition of her faithful, thoughtful helpfulness, Mrs. Edward R. Tanis, vice-chairman of the Board, presented Mrs. Gnade with a bound volume of appreciative letters received from all parts of our overseas missionary enterprise.

Among the letters in the bound volume was this poem by Daniel Y. Brink, president of the General Synod, 1955-1956:

> Dear Hazel:
>   The lens of your personality gathers the
>   concern of 200,000 people and focuses it on those who
>   otherwise might feel forgotten.
>   Thanks!

---

17. DWW *Minutes*, 1957. RCA Archives, Box 692, Folder 2.

18. The other honorees that evening were Luman and Amy Shafer, who were missionaries to Japan, 1912-1935. They were both teachers. When Ferris Seminary was destroyed by earthquake in 1923, Luman Shafer oversaw its reconstruction and became its principal. Both he and Amy taught there until 1935. At that time Luman Shafer was appointed secretary of the BFM with area responsibility for China, Japan, and eventually Africa. Following the end of World War II, he served in numerous capacities as consultant and resource person both for the government and for the church. For Luman Shafer's obituary, see *Church Herald*, January 31, 1958, 5.1

Chapter 9

Letters to Hazel

The letters reproduced in this chapter are arranged in alphabetical order. The list below indicates the original order of the letters as they appeared in the album presented to Hazel Gnade. The number in parentheses following the letter indicates the page on which the letter can be found. All writers are listed in the name index.

Harry L. Brower, April 6, 1955 (159)
Orville Jay Hine, April 7, 1955 (176)
Wilma Maassen, January 5, 1955 (192)
Frank Snuttjer, April 4, 1955 (210)
Daniel Y. Brink, April 2, 1955 (158)
Ruth Ransom, April 1, 1955 (202)
Luman J. Shafer, March 30, 1955 (207)
Mrs. Mike Tjoelker, n.d. (217)
Dirk and Minnie Dykstra, April 16, 1955 (213)
Barnerd Luben, n.d. (189)
Dorothy Van Ess, April 11, 1955 (219)
Chester Postma, April 20, 1955 (201)
Frances H. Gideon, n.d. (173)
Margaret Gibbons, n.d. (171)
Mary Geegh, n.d. (170)
Paul and Laurel, Lynn, Stephen, and Marybeth Arnold, May 2, 1955 (154)
John E. Buteyn, May 2, 1955 (161)
Galen and Maude Scudder, n.d. (205)
ElsieSchwager, April 26, 1955 (204)
Jim and Joyce Dunham, April 25, 1955 (168)
Margaret V. Babinsky, April 25, 1955 (155)
Mary W. S. Voskuil, April 29, 1955 (221)
Robert J. Block, April 21, 1955 (156)
Gertrude A.Wagner, April 29, 1955 (222)
Mae Slingerland, April 11, 1955 (209)
Isla G. Van Eenenaam, April 27, 1955 (218)
Mildred Howard, April 27, 1955 (180)
William C. De Jong, April 26, 1955 (165)
Theodore J. Jansma, April 25, 1955 (182)

Mary P. Sibley, n.d. (208)
Agnes Tanis, April 25, 1955 (214)
Jerry Pool, April 23, 1955 (200)
Louise J. and George J. Holler, April 21, 1955 (179)
Mamie S. Muyskens, April 22, 1955 (198)
Harvey B. Hoffman, April 22, 1955 (178)
M. Gerard Gosselink, Jr., April 22, 1955 (174)
M. J., Mary, and Mollie John, April 18, 1955 (183)
Staff, Board of Foreign Missions, n.d. (211)
Harriet Brumler, May 4, 1955 (160)
John D. Muyskens, May 9, 1955 (197)
Maurice A. TePaske, May 4, 1955 (215)
Paul E. Ammerman, n.d. (153)
Lilian Meury, n.d. (196)
Midge and Jay Kapenga, May 18, 1955 (185)
Lee and Kitty, Alan, Gary, and Ann Crandall, June 21, 1955 (162)
Wilma Piet, January 30, 1955 (199)
Marian and Blaise Levai, April 22, 1955 (188)
The Kortelings, n.d. (187)
Louise Decker, April 29, 1955 (167)
Lilian Meury, n.d. (194)

Woodmar Reformed Church
169th Street and Leland Avenue
Hammond, Indiana

Dear Mrs. Drade,

We do not always have an opportunity to express our heartfelt thanks and appreciation to people who are doing a worthy and faithful work. I do now express this thanks to you for having been the "official" greeter and hostess to the incoming missionaries for these several years. It has meant much to the work of the Foreign Mission in our beloved Church.

Knowing your gracious nature from the Schenectady days, we know that you found joy in the work. May the memories of these many meetings, acquaintances, new and renewed, bring you much satisfaction in the years ahead.

May God bless you and your family richly. When coming to South Holland, do stop in if you can.

Sincerely,

Paul E. Ammerman

On furlough in
New Paltz, New York

May 2, 1955

Dear Mrs. Gnade;

How wonderful it is to have this one chance to thank you again
for all you have done in making farewells and hellos pleasant for
missionary families. Your service is the kind that so often goes
unrecognized officially, and we're glad to be a part of a church
that bows to work of the heart like yours. Because it's the
real affection and complete selflessness and warmth of the things
you do that makes you so dear to us. I remember the first time
I saw you, you were feeding three restless Hoekstra children lunch
so that their mom and dad could have a peaceful meal alone in the
hotel. Arrivals and departures are always hectic, but the very
restfulness of your gracious assistance always refreshes frantic
missionaries and tearful parents alike. Thank you from the bottoms
of our hearts for loving Christ and his world-wide family so much,
we return that love on this occassion a hundred-fold.

In the name of our Lord,

Paul and Laurel Arnold
Lynn, Stephen and Marybeth

Ridgewood, N.J.

April 25,1955

Dear Mrs. Gnade,

It seems strange to be writing you a letter--you whom I can so easily call on the telephone. However, this is a real opportunity to tell you what you rarely give anyone a chance to say --thank you for all the thoughtful, patiently helpful things which you have been doing for folks all these weeks, months, years.

Your conversational reports have always been so full of amusing little sayings quoted from the hundreds of children you have cared for and the humorous coincidences involved in meeting the further hundreds of people at wharf and airport.

It is a particular gift of yours that you never mention the other things, neither humorous nor amusing, but wearing, aggravating which make up a schedule at the mercy of chance. I want you to know how much I love you for this gift. You have been a fine example when I needed it . I am one more of your appreciative friends.

Affectionately,

Margaret V. Babinsky

American School for Boys
Basrah, Iraq
April 21, 1955

Dear Mrs. Gnade:

It was September, 1952, when we met in the Board rooms. I had
been told that I would be "seen off," but at the time I was a
bit bewildered with all that was happening. My real concern
was to get on board the R.M.S. Queen Elizabeth, and when you
suggested that we see something in New York City, I was a bit
dazzled—I just hadn't thought of that. I remember going in
to have lunch and that good box of choclates. As I went to
the top of the Empire State building, you patiently waited
for me. The subway ride was fun and although I did not know
where we were going, you did. Your kindness and helpfulness
was very much appreciated.

Sincerely yours,

Robert J. Block

Robert J. Block

Kobe College, Okadayama
Nishinomiya, Japan
January 16, 1955

Dear Mrs. Gnade,

You didn't know I was going to be writing you twice in one day,
did you? By this time you've received the Christmas cards I sent, I suppose.

I think it is a wonderful idea--this folder of letters of appreciation
for all you've done and meant for us through the years. Of course, I know
you know that we appreciate it and you that you enjoy this type of service, but
it doesn't quite take the place of a concrete gesture just as this. It seems
strange that I, who usually come and go at the west coast and live in the Middle West should have been met by you in N.Y.C. It will probably be the only
time it will happen, but it was wonderful to have someone with the "know-how" to
get me through customs and on to the train in such hasty order. I shall remember that a life-time and ever be grateful.

I doubt that you will ever experience what it is to return to your homeland
after having been gone for a long time and feeling like a back number in your own
country. How terrific (and almost terrifying) it is to get back into the speed
of America, and N.Y.C. is the worst. The undergirding that you give at such a
time is heartening and certainly takes any unpleasant edge off the whole situation. You are performing a great duty and don't for one minute underestimate
it. May God give you strength to carry on for many more years to come.

Please be so kind as to extend my thanks to Dr. Gnade. I know that
there are sacrifices for him for the family bus also often stands by. He takes
it, too, in cold meals, no meals, or at least irregular ones. He's a great
sport to do it. You're a remarkable team.

See you the next trip.

Sincerely yours,

f. Belle Bogard

First Reformed Church

LAKE HILL

SCOTIA 2, NEW YORK

REV. DANIEL Y. BRINK, *Minister*
220 BALLSTON AVENUE
PHONE 6-7915

FOUNDED   NOV. 21, 1818

Office
224 BALLSTON AVENUE
PHONE 3-1521

April 2, 1955

Mrs. Gerard R. Gnade
156 Fifth Ave.
New York 10, New York

Dear Hazel:

The lens of your personality gathers the concern of 200,000 people and focuses it on those who otherwise might feel forgotten.

When you "lift your lamp beside the golden door", the crossing of the threshold becomes a never-to-be-forgotten experience, while the camera of memory snaps, by your light, a picture to be cherished through the years.

Thanks!

Daniel Y. Brink

EBENEZER REFORMED CHURCH
REV. HARRY L. BROWER, Minister • 311 EAST PARK • DIAL 2471 • MORRISON, ILLINOIS

April 6, 1955

Dear Mrs. Gnade:

Thank you so much, Mrs. Gnade, for the very valuable job of hospitality you have been doing in creating that personal Christian touch with our missionaries and their families which is so necessary and valuable.

I, like many other Board members, am not often in a position to meet or give that personal attention to our missionaries which I would like to give. Yet they must know that the "Board" is more than an efficient machine (granting that it is!), and it is thru you that many of our missionaries have for a long time become aware that we are personally interested in their problems, and that we as a group have a heart and personality as well as a bond of prayer, mutual interest, and fellowship in proclaiming with them the Gospel of our Lord. It is this personal interest in them and their work that enables them to carry on their work with greater fervor and zeal.

You have helped make know the heart, pulse, and felling of us all, as well as of myself, in your gracious, sacrificial, and prayerful contacts with our missionaries and their children. You have been of service wherever you were needed, and you did it out of love for our Lord and His workers.

So here is a simple "thank you" in appreciation as I see in you an exemplication of Paul's words in Romans 12:13, "Given to hospitality." I know you have received much joy as a reward for your work.

Yours in the Work of Christ,

Harry L. Brower

Harry L. Brower
Member of the Board of Foreign Missions,
R.C.A.

1940 Philadelphia S. E.
Grand Rapids, Mich.

May 4, 1955

Dear Mrs. Ganade:

I am writing to tell you how much it has meant to me to have you come to the boat to meet me.   I am sure only those who have returned from a foreign land can appreciate fully what it means to be met and welcomed back to U.S.A.   Six years ago when I returned to India you were at the docks and last year when I returned you were there again.

I want to say "thank you" for this thoughtful service and assure you of my great appreciation for all that you have done for me.

With cordial greetings

Sincerely yours

Harriet Brumler

First Reformed Church
ORGANIZED IN 1852
MINISTER
REV. JOHN E. BUTEYN

EAST MAIN STREET AT ALEXANDER
ROCHESTER 7, N. Y.

PARSONAGE
417 ALEXANDER STREET

PHONE
BAKER 1181

May 2, 1955

Mrs. Gerard R. Gnade
c/o The Board of Foreign Missions
The Reformed Church in America
156 Fifth Avenue
New York 10, New York

Dear Mrs. Gnade,

I consider it a real privilege to add a word of testimony and appreciation for the faithful and loving service you have rendered in "greeting and seeing off the missionaries" of The Reformed Church. I am sure that your warm smile and friendly presence has done much to give strength in those moments of arrival and departure that no doubt are such a mixture of joy and deep feeling.

Your service to the Board, to The Reformed Church, and especially to the Missionaries has been such an unobtrusive one, that many of us are only recently learning about it—your unnoticed service has been a real demonstration of love and loyalty.

Let me paraphrase a bit, a tribute on the Red Cross Column in Washington, D.C.—I'm sure it is true of you:

"You went where you were needed—
You did what you could—
You gave what you had—
And of such is the Kingdom of Heaven".

May God Bless you and best wishes from Mrs. Buteyn and myself.

Cordially,

John E. Buteyn

JEB:ng

Akobo, UNP, Sudan
June 21, 1955.

Dear Mrs. Goade,

I've vowed to write 2 letters a day 'til the steamer gets here and you have top priority. Aren't you flattered?!! The enclosed item is sorta a love gift through which I'm asking your forgiveness in neglecting to add our words of appreciation for all you do for us missionaries. I vaguely remember receiving a letter asking us to write to you through the Board but I promptly forgot it thinking how embarrassed I'd be if I got a bunch of letters telling how "sweet" I was (not that even such a thing could happen to me!) But now I see how nice it was and I'm truly sorry our words aren't in the "collection." It was a very thoughtful thing to do for one who is so deserving of it. The hours & hours of time & effort you've spent on our behalf shows clearly how you love the Lord and make every effort to show forth His self-less love & concern for others. It's wonderful knowing you! Wonderful having known you in our home church, too!

As I sit here writing I can hear wild shouts from boys playing soccer in three different games. The small fry are right in our back yard, the bigger school boys are playing an "official" game on the new field about 50 yards from our house and another group of boys are playing in front of the dormitories. This is the national sport; they love it. Because there is little team work in it and because they use only their feet & heads (ball can only be hit with feet or heads) we're teaching them volley ball. The school boys have it once a week and the teachers twice, once with the school boys + once with us missionaries; for it's part of our mission program to have tea + volley ball every Sat. afternoon from 4⁰⁰ to 6⁰⁰ for the government employees and our teachers. It's gone over very well. At first these folks have absolutely no hand coordination and the games are pretty wild. But they are catching on and fewer + fewer balls go sailing out to compete with flying saucers!

Our farmers (Vern Sikkema + Chuck Jordan) have really gone to town and have huge fields prepared this year. They're continuing their experiments with 58 various types of durra to see if the native grain can be improved. Lots of vegetables + fruits are in, too. It's pretty discouraging work though; let me tell you about their cantelope experiment. When sown, about 50% matured; the white ants or other bugs got the others. Then beetles got after the leaves + vines. It took almost daily spraying c̄ DDT powder. Cucumbers were near by + one day after our gardener was told to pick cucumbers in he came with a pail full of small immature cantelope. Few days later the cows got through the fence + ate a bunch. Along with these some got scorched by the hot sun. But we did get some cantelope on the table. They were delicious!!

The kids are fine. Alan + Gary spend most of their time outdoors going from toy cars + trucks, to sling shoting + fishing and David A. is with them all the time. Ann is doing well; she was just 6 mo. old the other day. Cute as a bug's ear -- but then I guess every mother thinks that of her baby.

Say hello to your hubby + Kenny for us. We think they're pretty nice, too!

With Christian love –
Alan, Gary, Ann, Lee + Kitty

The hanky was done by a Northern Sudanese in a U.P. Girl's School. Wilma's girls haven't prepared that far.

Katpadi, N. Arcot
S.India.
January 11, 1955.

Dear Mrs. Gnade:

Some of us married missionaries used to be a wee bit
jealous of the "Missies" in the old days of the Women's Board, because
somebody always seemed to make arrangements to meet them upon their
arrival in New York and speed them on their way when they sailed.
Whereas we would go to the Board Rooms ourselves and announce our
arrival and return. How times have changed and how we do appreciate
this change!

Remember when the DeBruin's decided to fly home for their
Joyce's wedding?Since this trip was no furlough, but strictly"on our
own", we just did not think the Board people would bother about
meeting us, especially when we were due to arrive at 5A.M. How very
chagrined we were later on to hear about your long trip to the air
port before dawn, only to find that the plane had arrived a couple hours
early, and we were nowhere to be found'. Had we only known what
trouble and anxiety we would cause by taxi ing over to Penn Station
and waiting here for morning to come. Again, our apologies to
both you and your good husband.

But not many have had the privelege of your help so often in
such a short time as we did in 1953. It was May when the "Queen Mary"
docked and we couldn't believe our eyes when we walked off the gang
plank right into the arms of your "Reception Committee" and then
marvelled at the ease with which you manoevered us through customs
and luggage and transportation and a congenial cup of coffee. Again
in October, the trip out to Idlewild was made so much easier because
of your thoughtfulness and understanding. We felt we had a real
friend with us that day, who shared our heartaches and loneliness
after our children had left us for Cairo, not India, as we had hoped.
How very grateful we were for your suggestion of rice and curry that
noon. It was a real life saver for us, but it made a change of plans
necessary for you. And again, less than a month later, when it was
impossible for you to see us off yourself, on our ship, you not only
made arrangements for Mrs. Schut to take your place, but you made a s
special trip into the city to take us out to dinner the previous
night. It is all these little extra and special things you do--not
in the course of duty-- that endear you to our hearts, and we are
very happy to have this opportunity to give this expression to our
appreciation. We hope that it will be possible for you to continue
working in this capacity for a long, long time.

Yours Sincerely,

Arnie and Frances De Bruin

Pella,Iowa
4-26-'55

Mrs. Gerard R. Gnade
156 Fifth ave.,
New York 10,N.Y.

My Dear Mrs.Gnade:

As a member of the Board of Foreign Missions I want to take
this opportunity of expressing to you our very sincere thanks for
the many acts of Christ-like service which you have rendered our
Board and its missionaries through the years. It has been a gracious labor of love in the name of Our Blessed Master and the man-
-ner in which it has been rendered has been such that it was a source
of comfort and inspiration to those inowhose behalf it was rendered.

May it be a source of joy and satisfaction to you that your
service has been appreciated and may that joy and satisfaction go
with you through the years and into eternity.

Yours Most Cordially,

Wm. C. De Jong

Arni, N. A. Dt.- S. Ind.
Jan. 30, 1955.

Our dear Mrs. Grade —

We are happy to have this opportunity to express our appreciation of your liberal help to our family.

That pre-dated Christmas party shortly before our sailing in December 1946 is still vividly in our minds and referred to in our conversation. It indicates how you and your family give of yourselves over and beyond the call of duty.

Your smiling and guiding presence on the docks when we landed in '53 greatly relieved our adjustment to the seemingly excess speed of the U.S.A.! Without your help it is doubtful we could have been able to leave by train only three hours after the ship docked!

Our experiences together at the Youth Camp at Lake Cassayuna have often been recalled with pleasure and with contrast as we compare it with other camps in the U.S.A. and here in India. May you receive and since continued joy in your peculiar and unique service.

Dr. Grade's help in bringing our car to the shippers saved us much time and simplified our departure.

Please accept our heartfelt thanks for all you have for us - as given by Part of your "India" family

With sincerity,
Benjamin and Mildred De Vries and their sons,
David
John
and
Robert.

46 Crescent Place
Yonkers, N.Y.
April 29,1955

My dear Mrs. Gnade,

    I am very happy to be a member of the Board of Foreign Missions, and I certainly have enjoyed your warm and contagious friendship.

    The place you have won in the hearts of all of our missionaries, as you bid each one "Bon Voyage" with Gods' blessing, and as each one returning you greeted with "that warm-hearted and genuinely sincere greeting," has been richly deserved.

    Your contribution, with your happy and cheerful disposition, with your deep and abiding faith, has been an inspiration to all of your associates.

    May Gods' richest blessing rest upon you, and may his peace and joy fill your cup to overflowing both now and forevermore.

        Sincerely,

        Mrs. Irving (Louise) Decker

        Louise Decker

Bahrain, Persian Gulf
April 25, 1955.

Dear Mrs. Gnade,

I don't know whose idea it was to have
someone on hand to receive and send off the missionaries, but it is a good one, and they couldn't have
found a better person to do it! You certainly have
a way with red caps and taxi drivers! By now you
must know all the ins and outs of all the railroad
stations, the docks and the airports of New York.

We greatly appreciated your help and
know-how at the docks when we met my parents two
years ago. And also your seeing us off royally
when we left from Idlewild Airport. We hope to see
you on the dock when we return to the States some
years hence.

Sincerely,

Jim & Joyce Dunham

Bishop Gwynne College

Mundri, via Juba

Feb. 14, 1955

Dear Mrs. Gnade,

It has made us very happy to hear that there is to be some official recognition of your wonderful work toward missionaries in New York. I am afraid that it must seem to you at times that we are ungrateful for your kindness as we hustle about and probably frequently don't take sufficient time to thank you properly for what you have done. This is not so and I can assure you that the one picture of New York that remains clear in our minds is one of you coming along Fifth Ave. with both our children on leashes and blowing tin horns for all they were worth.

Also, your assistance in getting taxis and the getting through the confusion at the docks is help of a sort that a "country bumpkin" can really appreciate.

We have enjoyed our work very much since coming out here and our prayer is that we can learn to be as unselfish in giving of ourselves as you are of giving of yourself in New York. This is a worthy goal and if we were all like Hazel Gnade, what a force we would be in the world today. Blessings on you in your chosen work.

With Christian Love

Lambert Ekster

The Ekster Family

"Thank ye" to Mrs Gnade

There'll be no one to meet me,
  Didn't get time to write _
What's that?! Loud speaker paging "Geep"
  The cloudy day turned bright!

There she stood — Mrs Gnade —
  So pleasant and cordial and gay;
Though I looked awful shoddy
  She treated me like the queen of May.

Furlough over. Again to the
                    "Anchor" Line.
  The eve would seem long in that hotel
                                      alone.
Telephone! Mrs Gnade! "Come with me to dine"
  So the eve went quickly and in high tone.

At breakfast, next morn,
Whom should I see but Mrs Gnade!
Just dropped in, lest I should be forlorn,
  To eat with me and chat with me.

Countless times she's lifted the load,
  Helped us smile, and waited the while
    On the crowded quay
Till the ship pulled out to the open sea,
  Her hand lifted high
    To wave us good bye.
And her upward nod
  Committed us to God.

      This isn't poetry —
        But just a "thank ye"
          To you and Mr Gnade
            from Mary Geegh.

<u>Greetings</u> !!

And gratitude from one who has benefitted by your labor of love which you have carried far "beyond the call of duty."

My mind goes especially to a last hectic day in New York. The packing days at home had been too full and so I had thrown into a box a lot of bits of movie film that I wanted to get off to various missionaries' relatives. You found me in my hotel room struggling over the little parcels & you just loaded them all in your bag & said "just give me your list of names & addresses, I'll tend to all that"! What a relief!

Then I think too of our Indian student Padma Sathya. You

not only met her, scared & lonely, &
got her through customs & brought
her door to door to her destination,
but you found two _more_ homeless
& confused Indian girls with her,
girls whose sending mission
didn't have any Mrs. Gnade
and though you had no responsibility for them (except the responsibility
of loving kindness) you took on their
problems too, and brought them to
their safe havens too.

   May there be a special angel
at the pearly gates when you get
there, to show you to your mansion!
      Gratefully yours.
      Margaret Gibbons.

To Mrs. Gnade

There is a Mrs. Gnade who lives near New York.
    She's not home very much, because more than likely
        she's down at a port
Meeting boats or planes from far-off terrains.
    The folks that she greets are our missionaries
        loaded down with bundles and books and
        children to carry.
Mrs. G. takes right over - no matter what time of day
    Gives the travellers a welcome - a nice place to stay.
She takes care of the children and lets the parents relax.
    It's often in <u>her</u> home where they rest their weary backs.

No matter when the freighters sail - on time or not,
    Mrs. Gnade will be there waiting on the dock.
Locating docks is often a problem too
    But Mrs. G. finds them with very little to-do.
It's to this wonderful woman we owe our many thanks.
    Thanks to her our missionaries aren't being stranded
        on banks.
For this service that you do
    Mrs. Gnade, we thank you!

                            Sincerely
                            Frances V. Gideon
                            (Mrs. M. Howard Gideon)
                            written by Zoe Gideon

Community Reformed Church of Baldwin

Joy Boulevard and Nelson Avenue
BALDWIN, NEW YORK

M. GERARD GOSSELINK, JR.
Minister
Study - 25 Joy Boulevard
Tel. BAldwin 3-3330

RESIDENCE
180 Kenneth Avenue
Baldwin, New York
Tel. BAldwin 3-4932

April 22, 1955

Mrs. Gerard R. Gnade
Ridgewood, New Jersey

Dear Mrs. Gnade:

Even though we have met only once, (and that appropriately at a meeting of the Board of Foreign Missions in Ridgewood) I want to add my word of appreciation for the unique and wonderful service you have rendered so faithfully and gladly to our missionaries.

I know that your real reward comes from Him who is the Head of His Church, but I am equally certain that countless numbers of His servants remember you with affection and joy.

May God's richest blessings continue to be yours.

Sincerely,

M. Gerard Gosselink, Jr.

The American Mission
Amarah, Iraq
Dec. 29, 1954

Dear Mrs. Gnade,

Elinor and I have often thought that we should write you and thank you
for the kind help that you showed us at the beginning and end of our
furlough. It set the proper basis for starting fifteen very happy months
in the States and it was the beginning of a very happy return to the
field. I wonder if you can full appreciate what all of the kind things
you do mean to a missionary. When we return we are no longer American,
our attitudes are changed, and we seem not to completely understand much
of what we first contact. You see, you, there have all changed a lot in
the five and one half years we are gone. The sincere acts you do when
we return bring us immediately into contact with something we do under-
stand-Christian love.

I once observed a senior missionary talking to a junior missionary about
sending children away to school. The junior of the two was not completely
convinced that the missionary experience should envolve sending children
away to school. Cold reason was not being well accepted. Finally the
senior missionary said"I covet for your children the opportunity to go
away to the school to which you now do not want to send them." Those
words struck deep into the mind of the person to whom they were directed
and his mind was immediately changed. Since that day I have been convinced
that in somethings we as Christians may be coveteous. And now as I close
this letter may I do it by saying that I covet for many the opportunity
to have you say good-bye to them when they leave for the field and also
to again have you meet them when they return!

In a lesser way please extend our thanks too to Rev. Gnade and your son.
They are indeed good drivers and know their way around where we would be
entirely lost. Their conversational ability is also first rate.

In Missionary Love,

Maurice and Elinor

Dr. and Mrs. Maurice Heusinkveld

The Warwick Reformed Church

Warwick, New York

ORVILLE J. HINE, Minister
16 Maple Avenue
Warwick, New York

TELEPHONES —
Study: Warwick 55-4522
Parsonage: Warwick 55-2247

April 7, 1955.

Mrs. Gerard R. Gnade,
c/o Miss Ruth Ransom,
Board of Foreign Missions, R.C.A.,
156 Fifth Ave., New York 10, N.Y.

My dear Mrs. Gnade:

I want to add a word of appreciation from Mrs. Hine and myself to you for the wonderful hospitality you have extended to so many, by meeting boats, caring for mission children, and in general acting as hostess to so many missionaries.

When Mrs. Hine and I took our trip around the world last year, we gained just a little inkling of what it means to be met, upon arrival, by a friendly host or hostess. When others around you are eagerly scanning faces and looking for friends, it is terribly lonesome to be all alone with no one to help with all the details of baggage and customs and children and transportation, etc. I know that you have filled this empty spot for so many and it has been a tremendous help to all whom you have served, as well as to the Kingdom of our Lord.

Our appreciation goes to you for this great service.

Sincerely yours,

Orville Jay Hine.

OJH:GW.

December 22, 1954
The American Mission
Gambela, Sudan

Dr. B. M. Luben
Board of Foreign Missions, R. C. A.
156 Fifth Ave.
New York, New York, U. S. A.

Dear Dr. Luben,

I wouldn't miss this opportunity to express our appreciation
for all the good that Mrs. Ganade has done for us missionaries
for anything in the world. It certainly is a grand thing of the
board to plan this sort of testimonial for her to treasure and to
keep.

I frankly don't know how she copes with all of us missionaries.
Most of us have fairly good size families, which means she
has to take care of the kids while we shop around frantically
that last hectic day before we leave. The kids are tired and
crabby usually, and you know what that means in a hotel room.
Or when we come home, we're usually so excited about meeting other
friends and perhaps loved ones that, I wouldn't be surprised if we
sometimes become careless in expressing our heartfelt thanks
to our dear friend Mrs. Ganade. And then, we mustn't forget
her husband either, because as I recall he's pretty active behind
the scenes too, and at others he's also on hand to meet the vessels.

Our thanks for Mrs. Ganade cannot be expressed in words.   On the
field here we have not infrequently talked of writing an article for
the Church paper to express our thanks andto tell the church at large
what a wonderful thing she does in meeting us when we come in
and in seeing us off. Frankly, without her I don't know just how
we'd be able to get through those hectic moments.

All I can say, and that goes for Lavina too, is " Thank you, Mrs.
Ganade from the depths of our hearts, and may your reward be
great in Heaven." I know she finds joy in this, and that her
sacrifices seem small to her, but she's really giving of her
love and devotion to Christ in a way that counts much, and must
at times bring much exhaustion to a tired body.

That's all then--just to add our sincere thanks which words so
ill express to a grand grand person and her husband for all
they mean to us Reformed Church Missionaries.

Very sincerely,

Harvey and Lavina Hoekstra and family

REV. HARVEY B. HOFFMAN
MINISTER

PARSONAGE: 291 CLINTON PLACE
TELEPHONE: DIAMOND 2-1805

The Second Reformed Church

HACKENSACK, NEW JERSEY

April 22, 1955

Dear Hazel,

No words can adequately express the appreciation of the members of the Board of Foreign Missions for the unselfish service you have rendered in the interest of our missionaries.

To leave a beautiful country for the first time, and to sail into the unknown, is indeed trying for the young missionaries. Their emotions, however, adjust themselves to a peaceful calm when you walk among them, demonstrating a warm motherly instinct, and when your countenance radiates an understanding smile.

As you know, it was my privilege last year to visit our missionaries in Iraq, Arabia and India. While there, numerous missionaries told me what strength and cheer they received when you were at hand on their sailing date, and when you were the first to greet them upon their furloughed return.

The wealth of appreciation which is contained in this book is what many people desire for inner peace and security. The reason most of them don't receive it is because it becomes at the expense of sacrifice and self-denial.

We hope you will frequently turn to these pages and drink deeply from these wells of love and gratitude.

Cordially yours,

Harvey B. Hoffman

American Mission Boys' School
Box 53
Basrah, Iraq
21 April, 1955

Letter of Remembrance for Mrs. Gnade

I first met Mrs. Gnade on August 9, 1949, the day I arrived home
from a short-term of work at the Basrah Boys' School. There was an
impression of pleasure and security in knowing that my needs were cared for
by this most gracious lady. There was a feeling of surprise and
admiration, too, in knowing that Mrs. Gnade was there to help others,
completely on her own, a volunteer to help her missionary friends through
the bewildering process of disembarkation in New York.

Again, on January 23, 1951, I had occasion to admire Mrs. Gnade's
work when she was at the Cunard Line's pier to see off my wife and me
for a full term of work in the Arabian Mission. She was there with a
going-away gift. Here again I knew that, in her person, the combined
thoughtfulness, support, and good wishes of the home churches were there
to wish our mission well. We could say sincerely that we sensed the spirit
of Christian giving in the way Mrs. Gnade gave unselfishly of herself to make
out going-away a good one.

We thank you, Mrs. Gnade, for the interest you have shown in us, and
for the help that you have given us. We shall remember you as the gracious
lady who stands at the threshold of our great homeland, welcoming the family
home, and wishing them well as they set off into the world to do the work
to which they are called.

Sincerely,

Louise   & George J. Haller

Louise J. and George J. Holler

Wynantskill, N.Y.
April 27, 1955

Dear Friend,

One of my first recollections of the department of Women's Work Meeting was a report you gave as hostess to our missionaries. Your heart just embraced every one of those little families as if they were your own. The love and thoughtfulness that went into that report touched every one of us.

Since then I know that you have duplicated this same thing an hundred times. We all love you for it. Many missionaries have learned through your acts of friendship and love that the Board of Foreign Missions has a heart.

We know that at times this must have cost you a great effort but we hope and pray that you have been blessed by Our Heavenly Father as well as by the love of many friends.

What a wonderful world this would be if there were more "Mrs. Snades"!

Most sincerely

Mildred Howard

Scotch Plains, N.J.
Jan. 14, 1955

Dear Mrs. Quade,

It's just a joy to add my note to your book. You are indeed one of those for whom at every remembrance of you we give thanks to our heavenly Father. The stories of your love and kindness and hospitality just to those whom I myself know would fill a book. I'm sure each one is written in a heart that treasures it.

I'll never forget the warmth that filled my heart when last June the first person I saw on entering the customs shed was your smiling self. It was 4.00 A.M. and the plane was an hour early so I thought no one could be there yet. I learned it was not yet but still, as you had been up all night. I remember too a very happy visit in your home with you and your good husband who has also been a helping friend to all.

May your good works follow you bringing the help and happiness you have so richly bestowed on others.

Lovingly,
Ruth Jackson
Bahrain
Arabia

Eighth Reformed Church

GRAND RAPIDS 9, MICHIGAN

REV. THEODORE J. JANSMA
841 Burton Street, S. W.
Office GL 2-9417
Residence 5-2054

April 25, 1955.

Dear Mrs. Gnade:

For all your kindness to our missionaries and their families
may I dedicate these lines from Tennyson to you :

> Thrice blest whose lives are faithful prayers,
>   Whose loves in higher love endure;
>   What souls possess themselves so pure,
> Or is there blessedness like theirs ?
>
>   - - -
>
> And so the Word had breath, and wrought
>   With human hands the creed of creeds
>   In loveliness of perfect deeds,
> More strong than all poetic thought.

Gratefully,

Theodore J. Jansma

Radio Broadcast Sunday 10 to 10:45 A.M. - WLAV, Grand Rapids - 1340

American Arcot Mission Agricultural Institute

In Co-operation with

World Neighbors, Inc. U. S. A.

KATPADI, N. A. Dt. S. INDIA

M.J.John, B.Sc.,(Ag) M.A.,M.S.,
Acting Principal.

April 18, 1955.

My Dear friends—

    A friend in need is a friend indeed. As I start writing this to you, many are the sweet reflections that come to my mind of my stay in your beloved country.

    I am reminded of the 9th of Sept.'53 when our ship pulled into the Harbour of New York. What a strange feeling to land in a strange country and not a single person whom I knew face to face to say hallo even. One of the Indian boys who had his Indian friend waiting for him said that "two American ladies are waiting for one M.J.John "for me" said I. I could not believe it. I walked on to the front main deck and there they were two angel in sweet smiling faces waving their handkerchief. I did not know who they were. In another half hour I got out of the ship to meet the good angels who took away the strange feelings of the stranger—Mrs. Hazel Gnade and Mrs. A. Teusink. What have they not done for me? 15th December 1953 when I enjoyed the Christian love and hospitality of yours in your home—a full eat of real chicken roast, the thought of which still waters the mouth—the laughter that followed Dr. Gnade jokes and stories made space for an extra bite all the time to enjoy it all again——? "well began half done" — but—"all is well that ends well". I completed my one year stay in the States on the 8th of Sept.'54 when I was to leave New York. The two angels who had to wait hours to greet me, spent hours with me to say the final goodbye——Mrs. Teusink with her two loving sons paul and Kenny my pals. Finally we all went to my cabin in Queen and we shared the lunch you had brought—— my last taste of American picnic lunch.

    My stay in U.S.A. has been a mountaintop experience to me the joy of which will only appreciate as years pass by—sweet happy instances. THANK YOU my friend THANK YOU for all you have done unto me which is much indeed. I shall ever remember with grateful heart my friends and happy associations in that country and of all you with Mrs. Teusink were the first to greet me into your land and to stay to the last and say goodbye. Ingratitude is the greatest of all sins in my contention, ingratitude to God and ingratitude to fellowmen through whom He works. THANK YOU.

    With our united love and regards,

                                  Yours in His love,

Mrs. Hazel Gnade,
Hostesses of R.C.A.,
C/o. Dr.B.M.Luben,
Secretary, Board of Foreign Missions,
156 Fifth Ave.,
New York 10, N.Y.,
U.S.A.

                                  M.J.John,Mary and Mollie.

A Big Thank You to "Tug-boat Annie"

What an "Angel of Mercy " you have been to me at various times when I arrived in and left New York, Mrs. Gnade. Always so ready to drop whatever you were doing to rush out to the Docks or Airport to take over charge. It has been such a relief to know you would be at hand.

I do recall all the various times you have met me and done the many lovely things to make my leaving easier and happier. But one time stands out very clear, when you met me at Newark to take me out to Blaise's and Marian Wedding. I had just arrived from the West and you met me at Newark. I had been suffering terribly with a bad ear. Without a moments hesitation you took me to Dr. Bosch, who contacted Dr. Keim, the Ear Specialist. Dr. Keim spoke over phone to Dr. Bosch telling him I could come sometime during the week. But you broke in and said "No, she must have treatment before we go to the Wedding." He agreed to see me that evening but still you insisted it must be at once. So at last he said, "Alright bring her over". We were in his office in a short time and he stopped all the line of patients to see me. He gave treatment and relief after 48 hours of suffering. So we went cheerfully off to the wedding and had a grand time. The next day Dr. Gnade took me over for another treatment. It was only through your prompt action and determination that I was able to keep to schedule and fly back to India a few days later.

I have so appresaited staying in your home after the long lonely, tiring ear trip from Iowa, enjoying the good Fellowship with you and your good Family, who also are so ready to make us feel at home, being entertained at an early Breakfast with a group of Women of the locality, and again at an evening party with Friends from Sioux County, rushing around at the last minute to get an extra suitcase to put the "extras" that had accumulated in the East for me to take out for other Missionaries, your rushing out to the airport after a busy day of Meetings to see me off in Sept.1949, your coming in to New York and having an early Breakfast with me before taking me out and getting me settled with Miss Aley Mathews in our wee little third class cabin way down in the Queen Mary in 1953. All these and many other nice,thoughtful things that you have done for me through the years when I have been so alone in New York before sailing and on arriving have always been and shall be most happy Memories for me. I do thank you and Dr. Gnade and your Mother for all that you have so willingly given and done for me through the years. Thank you most heartily,"Our Tug-boat Annie".

Affectionately Yours,

Mina Jongewaard

On Queen Mary 4

JAY R. KAPENGA
ARABIAN MISSION
MUSCAT, OMAN

Dar es Salaam
Kodaikanal, South India
May 18, 1955

Dear Mrs. Gnade,

A letter of Barney Luben's the other day reminded us of an "Occasion" to be celebrated which we very much wanted to be a part of. It is months ago that this "Occasion" was voiced abroad. And it is months ago that we were going to sit down and write our appreciation. Now at this late date we are embarrassed to be so late, and we are very sorry, but we MUST add our thanks to all the rest you must have received.

We can count up at least eight times that you or Mr. Gnade have met one or the other of us either coming into or going out of New York. And that doesn't cover a night spent at Idlewilde waiting for a late plane, a trip on the train to Philadelphia to see we made thetransfer to Pendle Hill alright, or an evening of baby sitting so we could see a show. I can remember an afternoon of shopping and the morning you sat with us at AMMO while we had our physical exams. We could go on and on. You are the first person of the Reformed Church I met in the States when I arrived just after Jay and I had been married in Teheran and I can still see Mr. Gnade running up to strange women in Penn station with a picture in hand to tell me there was no room at the hotel and I could stay with you.

We are sure we have never thanked you both properly for all these times of helping us out and spending literally hours so that our arrival or departure or stay in New York could be easier.

How to say it, I don't know, but we appreciate all the time you have spent for us and we wish to thank Mr. Gnade too, for letting his wife stay out all night and all hours for our benefit. We wish you could visit us somehow in Muscat so we could have the fun of meeting you at the boat!

Our heartfelt thanks for all you have done for us and our family.

Sincerely,

Midge and Jay Kapenga

American Mission,
Akobo, U.N.P.,
Sudan
Jan. 11, 1955

Dear Mrs. Snade:

I don't know if I approve of Barney's referring to you as "Tug-boat Annie" — it's not exactly a flattering nick-name! — but I certainly am grateful for this opportunity to say "thank you" to one whose self-less service and untiring devotion far exceeds any "ye old tug-boat" could ever give. How I appreciate all you did, not only for me, but for members of my family, too, — both when I left for Africa, and when I returned; — also, for your sending your good husband as your substitute when I left the second time. He does admirably as a "pinch-hitter" — though, of course, he neither pinches nor hits!!

Having made that train-bus-subway journey from New Jersey to New York myself a few times, I can appreciate just a little of the difficulties involved for you to be on hand to wave us off, and welcome us back. How glad I am that the Lord knows all about it, for I know He will reward you richly. Somehow I think He must have been thinking of you, too, when He said, so long ago, of Mary, who annointed

Him with oil, "She has done a beautiful thing to me, ... she has done what she could, ... this also that she has done shall be spoken of as a memorial of her."

With deep gratitude,
Wilma Kato

Dear Mrs. Grade,

although we have not had the happy privilege of seeing you at the docks, we do appreciate very much indeed the help you gave to our son Ralph last year. He joins us in sending you his grateful thanks. Yours sincerely,
The Kotelings

30 Arni Road
Vellore, North Arco
April 22, 1955

Dear Mrs. Gnade,

I hope this letter will reach you in time to join with the
hundreds of other well wishers at the May meeting of the Board of
Foreign Missions which you have served so faithfully, yet unosten-
tatiously, for so many years. I wonder if you will ever realize
to what extent you have given practical help, comfort and cheer
to those of us who while facing the excitement of an ocean voyage
have been under the strain of parting from loved ones and the un-
certainty of the immediate future whether first back in the States
or on the sea. Whether it was expressed through explanation of
customs or ordering a taxi or a word of sympathy or cheer, we are
all grateful to you for the help you have given to us.

I wonder if you will remember the little covered cup you gave
to Lynda when she was six months old and ready to start her first
journey across the world. Few others would think of the havoc a
stormy sea could do to a cup of milk, but this little gift was one
of the most practical we received. It has been in constant use
since then, and I certainly hope we will have it for the ocean
trip back again.

We wish we could be with you at the lovely ceremony planned by
the Board. But know that our thoughts and prayers will be with you.
May God bless you in your work for Him.

With affectionate regards,

Marian and Blaine Lewis

The Chronicle of Hazelia

In those days Roosevelt, he it was who was called Teddy, ruled the land; and he had armies, and navies, and he was a mighty man, and the nations were afraid of him, for his navies sailed far, and there was no sea where his navies did not sail. And the nations warred in those days, one against the other, but Roosevelt, he that is called Teddy, caused Rushi and Nipponi to cease fighting, and there was peace over all the earth, for the Rushites and the Nipponites warred no more.

Now it came to pass in those days, that the Lord appeared in a dream to a maid called Hazelia, of the daughters of Browna, of the Sect of the Methodists, in the country of Bergen. This maid feared the Lord, for she was of the strict sect of the Methodists who drank no strong wine, neither did they inhale the smoke of the tobacco, as was the custom in those days. And the Lord spake unto Hazelia, and the Lord said unto her, Blessed art thou, Hazelia, daughter of Browna, for I have a work for thee to do, when thou art come of years. And Hazelia praised the Lord for his word unto her.

But in those days, when the years were come, and Woodrow sat on the throne, the heart of Hazelia was smitten, and she did weep before the Lord, for he did not send her forth as one of his servants to a far country. For many went forth to speak the word of the Lord, even unto the uttermost parts of the earth, for the nations had forgotten the Lord, and gone after other gods, even after Mohammed, and Buddha and the Hindu, and the goddess of the Shekel; and they bound themselves unto strange gods, and set up idols in the market places, and went awhoring after them. And God sent forth his people, out of all the tribes of Israel, to speak of his Son, whom he had sent to save the nations from their sins. And they went forth, and preached mightily of his resurrection from the dead, and many heard, of all races, and the Lord added unto his church daily.

Now Hazelia, remembering the word of the Lord unto her, was troubled in spirit, for he sent her not forth, and she cried unto him, and sought to hear his voice. And again the word of the Lord came unto her, and the Lord spake unto her, and said, Hazelia, thou of little faith, doth the Lord not remember his word? Is he like man, whose words pass quickly, and whose thoughts are as the morning dew when the sun doth shine? I have a work for thee to do, and thou shalt do it. And Hazelia was no more sad, for she believed, and treasured these things in her heart.

There dwelt in those days, in the same country, a man of the house of Gnade, a Bergenite, of the course of Aaron, who first became a merchant of the south country but was called again to the north to do the work of a priest, and he was a priest in the synagogue of Schenectady until the high priest caused him to dwell in the temple. This Bergenite was called Gerhardus, and he sat at the treasury of the temple; the care of those priests who were full of years, and of the widows and orphans, was in his hands.

Now Gerhardus looked upon Hazelia, and saw that she was fair, and desired

her.   And the house of Browna looked with favor upon the Bergenite, and
Gerhardus took unto wife Hazelia, and they dwelt in the village of the woods
on the hill, after that they were no more in Schenectady.   And they begat
two sons, Gerrius the elder, and Kenneth the younger.   And Gerrius the first-
born took unto himself Edith, and begat sons and daughters, and these are the
generations of Gerhardus.

Now fear fell upon all the people, and they were greatly afraid, for the
Lord revealed his secrets to the wise men.   And men learned to do many things,
walking not as in the days of Abraham, nor riding in their chariots with fast
horses, for they had chariots made of iron that had no horses, chariots swifter
than the steeds of Arabia, and they had chariots with wings that made the eagles
slow.   And men left the earth, and flew like birds.   But for all those inven-
tions, men's hearts were faint, for the nations followed after strange gods,
and dwelt not in concord.   And God opened more mysteries, and taught his crea-
tures how he had put matter together, so man could take it apart.   And they
took it apart, with great sound.   They took it apart in the seas, and lo, the
isles were not.   Still men were afraid, for they feared not the Lord, and
there was war, and the nations took matter apart over their enemies, and their
cities were not.   And there was great dismay and much crying.   And people rose
against their rulers, and the nations changed; yet men knew not how the nations ought to go, for they sought after strange gods.

And God looked upon the nations, and he had compassion on them, for they
had little knowledge of him, and they were affrighted.   And he sent his servants
the more to say, Behold, your God.   And His servants labored mightily, so that
in the far countries they wearied, and sought to have rest, and would worship
again with their fathers in their own land.   So when they became weak, they
took sail to return to the promised land, the land that flowed with milk and
honey, where their fathers dwelt, and where the temple was.   But when they
neared port, they were dismayed, for they were as strangers, and no more knew
the customs of their land, for they had sojourned long.   And when they came in
the chariot of the air, and looked down on Manhattan, their joy was no more,
for the people were many, and the iron chariots filled the streets.

And the Lord appeared yet again to Hazelia, wife of Gerhardus, and said unto her, Hazelia, mother of Gerrius and Kenneth, I am pleased with thee.   Thou
hast brought forth sons and trained them in my way, and they shall serve me,
and their children after them.   Thou hast blessed thy husband, my servant, and
made him strong for my people.   In the synagogue of the village thy name is
blessed.   According to my promise, which I spake unto thee when thou was young,
I have given thee a work, and thou hast been faithful.   And now I call thee to
serve me yet again.   Behold, the servants whom I have sent to the nations, how
they need thee.   When they come again, their hearts faint at the ports.

And thus it came to pass, that when the chariots of the air put forth
their wheels, as a bird putteth forth its feet to land, and when the great ships
left the seas and were borne safely into the harbour, the envoys of God had no
dismay and their hearts were filled with joy, for Hazelia the daughter of God

welcomed them.   And when they left the land of their fathers to teach
all the families of the earth and speak peace to those afar off, they
were not afraid, neither were they cumbered with many things, for
Hazelia helped them.

From the lost book of The Chronicles of Modern Disciples,
recently discovered in the ruins of ancient Newyork, and
believed to have been written by an obscure scribe called
Barnabus who apparently lived, as deduced from an analysis
of the parchment, near the beginning of the atomic age.

DHOBIES AT WORK   I.R.WARREN

Sherman School
Chittoor, Andhra
S. India
January 5, 1955

Dear Mrs. Grado,

This afternoon my memory seemed to run wild and my thoughts went back two years ago to my departure from home and my arrival in this country. I recalled so vividly how I had dreaded that last day in New York — knowing very few people there, having no idea what I had to do or where I had to go — and then you came to the rescue. How I appreciated it! I was entertained royally. I've often seen signs advertising the movie "Million-Dollar Mermaid" and my immediate thought is "Oh, I saw that my last night in New York with Mrs. Grado." The next morning you arrived bright and early to see to it that I was delivered safely on the boat. What a joy it was to have someone with me who knew something about what was going on. I certainly felt like a "dumb-bell" at the time. You very patiently waited until the boat left so we could wave our fond farewells. Thanks so much.

In closing I want to send my best wishes for the

New year. It is my hope and prayer that God may continue to bless you as you do this important work for Him.

Love in Christ,

Wilma Meassim

Mrs. Calvin C. Meury

7601 Palisade Avenue, North Bergen, New Jersey

May 16, 1955.

Dear Hazel, —

Imagine my chagrin
on finding the enclosed carefully
stowed away in the desk. It was
in an envelope addressed to Miss
Ranson with a note telling her
why I could not be at the supper.
Later I had talked with her by
phone so didn't mail the note.

Everyone spoke so enthusi-
astically of the wonderful time they
had on Thursday evening. I was

sorry indeed that we coued not attend.

Even though this will not be bound in your book, I want you to know my intentions were good.

Cal Jr. is being married in Ann Arbor next month and I guess "Mamma's" mind has been too much on that.

Cordially,
Lilian

Nehemiah 8:10

---- for the joy of the Lord
is your strength.

Dear Hazel, -

What can I say that hasn't
already been said many times by the
hundreds of missionaries and their
families to whom you have given
your time, energy, gracious hospitality,
and helping hands?

You are certainly the one
matched to this responsibility – rendering
a remarkable service with a joyful
and untiring spirit. Blessings on thee!

Lilian Meury.

New Brunswick, N.J.
May 9, 1955.

Dear Mrs. Gnade:

Mrs. Muyskens and I want to add our expression of appreciation of your fine service extended to us missionaries, our Board, and to the glorious cause of Missions. How wonderful it is that people like you give themselves in the various forms of service which you have been rendering for so many years. Among the many happy memories of that service which you will treasure we trust that the occasion of this recognition of that service will be one of the happiest and most meaningful. May God continue to bless you and use you to His Glory.

Yours sincerely

John D. Muyskens

109 East Morris
Morrison Ill.
April 22, 1955

Dear Mrs. Gnade,

It is indeed a pleasure for me to add my note of appreciation to you for the many services you have rendered to our board.

I have often tho't that we in the West owe a debt of gratitude to our loyal "sisters" in the East who so faithfully carry on the various services that are so necessary if our boards are to carry on efficiently – and which we cannot share due to distances –

I feel confident that the cheer that you have bro't and the confidence that you have inspired upon meeting the missionaries and their families and in taking care of them is a work that shall never be forgotten by them, nor by us who have had a part in sending them forth to bring the gospel of Jesus Christ to all parts of the world.

You were a living example of that wonderful way of living that Christ has taught us and as such I thank you most sincerely

Since you and your husband have been such good friends of my brother George D. Dikkolter I have often heard of your family and so have a slight "connection"

Sincerely yours –

[Mrs. Jo. C.] Maxine S. Muysken

Vellore, India
January 30, 1955

Dear Mrs. Grade,

Although it is almost seven years ago since you saw us safely off on the "Kota Agoeng," the memories of our last few days in New York are vivid. We were not complete strangers to the Big City, but it was wonderful to be greeted on the sidewalk in front of the Prince George as we completed the long drive from Michigan. We will never forget your kindness in taking John and David to the Bronx Zoo for a whole day, my insisting on our having a last night "a-t," and your taking us to the Brooklyn docks. While we were riding in the taxi, you remarked how the circle of friends — the community, the church, the relatives, the parents, sisters and brothers — continued to decrease as the missionary left the homeland. Although you were the only person to "see us off," you seemed like a dear friend — not a representative of the board fulfilling her duty. That meant a great deal to us that day and we will always cherish it as a happy memory.

I am enclosing a snap of John and David with their propeller-beanie caps purchased on that memorable outing.

With love,
Wilma Piet

REV. GERARD C. POOL
2607 Palisade Avenue
Union City, N. J.
Phone, UNion 7-2544

First Reformed Church

Palisade Avenue and 28th Street
Union City, New Jersey

April 23, 1955

Dear Hazel,

It is a pleasure to add a word of appreciation to the many that are gathered in this book. Only by a number of such expressions could there be any approach to an adequate statement of the feeling of all of us who thank you for helping the missionaries. You have been unsparing of time and effort, and always have added the quality of gracious friendship to the practical help you gave.

New York City has an official "Greeter," working on a substantial budget. He often does things with a brass band and a flourish. But he doesn't do anything that is more important than what you have done for the missionaries and their families. You have made glad their hearts by your genuine love of people and by your devotion to the work which they represent. All who know of your kindness are deeply grateful.

Sincerely yours,

Jerry

Emmanuel Reformed Church

C. POSTMA, Minister

Telephone 264-R
Church Study 264-W

302 Bly Street
Waupun, Wisconsin

April 20, 1955

Dear Mrs. Gnade:

As a member of the Board of Foreign Missions, R.C.A., I would like to convey my personal thanks to your for your wonderful hospitality shown to our missionaries upon their arrival and departure from our country. So often we take these matters for granted and do not stop to consider just how much it means to those who are leaving for Foreign countries or returning from them. At our Board meetings we have heard how you were willing to spend a great deal of time, sometime long hours of the night, to meet delayed planes and boats. Certainly you have endeared yourself to the missionary families and undoubtedly they and their children constitute your closest friends. When one has such interest in others as you have displayed, certainly God's choicest blessings will rest upon such gracious acts of kindness.

Again may I say "Thank-you". May the Lord continue to give you added strength and health to perform this service.

Cordially Yours,

Chester Postma

Chester Postma

BOARD OF FOREIGN MISSIONS
OF THE
REFORMED CHURCH IN AMERICA
156 FIFTH AVENUE
NEW YORK 10, N. Y.

CABLE ADDRESS: SYNODICAL   TELEPHONE: CHELSEA 2-3650

April 1, 1955

Dear Mrs. Gnade:

If I were to name one volunteer worker who has helped me most since I have been a secretary of the Board of Foreign Missions, it would be Hazel Gnade. Many of the other women of the former Woman's Board of Foreign Missions and the Department of Women's Work have given great leadership and helped in many ways, but you have given me a feeling that our missionaries are well cared for when they come to big and busy New York City. It is so important that we be hospitable, but when we get busy in an office we find ourselves caught in a whirlwind of duties and we cannot be the calm hosts and hostesses that we want to be. You have done the things that I have wanted to do and done them so well. Thank you.

You could never have done the many things you did - and which I hope you will continue to do, unless you had had an understanding and cooperative family. Your mother; your children; your husband who was ready so many times to drive the car for "Little Hazel". We do appreciate their sacrifice and also their cooperation so that you could do the work that means so much. I know that you will thank each one of them for me.

Some day when you get old - and that will be a long time from now - I wish that you would write a booklet telling of the sad, the serious and the funny things that have happened to you. It would be a best seller and even a Book-of-the-Year among the missionaries.

My love and best wishes to you as you continue in this great service.

Gratefully,

Ruth

Harrison, South Dakota
January 17, 1955

Dear Mrs. Gnade,

As one of your more recent arrivees, the memory of your welcome is still very fresh in my mind. To find you, and Galen and Maude Scudder, waiting for me was one of the nicest things about arriving in New York.

I remember staying in your home one night on my first visit to New York. That, too, was an experience to be remembered for there I found you not only a friend quickly made but a gracious and clever hostess as well. Your home was just the kind of place that had all you would want in a home. I have never forgotten one funny little thing that happened that night. I was to sleep, it seemed, in your young son's room and his father informed him when he went to retire that he was to sleep in the top story. "And", concluded Dad, "Don't forget to say your prayers". "Okay", replied Sonny cheerfully, "I won't have to say them so loud tonight, I guess, because I'll be up closer to God."

So I do want to join many others in saying from the bottom of my heart, Thank you for the many little things you do and for what you are, most of all, which enables you to make our visits to New York easier and happier. Especially, I appreciated your coming out and staying until all was cared for even when you had cares at home which demanded your attention. If you weren't there, I assure you, we would miss you because of what you are more than for what you do, even. I hope that my staying in America doesnt need to mean that my acquaintance with Mrs. Gnade is over.

Sincerely and Gratefully,

Lois E. Rozendaal

ALFRED W. SCHWAGER
ONE LEFURGY TERRACE
HASTINGS ON HUDSON, NEW YORK

April 26, 1955

Dear Mrs. Gnade:

I believe my first personal contact with you was
in connection with Sewing Guild. Since you did not have
enough to do at home and on the waterfront, you came to
the warehouse in Jersey City to help with the packing
many times.

May I add a word of appreciation for all you have
done to help us and thank you for the opportunity of
knowing you since I have been with the B.F.M.

Affectionately yours,

Elsie Schwager

My dear Mrs Snade—

My wife and I want to
add our words of gratitude
and thanks to all the many others
that you will receive at this time.
You have been a blessing and joy
to many missionaries. You have
saved us many an anxiety. We
wish you could carry on your
beneficent service for many many
more long years. But if you

feel some other must take over we
can only hope that you will thoroughly
instruct your successor in all
the intracacies of New York Piers
and Customs and allow your
mantle to fall upon broad
shoulders.

    Yours in gratitude

     Galen & Mantle Scudder

LUMAN J. SHAFER
SECRETARY FOR JAPAN,
CHAIRMAN OF BOARD STAFF

RUTH RANSOM
SECRETARY FOR THE PHILIPPINES,
HOME DEPARTMENT, PERSONNEL
AND WOMEN'S WORK

BARNERD M. LUBEN
SECRETARY FOR INDIA, ARABIA,
AND AFRICA

BOARD OF FOREIGN MISSIONS
OF THE
REFORMED CHURCH IN AMERICA
156 FIFTH AVENUE
NEW YORK 10, N. Y.

CABLE ADDRESS: SYNODICAL   TELEPHONE: CHELSEA 2-3650

HENRY G. BOVENKERK
TREASURER

EDWINA PAIGE
ASSOCIATE TREASURER,
PURCHASING AND TRAVEL

EDWIN W. KOEPPE
ACTING FIELD SECRETARY
1848 GODFREY AVE. S.W.
GRAND RAPIDS, MICHIGAN
TEL. GLENDALE 2-2391

March 30, 1955

Mrs. Gerard R. Gnade
148 North Maple Street
Ridgewood, New Jersey

Dear Hazel:

As one of those who has received kindness and courtesy from you as a missionary, I would like to be included in this very creditable plan of letting you know something of how we feel about you. I remember your meeting us in Brooklyn and driving us over to New York when we came back from Japan in the middle of a hot summer day. It was a very warm experience to find someone on the dock who knew the ropes and was there to welcome us.

I am continually astonished by the amount of energy that you display in carrying on this program. Apparently you have a motto of never failing, no matter what the weather or the time or circumstances. That motto on the United States Post Office Building on Eighth Avenue ought to be over your door lintel.

Well, it has been a wonderful service that you are doing and one cannot say enough about it. At the same time, being a husband myself, I think a word should be said about the good man who not only is ready for you to take this responsibility but also personally shares in it many times.

Long may you wave!

Yours, sincerely,

Luman

L. J. Shafer

LJS:eh

Dear Mrs. Gnade,

It is a pleasure to have a chance, with many others, of saying "thank you" for all you have done. You have given generously and unselfishly of your time and energy. But more than that, you have given friendliness and caring to your task. I know that many times it must have been inconvenient for you to meet ships, but you did it cheerfully.

This work of yours is important because the arriving or departing missionary feels that someone representing the Board of Foreign Missions is there to meet or see him off. But you have gone far beyond the requirements of your task, as you kept the missionaries' children while they shopped or visited, and helped the missionaries in so many unexpected ways. And you have done it all with a graciousness and devotedness for which we can never adequately thank you, but we are grateful.

Sincerely yours,

Mary P. Sibley

Protestant Dutch Reformed Church of Flatlands

FOUNDED, FEBRUARY 9, 1654

KINGS HIGHWAY AND EAST 40TH STREET
BROOKLYN 10, NEW YORK

Celebrating 300 Years of Christian Service in 1954

STANLEY S. SLINGERLAND
Minister

PHONE CLOVERDALE 2-3790

April 11, 1955

Dear Mrs. Gnade,

Your kind efforts in behalf of our Missionaries
and their families has been deeply appreciated, and we
want you to know about it.

You have been a wonderful Hospitality Chairman
doing with a loving heart far more then the job required
of you. We have learned of the night vigils you have
kept in order that some little family mighty find warmth
and welcome on the return from a far country. We know,
too, of the risk to your own safety on the dark water fronts as
you send off the Lord's Ambassadors with loving farewells.

For these things and for all of your fervant efforts
for the Reformed Church, we want to thank you. Surely the
Lord Himself shall say to you, "well done thou good and
faithful servant!"

Most sincerely yours,

Mae Slingerland

Mae Slingerland.

Little Rock, Iowa
April 4, 1955

Mrs. Gerard R. Gnade
% Board of Foreign Missions
Reformed Church in America
156 Fifth Avenue
New York 10, N.Y.

Dear Mrs. Gnade:

As a member of the Board of Foreign Missions, I am happy for this special opportunity of saying, "Thank you so very much" for all that you have done in hospitality, in meeting the boats, taking care of missionaries' children and helping generally as a wonderful hostess to our missionaries. It is a great service that you have rendered to these servants of the Lord, but a service that you have cheerfully rendered because you love the Lord and His people.

I had heard a great deal about you and this gracious service you were rendering before I met you at the Board Meeting at Ridgewood, New Jersey. It was there that I learned to know you and appreciate your charming personality and gracious ways. I could more fully understand then why so many of the Board members spoke frequently with deep appreciation of this service of hospitality that you were rendering to the missionaries of the Cross.

Thank you again, Mrs. Gnade. May the Lord continue to bless you as you continue to serve Him.

Cordially yours,

Frank Snuttjer

Frank Snuttjer, pastor
Salem Reformed Church
Little Rock, Iowa

From the Staff
of the
Board of Foreign Missions

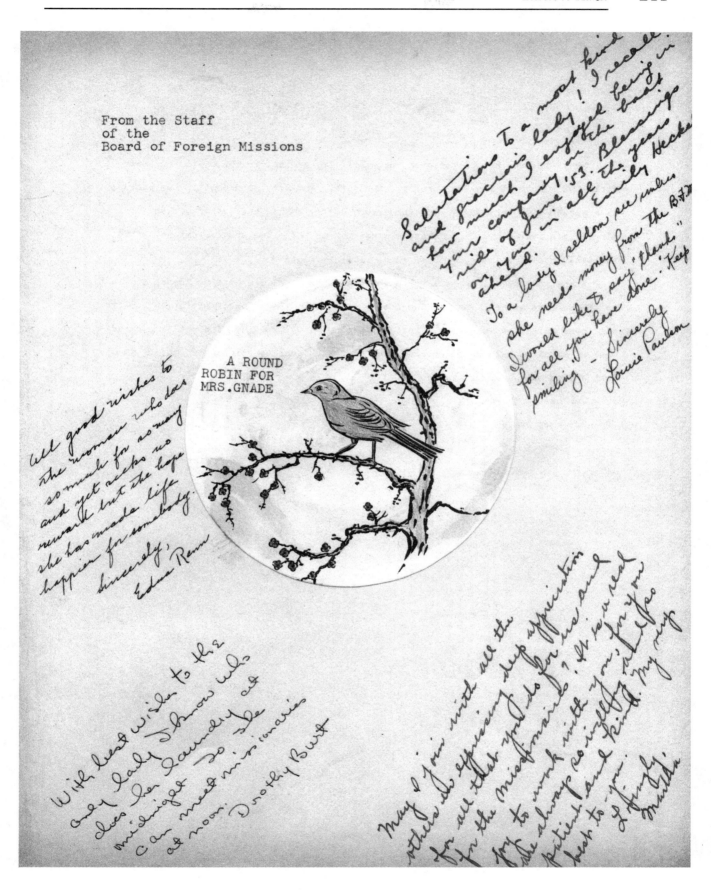

A ROUND
ROBIN FOR
MRS. GNADE

Salutations to a most kind
and gracious lady! I recall
how much I enjoyed being in
your company on the boat
ride of June '53. Blessings
on you in all the years
ahead.

To a lady I seldom see unless
she need money from the B.F.M.
I would like to say "thanks"
for all you have done. Keep
smiling. — Sincerely,
Louise Paulson

All good wishes to
the woman who does
so much for so many
and yet seeks no
reward but the hope
she has made life
happier for somebody.
Sincerely,
Edna Renn

With best wishes to the
one lady I know who
does he laundry at
midnight so she
can meet missionaries
at noon. Dorothy Burt

May I join with all the
others to express my deep appreciation
for all that you do for us and
for the missionaries? If you ever need
to work with you, for you
she always so willingly, helps
try patient and kind. My my
best to —. Firstly,
Martin

American Mission
Pibor Post, A.E.Sudan
Feb. 4, 1955

Dear Mrs. Gnade,

Many times we have lived over that thrilling arrival in the States in early April '52 - home at last on our first furlough. And very prominent in the picture is a person with very merry eyes and a very lovely smile, and two of our children are already captivated by her and have claimed her as their own special friend. That in itself speaks volumes.

Thank you for all the times you've been there - and for getting there; it isn't as if you have an apartment at the pier. It must take much careful planning to fit all those missionary excursions into an already busy life. You are the very embodiment of American warmth and welcome, and of Christian cheerfulness and love. It all just shines out.

Our hearts to you!

God keep you!

Gratefully and affectionately yours,

Bob and Morrie Swart

Route 5
Holland, Mich.
April 16/1955

Dear Mrs. Gnade:

Mrs. Dykstra and myself would like to take this opportunity to express to you our appreciation of your many kindnesses you showed us in our comings and goings to our field in Arabia.

Never have we forgotten how your husband and yourself came to our rescue when we had to board the Queen Elizabeth in that terrific blizzard in February 1947. Nor can we forget your helpfulness and patience when we returned from the field in May 1952, and the many hours you spent on that pier, and the many things you were able to do for us in our need.

We truly thank you again for all that you have been and done for us, and the highest praise we can give is to say that you always reminded us of the gracious lady that for so many years met and escorted the Arabian Missionaries during their passage through New York. She has long since gone to glory, but her memory abides, and your kindnesses have always refreshed our memory of her.

Sincerely Your Friends,

Dirk and Minnie Dykstra

Faith Reformed Church

Zeeland, Michigan
April 25, 1955

Dear Mrs. Gnade:

We are trying to express our sincere gratitude to you in the
following lines:

T   THANK YOU again and again for all your

H   HELPFULNESS to the outgoing and incoming missionaries and
                    their families.

A   ALWAYS dependable, no matter what time of day or night a
                    boat is due.

N   NICE, (for lack of a better word) for this does not fully
               describe your every

K   KINDNESS, thoughtfulness and cheerful personality, as

Y   YOU take the place of parents, loved ones and friends;
             when they are especially in need of someone to stand
            by, as they leave

O   OR as they return to these

U   UNITED STATES.

                    Sincerely,

                    (Mrs. E. H.) Agnes Tanis

Daily in our prayers

Miss Eunice Post
American Mission
Bahrain, Persian Gulf

"Go ye into all the world

Ila De Boer
Muriel Raak
Gloria Mouw
Elsie Schaap
Ruth Vermeer
Frances Wynia
Clarene Kroon
Norma De Boer
Arlene Franken
Esther Roghair
Arthea Hulstein
Audrey Dykshorn
Darlene Doornink
Grada Schuiteman
Virginia Bartels
Connie Cleveland
Maria Van Roekel
Ellen Van Roekel
Jane Ann De Jong
Caroline Vermeer
Dorothy Lockhorst
Wilemina Kaemingk
Margaret Kaemingk
Adrianna Lockhorst
Aldeane Cleveringa
Jeanette Lockhorst
Wilma Cleveringa, Class sec'y.

Maurice A. Te Paske, Teacher.

GIRLS TEACHER TRAINING CLASS
SUNDAY SCHOOL
First Reformed Church
SIOUX CENTER, IOWA
Rev. Peter A. De Jong, Pastor

Daily in our prayers

Miss Marianne Walvoord
American Mission
Bahrain, Persian Gulf

May 4, 1955

Dear Mrs. Gnade,

Those who have been fortunate enough to know of your dedicated efforts more directly have doubtless expressed appreciation much more adequately than I can.   But your cheerful and radiant spirit has been a benediction for all of us---p_utting into practice and demonstration the spirit and the grace which we can only hope to emulate.

Some years ago in the Reader's Digest there appeared an article by Gillette Burgess entitled "An Educated Heart." It described personality characteristics which make certain individuals stand out from the crowd, particularly in reference to thoughtfulness and kindness in practice.

How often I have thought of that article in reference to the reports of your gracious work of hospitality toward those who appreciated and deserved it so much.   All of us are your debtor for having so served with a full measure of devotion.

Reverently we say "God bless you for your 'educated heart!"

Respectfully yours,

Maurice A. TePaske

Maurice A. TePaske

JAN 1 9 1955

Jan. 4th. '55.

Dear Miss Ransom;

Beth and I want you and Mrs. Gnade to know how much
we appreciated being met by her at the Jersey City pier in August
1948 and seen off by her at the Brooklyn pier in December '49.
She has aarried on the wonderful tradition established by Mrs. E.E.
Olcott of welcoming in-coming missionaries and giving them a cheerful
farewell when the time comes for them to go back to the field.
Since our childhood Beth and I have felt the close family tie that
has always existed in the Reformed Church , between the sending churches
and the ones sent, Between the secretaries and board members and the
missionaries.. " Tugboat Annie" as Mrs. Gnade is affectionately
called by many of us gave our four children the same sense of being
welcomed back to the "homeland" that Mrs. Olcott gave us when we
were missionary children returning to America with our parents.
Mr. Gnade did his share of heart warming when we visited their homw
the day after arriving in"the States" . We are looking forward to
seeing Mrs. Gnade at the pier when Beth and Lois and I reach New York
City about the first of June on board the Queen Elizabeth.

All of you who have had to do with getting out the
November Memo for Missionaries did a grand job. By the way you can
use anything that you think useful in any letters that I write to you
or to the supporting churches. I can just hear your comment" we have-
n't had had many letters from him to use. " Thats true I am sad
to say. We have not written many letters. We have just had a wonderful Christmas season . We have a grand bunch of native and our Europ-
ean Christians who love to sing carols.. The event that I cherish the
most was the night after Christmas when all the staff members of the
men's and women's hospital walked over in a group to the home for leprosy patients at night carrying lighted lanters . The ten male patients
and one woman, dear old Sharbanoo , were dressed up in new clothes
waiting for use on the veranda of their home,which they had helped
to decorate that afternoon , and their faces beamed with pleasure
when we sang them the Christmas hymns and then gave each patient a
lantern as his gift from the American Leprosy Mission and some candy
and fruit from the Christians on the staff..

We are so glad to have Marianne Walvoord with us as our
first missionary nurse in charge of the nursing in the Knox Memorial
Hospital. We will soon welcome the Bosches here. Beth is almost her
old healthy , energetic self again and Lois is flouringshing. We have
so much to be thankful for. We are looking forward to our coming full
lough .   Sincerely yours,   Wells Thoms

With apologies to Arthur Chapman
Author of "Out Where The West Begins."

To make the hand clasp a little stronger,
To make the smile last a little longer,
    And "The Tie That Binds" is tighter tying
      Thru the work Gnade does.
For hoary heads grown a trifle ——   *Mrs. Mike Tjoelker*
For heavy hearts that should be lighter,
    That's the way Gnade begins.

To meet in-comers from ocean bluer,
To assure them our friendship's a little truer,
    Is the way Gnade acts;
To wave farewell with breezes blowing,
For cheer to those who are outward going
To the fields now open in need of sowing,
    Is the way Gnade acts.

Out where the West is in the making,
We hear reports of the time she is taking,
    Of the work Gnade does.
How there's more of singing and less of sighing
How there's more of giving and less of buying,
And "The Tie That Binds" is tighter tying
    Thru the work Gnade does.
      — *Mrs. Mike Tjoelker*

Dear Mrs. Grade,

Long before I became a member of the Board of Foreign Missions, I heard glowing reports from travel weary missionaries, of an angel, who regardless of time, place or season, was always on hand at the dock to welcome them home.

How heart warming to find someone who in a world of deadlines, finds and takes the time for the gracious thoughtful gesture.

Some day, I hope I may have the opportunity to thank you personally for representing the Church, the Board of Foreign Missions and me in these kind ministration. May God richly bless you.

Most Sincerely,

(Mrs. G.) Isla G. Van Eenenaam

Muskegon
Wednesday
April 27, 1955.

American Mission,Basrah,Iraq.

April 11,1955.

Dear Mrs.Gnade:

It is a privilege to add my word of appreciation for all you do for the missionaries in the way of "Hail and Farewell".

Mine was a farewell,I have always remembered with pleasure our lunch together at Pan American's expense,as I was waiting at La Guardia Airport for my plane to bring me back to the Near East last time.

I don't know how you manage to convey that sense of leisure,you gave the impression that you could cheerfully wait there all day with the departing traveller so to bid"Godspeed" when I actually was on my way.

It gives a warm glow to the heart of the one who is about to take off, to have such a friend at hand.

I am happy to join in a big "Thank You" !

Cordially and gratefully yours,

Dorothy Van Ess.

(Mrs.John Van Ess)

Ranipet
North Arcot District
South India
Thursday 17th December 1954

Dear Friends: —

    We wish to add our note of appreciation for Mrs Hazel Gnade's tireless efforts on behalf of bewildered Missionaries, coming and going.

    We admire her resourcefulness and energy. It gives one a sense of relief to have help at such a time. Coming from an "Underprivileged" country one's breath is taken away by the sudden change of climate.

    She carries weight around that turbulent waterfront. With her smiling face and quiet speech; —somewhat different from Tugboat Annie's colloquial— Hazel accomplishes much for the comfort of all who come under her care.

    Dr "Gary" Gnade, too, must be thanked for his part in allowing her to be away from household duties as well as for personally lending a hand.

Cordially,
Marge, Tess and Herb.

419 W. Saddle River Road
Ridgewood, N.J.

April 29,1955.

Dear Mrs. Gnade,-

When first I heard of this collection of apprecia-
tions, I thought I couldn't qualify,- not being a member of
Board or Staff, nor yet one of those lucky missionaries who
have been so wonderfully served by you,- but perhaps as a former member of your Hospitality Committee, called to help you now
and then, I can appreciate a little of the demands and triumphs
of your continual service.

There isn't room here to do more than remind you of families needing a baby sitter while the parents shopped; of child-
dren comforted and entertained,- not to mention being fed and put t
to bed. (I can see Laila yet, climbing up the furniture like a
little monkey.) It was miraculous how small toys or candy appeared
just in time to avert a crisis!   Then there were days of waiting because steamer sailings were delayed; wandering luggage to be
located and brought to the pier in time; arrivals to be met, who
didn't arrive at all; and always the need for understanding and
comfort and loving cooperation,- in all of which I have seen you
(and Dr.Gnade) busy and devoted and untiring.

So with all my heart I salute your "steadfast love", like
that of our God Himself whose grace is upon you.

With loving admiration,

Mary W. S. Voskuil-

514 Wyndham Road,
Teaneck, New Jersey.
April 29, 1955.

Dear Mrs. Gnade,

As a newcomer in the Department of Women's Work I
was acquainted with very few of the members. One of my earliest
recollections was meeting you and feeling completely at home in
the warmth of your welcome and your encouraging smile. At subsequent
meetings I was always impressed anew with your friendliness. Your
monthly reports were something to look forward to; we actually missed
them, as well as you, the times you were absent.

I pleasantly recall the trips we took together back and
forth to Ficken's in Jersey City, and the hours we spent bending over
the boxes, being sure we counted the thousands of bandages correctly,
laughing over some of the odd things that had been sent in, enjoying
the beauty of the loving handwork in many of the articles, wondering
what the children would look like who eventually would wear the lovely
little dresses. It is hard work, but satisfying too, isn't it?

The few trips I took with you to see some of our missionaries off are firmly pictured in my mind. They are a part of the
whole picture of the work of the Board of Foreign Missions and as such
rounded out my education. I note too, how much of yourself you give
to everything you do. As a fine example of loving Christian service
I can think of none better than yours. I know that God blesses you
richly in and through all you do.

It is my happy privilege to join in this tribute to your
faithful, cheerful and selfless service, and my prayer is for God's
continued blessing upon you and yours.

Affectionately,

Gertrude A. Wagner

Beattie M. Training School

Chittoor, Andhra State

So. India

Jan. 2, 1955

Dear Mrs. Gnade,

The interval between the ship and the arrival in
the bosom of your family can be one of worry and concern over
endless little things at a new dock, customs, a broken trunk,
a parcel to be sent to someone direct from the dock, an urgent
telephone call or a railway reservation, but since you have been
meeting us at the dock or airport, these minor irritations melt
away as you calmly deal with each one. You welcome us, old
clothes and all, and never seem to mind the things our families
quickly insist upon sending to the "Goodwill" or just throwing
in the rag bag. You know where to find us a cup of coffee or a
quick lunch, and most of all are just the friend who is always
ready with a word of cheer and you are so understanding of one's
feelings at arrivals and departures. For most of us life is made
up of "good byes" and "greetings". This is the privilege and the
burden of those of us who love people in many parts of the world.
Each time we step aboard a train, plane or ship, we bid farewell
to many who are very dear to us not knowing when we'll meet again.
Sensing all of these emotions, you so quietly wait while we
make a last minute telephone call, or slowly pack up our belongings
after the customs inspection. We wonder how you can spend so
many hours on the cold draughty docks at all hours of day and
night, sleeping on a bench or justt sitting up all night when
a plane is late so that you'll be sure to be there when one of
us arrives.

2.

You have a very sympathetic husband in Dr. Gnade who drives you to the docks when possible or just takes care of himself when you suddenly find a weary mother and children who need your companionship and help part of the way to their destination. I'm sure the Ridgewood bus drivers must all know you as you make your frequent trips from your delightful home to dull uninteresting railway stations, and airports. Even for some of us who know New York and tell you that we can really save you a trip to the airport as we have friends who will see us off and thus save your energy for someone else, you just come along to be sure that all is well and we are safely aboard the plane for the first time. You know how much we like to meet our Mission friends and bother to get us passes that we may share in meeting ships too.

I wish that the Board could send you and Dr. Gnade to all of our Mission stations so that we could show you two grand folk a little of the care and love that you have showered on us over the years. We'd welcome you with garlands at every turn, and lose no chance to give you a royal welcome.

With loving appreciation to a very dear
friend,

Doris A. Wells

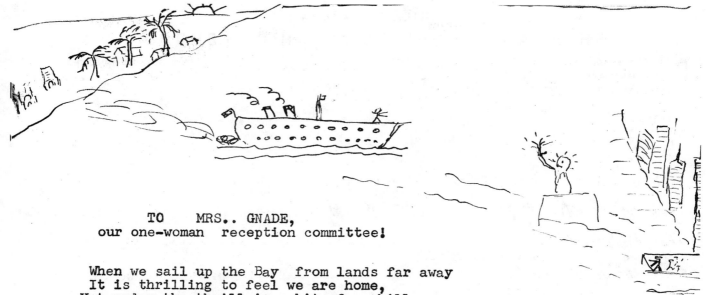

TO   MRS.. GNADE,
our one-woman reception committee!

When we sail up the Bay from lands far away
It is thrilling to feel we are home,
Yet under the thrill is a bit of a chill
As we wonder just why we have come.
Will our speech sound strange? Have our habits quite changed?
Are our clothes now dated? And will those related
To us recognise us or not?
In all of the flurry there's a bit of a worry,--
It's quite a transition to come home ~~home~~ from a mission
In Afric' , Arabia, Arcot.

As we sail up the Bay from lands far away
We're thrilled to see Liberty's light,
But there on the pier is a figure more dear,--
Day and night she may wait, but she'll never be late;
She'll be first to meet us and greet us and treat us,
And for us through Customs to fight.

And when, after a year, again on the pier,
Figures trimmed, eyes tear-dimmed, we meet,
She is with us again, our dear mother-hen,
Concerned for her chicks to the end.
The last down the plank, she stands waving her han'k--
Till the shores fade away and we're off down the Bay.

Dear Mrs. Gnade, for the efforts of body
And mind for our comfort you spend,
We thank you and bless you and herewith address you
As in time of need our best friend!

*Love and grateful thanks
from Charlotte C. Wyckoff*

MAHILA VIDYAVARAM
SHERMAN MEMORIAL GIRLS' HIGH SCHOOL.

MRS S. W. ZWEMER, M. A.,
MANAGER & CORRESPONDENT.
MISS STELLA D. SOURI, B. A., L. T.,
HEADMISTRESS,
MISS G. SHADRACH,
HOSTEL SUPERINTENDENT.

AMERICAN ARCOT MISSION.
CHITTOOR. Andhra
S. India.
Jan. 4, 1955.

Mrs. Gerard R. Gnade,
% Board of Foreign Missions, R.C.A.,
156 Fifth Avenue,
New York 10, N.Y., U.S.A.

Dear Mrs. Gnade,

It gives me great pleasure to be able to add my bit to the chorus of "Thank you's!" which are now going to you from many parts of the world. I appreciated very much your taking me from my New York hotel to the boat the last time I left the States. There was first a good meal and then a long ride somewhere, I remember, with flowers and something to read, and the assurance of personal interest which meant a great deal.

Thank you very much! May you be strengthened and encouraged in this labour of love for our Lord, and be warmed in heart as you have so often cheered others.

Looking forward to meeting you again in a few months,

I remain,

Cordially yours,

Sara W. Zwemer.

Appendix A

WBFM Constitution

Article 1

This association shall be called the Woman's Board of Foreign Missions of the Reformed Church in America, and its central point of operations shall be in the City of New York.

Article 2

Its object shall be to aid the Board of Foreign Missions of the Reformed Church in America, by promoting its work among the women and children of heathen lands, and for this purpose it shall receive and disburse all money which shall be contributed to this society, subject to the approval of the Board, in the appointment of missionaries supported by this association, and in fixing their locations and salaries.

To the furtherance of this end, it shall also endeavor to organize similar associations in all Reformed Churches, and these associations shall bear the name of Auxiliary Societies to the Woman's Board of Foreign Missions of the Reformed Church in America, and shall report their work to this Board at such times as the by-laws may direct.

Article 3

Each person paying one dollar annually, through an auxiliary, or directly to the treasury, shall become a member of this association. The payment of twenty-five dollars by one person, at one time, shall constitute a life membership.

Article 4

The business of this Board shall be conducted by thirty Managers, each of whom shall be a member of an auxiliary society. They shall be elected annually by the members of the Board, who may be present at the annual meeting, and shall organize on the first Tuesday after their election, by selecting from their number a President, two Vice-Presidents, a Recording Secretary, two or more Corresponding Secretaries, and a Treasurer. They shall have power to elect not more than twelve Honorary Vice-Presidents, and to appoint corresponding members, when the object of the Board can be promoted thereby; they shall also have authority to fill vacancies occurring in their body during the year.

Article 5

There shall be an Executive Committee, composed of the officers and two other Managers, to be elected annually. This committee shall have power to transact such business as may require attention in the intervals between the stated meetings of the Managers. Five members shall constitute a quorum.

Article 6

The annual meeting of the Board shall be held on the second Tuesday in May, in the City of New York, at which time the Managers shall report to the association the operations, condition, and prospects thereof, and an election shall be made of Managers for the ensuing year.

Article 7

A special meeting of the Board may be called at any time by the President, upon the request of the managers.

Article 8

This Constitution may be altered at any regular meeting of the Board, by a vote of two-thirds of the members present, notice of the intended alteration having been given at a previous meeting.

By-Laws

Article 1

The Managers shall hold their stated meetings on the second Tuesday of February, May, August, and November, at eleven o'clock A.M., at such place as they shall appoint. Seven members shall constitute a quorum. Special meetings may be called by the President, upon the request of five members.

Article 2

The Executive Committee shall meet once a month, at such time and place as the committee shall decide.

Article 3

The President shall preside at all meetings of the Board and of the Managers, appoint all committees not otherwise provided for, and perform such other duties as are incident to the office, and shall sign all drafts upon the treasury before they are paid.

Article 4

A Vice-President shall perform, in the absence of the President, all the duties of her office. The Honorary Vice-Presidents shall have all the privileges of Corresponding Members.

Article 5

The Treasurer shall receive and hold, and keep an account of, all money given to the Board, and shall disburse it as the Managers shall direct. She shall report the state of the treasury at each regular meeting of the Executive Committee, and make a quarterly report to the Managers. Her annual report shall be examined by an auditor appointed by the Managers.

Article 6

The Recording Secretary shall keep a full record of the proceedings of the Board and Managers, which shall be read for correction at the close of each meeting, and she shall give proper notice of special and stated meetings.

Article 7

It shall be the duty of the Corresponding Secretaries for the foreign field to conduct the business of this Board with the Board of Foreign Missions, and also with the Missionaries, Teachers, and Bible-readers supported by this association. They shall prepare the annual report of the Managers; and missionaries supported by this association shall report to them.

Article 8

The Corresponding Secretaries for the home field shall correspond with the churches, and propose the organization of auxiliary societies wherever it is possible to awaken an interest in the work for which this association is formed.

Article 9

Auxiliary societies shall be required to make an annual report to the Managers through the Corresponding Secretaries, on or before the first Tuesday in April.

Article 10

Any Manager who shall be absent from three successive meetings, without giving notice of the reason of her absence, shall forfeit her position, and her place may be filled.

Article 11

These By-Laws may be amended at any meeting of the Managers, by a vote of two-thirds of the members present; but notice of the proposed amendment must be given in writing at the meeting preceding such vote.

The following constitutions are recommended for adoption. They can be modified and adapted to the circumstances of different localities:

Constitution
for an
Auxiliary to the Woman's Board of Foreign Missions
of the
Reformed Church in America

Article 1

This Society shall be called the _____ of the Woman's Board of Foreign Missions of the Reformed Church in America.

Article 2

Its object shall be to aid the Board in sending out and maintaining Female Missionaries, Bible-readers, and Teachers, who shall work among heathen women and children.

Article 3

Any person may become a member of this Society by the payment of _____ annually.

Article 4

The officers of this Society shall be a President, Secretary, and Treasurer, who shall be elected annually.

Article 5

The duty of these officers shall be as follows: The President shall preside at all meetings, and have a general oversight of the work of the Society. The Secretary shall give notice of meetings, shall record the minutes of each session, and shall prepare the Annual Report. It shall also be her duty to transmit to the Woman's Board the names of the officers of this Auxiliary, a report of its proceedings and condition, whenever necessary, and the Annual Report with that of the Treasurer. The Treasurer shall report the state of the Treasury at every meeting, and shall remit the funds obtained, at least once a year, on or before the tenth day of April, to the Treasurer of the Woman's Board.

Article 6

This Society shall hold regular meetings on the _____, and an annual meeting on the _____, to receive and adopt the Annual Report, and to elect officers.

Directions for Forming Mission Bands

1. An association of young ladies, formed to aid the Woman's Board of Foreign Missions of the Reformed Church in America, shall be called a "Mission Band," and shall be auxiliary to the Missionary Society of the Church in which it is formed, or to the Woman's Board.
2. Each Band shall be responsible for at least $20 each year.
3. Any young lady may become a memer of a Mission Band by the payment of twenty-five cents yearly. Each member shall be entitled to a certificate of membership, to be furnished by the Woman's Board.
4. The officers of a Band shall be a President, Secretary, and Treasurer, who shall be elected annually.
5. The President shall preside at all meetings, and shall have a general oversight of the work of the Band. The Secretary shall keep a record of the proceedings of the Band, and shall make an Annual Report to the Society to which it is auxiliary, or to the Woman's Board of Foreign Missions of the Reformed Church. The Treasurer shall receive and hold all sums contributed, paying the same, at least once a year, to the Treasurer of the Auxiliary of the Church in which the Band is formed, or to the Treasurer of the Woman's Board of Foreign Missions of the Reformed Church.
6. Each Mission Band must select an appropriate name, not already in use, and report the same to the Society to which its money is sent.

Mission Circles of Children

1. An association of children, remitting yearly not less than five dollars to the Woman's Board of Foreign Missions of the Reformed Church in America, shall constitute a "Mission Circle."
2. Each Circle shall be designated by an appropriate name, and shall appoint a Secretary and Treasurer, to whom due acknowledgment can be returned by the Woman's Board.

Or, if preferred, the following can be adopted:

Pledge for Mission Circles

We desire to help in sending the Gospel to heathen children, that they may hear of Christ, who died to save them. We promise to give one cent a week to the missionary box, and to come together once a month to hear about missions, and to work for the cause.

Appendix B

RCA Women's Triennials

Format:

Events	Dates	Location
Triennial Chair		
National President		
National Staff		

First National Women's Assembly   April 23-25, 1957   Buck Hill Falls, PA
   Irene Dykstra (Rev. John A.)
   Ruth Dickson (Rev. Robert) 1957-1960
   Alma Resch (Mr. Arthur) 1951-1957

First Triennial   April 4-6, 1962   Holland, MI
   Ruth Dickson/Cornelia Neevel (Rev. Alvin) 1960-1962
   Mina Buys (Mr. Ekdal) 1962-1965
   Anita Welwood (Rev. Foster) 1957-1972/Remi Flikkema (Rev. John) 1960-1980

Second Triennial   April 20-22, 1965   Chicago, IL
  Julia Van Wyk (Rev. Herbert)
  Marie Walvoord (Rev. Christian) 1965-1968
  Anita Welwood/Remi Flikkema

Third Triennial   April 23-25, 1968   Philadelphia, PA
  Mina Buys
  Celeste Van Zyl (Rev. Robert) 1968-1971
  Anita Welwood/Remi Flikkema

Fourth Triennial   May 4-6, 1971   Cleveland, OH
  Marie Walvoord
  Alice Redeker (Rev. Russell) 1971-1974
  Anita Welwood/Remi Flikkema

Fifth Triennial   April 23-25, 1974   Long Beach, CA
  Mary June (Mr. Willard)
  Margaret Wormuth (Mr. Wilbur) 1974-1977
  Beth Marcus 1973-1986/Remi Flikkema 1960-1980

Sixth Triennial   April 20-22, 1977   Minnaepolis, MN
  Cornelia Poppen (Rev. Henry B.)
  Betty Boerman (Dr. Walter) 1977-1980
  Beth Marcus/Remi Flikkema

Seventh Triennial   May 5-9, 1980   Miami Beach, FL
  Jean Cook (Rev. James)
  Helen DeBoer (Mr. Keith) 1980-1983
  Beth Marcus/Remi Flikkema

Eighth Triennial   May 23-27, 1983   Holland, MI
  Betty Boerman
  Jacqueline Droog (Rev. Chester) 1983-1986
  Beth Marcus/Louise Birkelbach (Rev. Clement) 1980-1993

Ninth Triennial   July 8-11, 1986   Garden Grove, CA
  Eloise Van Heest (Rev. Gerard)
  Ruth Wilson (Mr. Walter J.) 1986-1989
  Beth Marcus/Louise Birkelbach

Tenth Triennial   May 23-26, 1989   Holland, MI
  Trudy Vander Haar (Rev. Delbert)
  Audrey Den Herder (Mr. Roger) 1989-1992
  Diana Paulsen (Rev. Peter) (1986-1994)/Louise Birkelbach

Eleventh Triennial   July 12-15, 1992   Estes Park, CO
   Barbara Neevel (Rev. James)
   Beula Maris (Rev. David) 1992-1995
   Diana Paulsen/Louise Birkelbach

Twelfth Triennial   July 8-12, 1995   Saratoga Springs, NY
   Mary Clark (Rev. Stuart)
   Sheri Vander Eyk (Mr. Cornelius) 1995-1998
   Christine Van Eyl (Mr. William Godin) 1994-1996/Louise Birkelbach

Thirteenth Triennial   August 1-5, 1998   Grand Rapids, MI
   Gloria Nollen (Mr. Keith)
   Barbara Boss (Dr. Richard) 1998-2001
   Arlene Waldorf (Mr. William) 1996-2001

Fourteenth Triennial   July 27-30, 2001   Sioux Falls, SD
   Nancy Matthews (Mr. Clark)
   None
   Arlene Waldorf

Fifteenth Triennial   July 22-24, 2004   Garden Grove, CA
   Gerry Wakeland (Mr. Donald E.)
   None
   None

Bibliography

A Brief History of the Woman's Board of Foreign Missions of the Reformed Church in America and A Little Journey to our Mission Fields with Illustrations. [W.B.F.M. 1875-1900] New York: Press of Styles and Cash, n.d.

The Acts and Proceedings of the General Synod of the Reformed Church in America. Vols. 1-50 inclusive. New York: Board of Publication of the Reformed Church in America, 1771-1970.

Annual Reports of the Woman's Board of Foreign Missions. New York: Board of Publication of the Reformed Church in America, 1875-1939. Imprint varies.

Armerding, Paul. "A Doctor for the Kingdom." *Church Herald*, December, 2003.

Armerding, Paul. *Doctors for the Kingdom: The Work of the American Mission Hospitals in the Kingdom of Saudi Arabia 1913-1955.* The Historical Series of the Reformed Church in America, no. 43. Grand Rapids: Eerdmans, 2003.

Beardslee, John W. III. "The Dutch Women in Two Cultures: Looking for the Questions?" in Renée House and John Coakley, eds. *Patterns and Portraits: Women in the History of the Reformed Church in America.* The Historical Series of the Reformed

Church in America, no. 31. Grand Rapids: Eerdmans, 1999.

Beaver, R. Pierce. *All Loves Excelling: American Protestant Women in World Mission.* Grand Rapids: Eerdmans, 1968.

Beaver, R. Pierce. *American Protestant Women in World Mission: History of the First Feminist Movement in North America.* Grand Rapids: Eerdmans, 1968.

Benson, Mary S. "Sarah Platt Haines Doremus," in Edward T. James ed., *Notable American Women 1607-1950: A Biographical Dictionary*, vol. 1. Cambridge: Belknap, 1971.

Biographical Notes of the Graduates of Rutgers College. New Brunswick: n.d., n.p., ca. 1908.

Board of Foreign Mission Minutes, November, 1955.

Boersma, Jeanette. *Grace in the Gulf: The Autobiography of Jeanette Boersma, Missionary Nurse in Iraq and the Sultanate of Oman.* The Historical Series of the Reformed Church in America, no. 20. Grand Rapids: Eerdmans, 1991.

Brackney, William H. "The Legacy of Helen B. Montgomery and Lucy W. Peabody," *International Bulletin of Missionary Research* 15, no. 1 (January, 1991).

Brouwer, Arie R. *Reformed Church Roots: Thirty-five Formative Events.* New York: Reformed Church Press, 1977.

Brown, Willard Dayton. *A History of the Reformed Church in America.* New York: Board of Publication and Bible School Work of the Reformed Church in America, 1928.

Bruins, Elton J., Karen G. Schakel, Sara Fredrickson Simmons, and Marie N. Zingle. *Albertus and Christina: The Van Raalte Family, Home, and Roots.* Grand Rapids: Eerdmans, 2004.

Brumberg, Joan Jacobs. *Mission for Life: The story of the family of Adoniram Judson, the dramatic events of the first American foreign mission, and the course of evangelical religion in the nineteenth century.* New York: The Free Press, 1980.

Brumberg, Joan Jacobs. "The Case of Ann Hasseltine Judson," in Rosemary Skinner Keller, Louise L. Queen, and Hilah R. Thomas eds., *Women in New Worlds: Historical Perspectives on the Wesleyan Tradition*, vol. II. Women's History Project General Commission on Archives and History, The United Methodist Church, Nashville: Abingdon, 1982.

Brumberg, Joan Jacobs, and Nancy Tomes. "Women in the Professions: A Research Agenda for American Historians," *Reviews in American History*, 10 (June, 1982).

Burt, Dorothy. *I Call to Remembrance My Song.* New York: Reformed Church Women, 1970.

Campbell, Rev. W.H. "Its System of Catechetical Instruction," in *Centennial Discourses: A Series of Sermons Delivered in the Year 1876, By Order of the General Synod of the Reformed (Dutch) Church in America*, 2nd ed., New York: Board of Publication of the Reformed Church in America, 1877.

Cattan, Louise Armstrong. *Lamps Are for Lighting: The Story of Helen Barrett Montgomery and Lucy Waterbury Peabody.* Grand Rapids: Eerdmans, 1972.

Centennial Book First Reformed Church of South Holland, Illinois:1848-1948. N.p., n.p., n.d.

Centennial of the Theological Seminary of the Reformed Church in America (Formerly Ref. Prot. Dutch Church) 1784-1884. New York: Board of Publication of the Reformed Church in America, 1885.

Chamberlain, Mary Anable (Mrs. W.I.). *Fifty Years in Foreign Fields, China, Japan, India,*

Arabia: A History of Five Decades of the Woman's Board of Foreign Missions Reformed Church in America. New York: Abbott Press, 1925.

The *Christian Intelligencer* and the *Intelligencer-Leader.*, 1830-1944.

The *Church Herald.*, 1944-2004.

Coakley, John. "Women in the History of the Reformed Church in America," in Renée House and John Coakley, eds., *Patterns and Portraits: Women in the History of the Reformed Church in America.* The Historical Series of the Reformed Church in America, no. 31. Grand Rapids: Eerdmans, 1999.

Cobb, Henry N. *Far Hence.* New York: Woman's Board of Foreign Missions, Reformed Church in America, 1893.

Corwin, Edward Tanjore. *A Digest of the Constitutional and Synodical Legislation of the Reformed Church in America.* New York: The Board of Publication of the Reformed Church in America, 1906.

Corwin, Edward Tanjore. *A Manual of the Reformed Church in America, 1628-1902*, 4th ed. New York: Board of Publication of the Reformed Church in America, 1902.

Dalenberg, Cornelia. *Sharifa.* The Historical Series of the Reformed Church in America, no. 11. Grand Rapids: Eerdmans, 1983.

David, Immanuel. *Reformed Church in America Missionaries in South India, 1839-1938: an Analytical Study.* Bangalore, India: Asian Trading Corporation, distributers, 1986.

DeBerg, Betty A. *Ungodly Women: Gender and the First Wave of American Fundamentalism.* Minneapolis: Fortress Press, 1990.

De Jong, Gerald F. *The Dutch in America, 1609-1974.* Boston: Twayne Publishers, 1975.

De Jong, Gerald F. *The Reformed Church in China 1842-1951.* The Historical Series of the Reformed Church in America, no. 22. Grand Rapids: Eerdmans,1992.

Department of Women's Work Executive Committee Minutes. December 3, 1957, 1. RCA Archives, Box 1.

Department of Women's Work Minutes. 1954, RCA Archives, Box 1.

"Department of Women's Work Statement of Purpose, April 48, 1950." RCA Archives, Box 712, Folder 2.

Dickson, Ruth. *Glory Be . . ..* New York: Half Moon Press, 1966.

Edland, Elisabeth. *The Tercentenary Pageant 1628-1928: A Dramatic Representation of the History of the Reformed Church in America.* Mecca Temple Auditorium, New York, New York, 4 May 1928.

Fabend, Firth Haring. *Zion on the Hudson: Dutch New York and New Jersey in the Age of Revivals.* New Brunswick: Rutgers University Press, 2000.

Fassler, Barbara. "The Role of Women in the India Mission, 1819-1880," in James W. VanHoeven, ed., *Piety and Patriotism: Bicentennial Studies of the Reformed Church in America, 1776-1976.* Grand Rapids: Eerdmans, 1976.

Farley, Tom. http://www.privateline.com/TelephoneHistory2A/Telehistory2A.htm and http://www.privateline.com/TelephoneHistory2/History2.html.

Flemming, Leslie A. "Introduction: Studying Women Missionaries in Asia," in Leslie A. Flemming ed., *Women's Work for Women: Missionaries and Social Change in Asia.* Boulder: Westview Press, 1989.

Flemming, Leslie A., ed. *Women's Work for Women: Missionaries and Social Change in Asia.* Boulder: Westview Press, 1989.

Flexner, Eleanor. *Century of Struggle: The Woman's Rights Movement in the United States.* New York: Atheneum, 1974.

First Reformed Church Centenary 1854-1954 Cedar Grove, Wisconsin. Port Washington, Wis.: Pilot Print, 1954.

Founders of Church and State Represented in the Women's Tercentenary Committee Reformed Church in America June 13, 1928. Comp. Alma Rogers Van Hoevenberg. Amityville, N.Y.: Waldau's Printing, n.d.

Gasero, Russell L. *Historical Directory of the Reformed Church in America 1628-1992.* The Historical Series of the Reformed Church in America, no. 23. Grand Rapids: Eerdmans, 2001.

Gasero, Russell L . *Historical Directory of the Reformed Church in America 1628-2000.* The Historical Series of the Reformed Church in America, no. 37. Grand Rapids: Eerdmans, 2001.

Georgia, Jennifer. *Legacy and Challenge: The Story of Dr. Ida B. Scudder.* Saline, Mich.: McNaughton & Gunn, 1994.

Glassberg, David. *American Historical Pageantry: The Uses of Tradition in the Early Twentieth Century.* Chapel Hill: Univ. of North Carolina Press, 1990.

Golden Years in Miniature: A History of the Women's Board of Domestic Missions of the Reformed Church in America from the Time of Its Organization in 1882 as the Women's Executive Committee of the Board of Domestic Missions to Its Present Golden Anniversary Year. 1932.

Good, Rev. James I. *Women of the Reformed Church.* N.p., 1901.

Gram, Robert L. An Original Play: in celebration of the Bicentennial of New Brunswick Theological Seminary [1984]. New Brunswick Theological Seminary Archives, Gardner A. Sage Library, New Brunswick, New Jersey.

Hageman, Carol W. "The Decline, Fall, and Rise of Women in the Reformed Church in America, 1947-1997" in Renée House and John Coakley, eds., *Patterns and Portraits: Women in the History of the Reformed Church in America.* The Historical Series of the Reformed Church in America, no 31. Grand Rapids: Eerdmans, 1999.

The Handbook for Women's Organizations, RCA. N.p., 1960.

Hardesty, Nancy A. *Women Called to Witness: Evangelical Feminism in the 19th Century.* Nashville: Abingdon Press, 1984.

Harmelink, Herman III. "World Mission" in James W. Van Hoeven ed., *Piety and Patriotism: Bicentennial Studies of the Reformed Church in America, 1776-1976.* The Historical Series of the Reformed Church in America, no. 4. Grand Rapids: Eerdmans, 1976.

Heideman, Eugene P. *From Mission to Church: The Reformed Church in America Mission to India.* The Historical Series of the Reformed Church in America, no. 38, Grand Rapids: Eerdmans, 2001.

Heideman, Eugene P. *A People in Mission: The Surprising Harvest.* The Heritage and Hope Series of the Reformed Church in America, Focus Three: Missions. New York: Reformed Church Press, 1980.

Henreeta, James A., W. Eliot Brownlee, David Brody, Susan Ware, and Marilynn S. Johnson. *America's History.* 3rd ed. New York: Worth, 1997.

Hill, Patricia R. *The World Their Household: The American Woman's Foreign Mission Movement and Cultural Transformation, 1870-1920.* Ann Arbor: Univiversity of

Michigan Press, 1985.

Historical Sketch of the South Church (Reformed) of New York City. Comp. Frederic C. White and Roderick Terry, for the 75th Anniversary of the Separation of the Church from the other Collegiate Churches. New York: Gilliss Brothers and Turnure, 1887.

Hoff, Marvin. *The Reformed Church in America: Structures for Mission.* The Historical Series of the Reformed Church in America, no. 14. Grand Rapids: Eerdmans, 1985.

House, Renée S. "Women Raising Women: The Urgent Work of the *Mission Gleaner,* 1883-1917," in Renée House and John Coakley eds., *Patterns and Portraits: Women in the History of the Reformed Church in America.* Historical Series of the Reformed Church in America, no. 31. Grand Rapids: Eerdmans, 1999.

House, Renée S. and John W. Coakley, eds. *Patterns and Portraits: Women in the History of the Reformed Church in America.* Historical Series of the Reformed Church in America, no. 31. Grand Rapids: Eerdmans 1999.

Japinga, Lynn. "Differences in Theory, Friends at Sight: Conflict in the RCA." Presented at Hope College, Holland, Michigan, March 27-29, 1998.

Kansfield, Mary. "Dutch Immigration." Presented to the Raritan Millstone Heritage Alliance, New Brunswick, New Jersey, April 27, 2003.

Kansfield, Norman J. "Christian Education and the Ten-Year Goal," *Reformed Review,* 57, no. 1 (Autumn, 2003).

Keller, Rosemary Skinner. "Lay Women in the Protestant Tradition," in Rosemary Radford Ruether and Rosemary Skinner Keller, eds., *Women and Religion in America: Volume 1: The Nineteenth Century.* San Francisco: Harper & Row, 1981.

Keller, Rosemary Skinner. "Patterns of Laywomen's Leadership in Twentieth-Century Protestantism," in Rosemary Radford Ruether and Rosemary Skinner Keller, eds., *Women and Religion in America: Volume 3: 1900-1968.* San Francisco: Harper & Row, 1986.

Kerber, Linda K. and Mathews, Jane De Hart, eds. *Women's America: Refocusing the Past.* New York: Oxford Univ. Press, 1982.

Lerner, Gerda. *The Grimké Sisters from South Carolina: Pioneers for Woman's Rights and Abolition.* New York: Houghton Mifflin, 1967.

Lindley, Susan Hill. *"You Have Stept Out of Your Place:" A History of Women and Religion in America.* Louisville: Westminster John Knox, 1996.

Livingston, John L. "The Everlasting Gospel," in John W. Beardslee III, ed., *Vision from the Hill.* The Historical Series of the Reformed Church in America, no. 12. Grand Rapids: Eerdmans, 1984.

Luidens, Donald A. "National Engagement with Localism: The Last Gasp of the Corporate Denomination?" Paper delivered at New Brunswick Theological Seminary, April, 2002. Soon to appear in David Roozen, ed., *Denominational Identities in Unsettled Times: Theology, Structure, and Change.* Grand Rapids: Eerdmans, forthcoming.

Luidens, Donald A. "'The Rest of the Story . . .': Hope Alumnae and International Missions," in Robert J. Donia and John M. Mulder, eds., *Into All the World: Hope*

College and International Affairs: Essays in Honor of Paul G. Fried. Holland, Mich.: Hope College, 1985.

Lucking, F. Dean. "The Legacy of R. Pierce Beaver," *International Bulletin of Missionary Research*. 14 (January, 1990).

Mason, A. DeWitt. "The Missionary Periodicals of the Reformed Church," in Edward Tanjore Corwin, *A Manual of the Reformed Church in America, 1628-1902*, 4th ed. New York: Board of Publication of the Reformed Church in America, 1902.

Mason, Caroline Atwater. *World Missions and World Peace: A Study of Christ's Conquest*. West Medford, Mass.: The Central Committee on the United Study of Foreign Missions, 1916.

Mathews, Winifred. *Dauntless Women: Stories of Pioneer Wives*. New York: Friendship Press, 1947.

Mieder, Wolfgang, Stewart, A. Kingsbury, and Kelsie B. Harder, eds. *A Dictionary of American Proverbs*. New York: Oxford Univ. Press, 1992.

Mintz, Steven, and Susan Kellogg. *Domestic Revolutions: A Social History of American Family Life*. New York: The Free Press 1988.

Minutes of the Department of Women's Work.

Minutes of the Woman's Board of Foreign Missions, 1875-1946 inclusive.

The *Mission Gleaner*. November 1883 to January 1918 inclusive.

The *Missionary Link for the Woman's Union Missionary Society of America for Heathen Lands*. 9 (March 1877) no. 2.

Montgomery, Helen Barrett. *Western Women in Eastern Lands: An Outline Study of Fifty Years of Woman's Work in Foreign Missions*. New York: Macmillan, 1910.

Nemeth, Roger J., and Donald A. Luidens. "The RCA in the Larger Picture: Facing Structural Realities," *Reformed Review* 47 (Winter, 1993-1994), no 2.

The New Encyclopedia Britannica Micropaedia. Chicago: Helen Hemingway Benton, 1974, 91.

Norton-Levering, Abigail. "Women Writing History: The Tercentenary Celebration of 1928." Independent Study Project for Prof. John Coakley, December 2002, New Brunswick Theological Seminary. Paper available in NBTS Archive Collection at Gardner Sage Library.

Opdycke, Sandra. *The Routledge Historical Atlas of Women in America*. New York and London: Routledge, 2000.

Parsons, Ellen C. "History of Woman's Organized Missionary Work as Promoted by American Women," in E. M. Wherry, comp. *Woman in Missions: Papers and Addresses Presented at the Woman's Congress of Missions*. New York: American Tract Society, 1894.

Platt, Mary Schauffler. *A Straight Way Toward Tomorrow*. Cambridge: The Central Committee on the United Study of Foreign Missions, 1926.

Ratmeyer, Una H. *Hands, Hearts, and Voices: Women Who Followed God's Call*. New York: Reformed Church Press, 1995.

Reece, Jennifer M. "They Published Glad Tidings: American Women in Mission and the Evangelical Sisterhood of Letters in the United States and Japan, 1861-1911." Ph.D. diss. Princeton Theological Seminary, 2002.

Robert, Dana L. *American Women in Mission: A Social History of Their Thought and Practice*. Macon: Mercer Univ. Press, 1977.

Romig, Edgar Franklin. *The Tercentenary Year: A Record of the Celebration of the Three Hundredth Anniversary of the Founding of the First Church in New Netherland, Now New York, and the Beginning of Organized Religious Life Under the Reformed (Dutch) Church in America Held under the Auspices of the General Synod, R.C.A., A.D. 1928*. New York: Reformed Church in America, 1929.

Romig, Ella Dutcher. "The Seventh Decade in the Home Base," in *The Story of the Seventh Decade 1935-1945*. New York: Woman's Board of Foreign Missions, 1945.

Sangster, Margaret E., ed. *Manual of the Missions of the Reformed (Dutch) Church in America*. New York: Board of Publication of the Reformed Church in America, 1877.

Schuppert, Mildred W. *A Digest and Index of the Minutes of the General Synod of the Reformed Church in America 1906-1957*. The Historical Series of the Reformed Church in America, no. 8. Grand Rapids: Eerdmans, 1982.

Schuppert, Mildred W. *A Digest and Index of the Minutes of the General Synod of the Reformed Church in America 1958-1977*. The Historical Series of the Reformed Church in America, no. 7. Grand Rapids: Eerdmans, 1979.

Scudder, Dorothy Jealous. *A Thousand Years in Thy Sight: The Story of the Scudder Missionaries of India*. New York: Vantage Press, 1984.

Scudder, Lewis R. III. *The Arabian Mission's Story: In Search of Abraham's Other Son*. The Historical Series of the Reformed Church in America, no. 30. Grand Rapids: Eerdmans, 1998.

Sinke, Suzanne M. *Dutch Immigrant Women in the United States, 1880-1920*. State of Liberty-Ellis Island Centennial Series, Urbana: Univ. of Illinois Press, 2002.

Stewart, Sonja Marie. "John Heyl Vincent: His Theory and Practice of Protestant Religious Education from 1855-1920." Ph.D. diss., Univ. of Notre Dame, 1977.

The Story of the Seventh Decade 1935-1945. New York: Woman's Board of Foreign Missions Reformed Church in America, n.d.

Swart, Morrell F. *The Call of Africa: The Reformed Church in America Mission in the Sub-Sahara, 1948-1998*. The Historical Series of the Reformed Church in America, no. 29. Grand Rapids: Eerdmans, 1998.

Swierenga, Robert P. *Dutch Chicago: A History of the Hollanders in the Windy City*. Grand Rapids: Eerdmans, 2002.

"Temporary Rules of Organization Department of Women's Work of the Board of Foreign Missions." March 25, 1946. RCA Archives Box 710.1.

Tercentenary Studies 1928 Reformed Church in America: A Record of Beginnings. Compiled by the Tercentenary Committee on Research and Publication, New York: Reformed Church in America, 1928.

Te Winkel, Sarella. *The Sixth Decade of the Woman's Board of Foreign Missions Reformed Church in America 1926-1935*. New York: Woman's Board of Foreign Missions, 1935.

Twenty-four Missionary Travelogues. The Joint Committee on Mission Study of the Mission Boards of the Reformed Church in America. New York: Board of Publication and Bible School Work of the Reformed Church in America, 1919.

Underwood, Lillias H. *Underwood of Korea*. New York: Revell, 1918.

VandenBerge, Peter N. *Historical Directory of the Reformed Church in America 1628-1978*. The Historical Series of the Reformed Church in America, no. 6. Grand Rapids: Eerdmans, 1978.

Van Ess, Dorothy F. *Pioneers in the Arab World*. The Historical Series of the Reformed Church in America, no. 3. Grand Rapids: Eerdmans, 1974.

W. S. "Woman as a Christian Factor," in *Woman's Work for Woman*. December 11, 1881.

Walker, Mrs. Harry Leslie and LaMont A. Warner, eds. *A History of the Reformed Church of Bronxville in Commemoration of its Centenary, November 5, 1950*. Bronxville, N.Y.: Published by the Consistory, 1951.

Weddell, Sue. *Roadbuilders: A Study of the Foreign Mission Program of the Reformed Church in America*. New York: Department of Missionary Education, Reformed Church in America, 1932.

Welch, Ransom Bethune. "The Hereditary Interest of the Reformed (Dutch) Church in Education, Common and Collegiate," in *Centennial Discourses: A Series of Sermons Delivered in the Year 1876, By Order of the General Synod of the Reformed (Dutch) Church in America*, 2nd ed. New York: Board of Publication of the Reformed Church in America, 1877.

Welter, Barbara. "The Cult of True Womanhood: 1820-60," *American Quarterly*. XVIII (summer 1966).

Welter, Barbara. "The Feminization of American Religion: 1800-1860," in Mary S. Hartman and Lois Banner, eds., *Clio's Consciousness Raised: New Perspectives on the History of Women*. New York: Harper Torchbooks, 1974.

Welter, Barbara. "She Hath Done What She Could: Protestant Women's Missionary Careers in Nineteenth-Century America," in Janet Wilson James, ed., *Women in American Religious History*. Philadelphia: Univ. of Pennsylvania Press, 1980.

Whately, E. Jane. "The Society for Promoting Female Education in the East," in E. M. Wherry, comp., *Woman in Missions: Papers and Addresses Presented at The Woman's Congress of Missions October, 2-4, 1893, in the Hall of Columbus, Chicago*. New York: American Tract Society, 1894.

Willims, Delores S. *Sisters in the Wilderness: The Challenge of Womanist God-Talk*. Maryknoll: Orbia Books, 2000.

"Women and Temperance," *Christian Intelligencer*, December 17, 1874.

Wyckoff, Charlotte. *A Hundred Years with Christ in Arcot: A Brief History of the Arcot Mission of the Reformed Church in America*. Printed for the Arcot Mission Centenary Celebration, 1953.

Zandstra, Gerald L. *Daughters Who Dared: Answering God's Call to Nigeria*. Grand Rapids: Calvin Theological Seminary and CRC Publications, 1992.

Name Index

The entries in this index are in continuous alphabetical order. There is no separation between words of the last name such as Van and Van der; titles such as Miss, Mr., Mrs., and Dr. are ignored. Entries referring to illustrations are in italic type and entries referring to the letters written to Hazel are in bold type.

Subject Index

The Historical Series of the Reformed Church in America

Books in print, William B. Eerdmans, publisher

Dorothy F. Van Ess
Pioneers in the Arab World

James W. Van Hoeven, editor
Piety and Patriotism

Mildred W. Schuppert
Digest and Index of the Minutes of General Synod, 1958-1977

Mildred W. Schuppert
Digest and Index of the Minutes of General Synod, 1906-1957

Gerald F. De Jong
From Strength to Strength

D. Ivan Dykstra
"B. D."

John W. Beardslee III, editor
Vision From the Hill

Howard G. Hageman
Two Centuries Plus

Marvin D. Hoff
Structures for Mission

James I. Cook, editor
The Church Speaks: Papers of the Commission on Theology of the Reformed Church in America, 1959-1984

James W. Van Hoeven, editor
Word and World

Gerrit J. tenZythoff
Sources of Secession: The Netherlands Hervormde Kerk on the Eve of the Dutch Immigration to the Midwest

Gordon J. Van Wylen
Vision for a Christian College

Jack D. Klunder and Russell L. Gasero, editors
Servant Gladly

Jeanette Boersma
Grace in the Gulf

Arie R. Brouwer
Ecumenical Testimony

Gerald F. De Jong
The Reformed Church in China, 1842-1951

Russell L. Gasero
Historical Directory of the Reformed Church in America, 1628-1992

Daniel J. Meeter
Meeting Each Other in Doctrine, Liturgy, and Government

Allan J. Janssen
Gathered at Albany

Elton J. Bruins
The Americanization of a Congregation, 2nd ed., by Elton J. Bruins (1995)

Gregg A. Mast
In Remembrance and Hope: The Ministry and Vision of Howard G. Hageman

Janny Venema, translator & editor
Deacons' Accounts, 1652-1674, First Dutch Reformed Church of Beverwyck/Albany

Morrill F. Swart
The Call of Africa

Lewis R. Scudder III
The Arabian Mission's Story: In Search of Abraham's Other Son

Renée S. House and John W. Coakley, editors
Patterns and Portraits: Women in the History of the Reformed Church in America

Elton J. Bruins & Robert P. Swierenga
Family Quarrels in the Dutch Reformed Churches in the Nineteenth Century

Allan J. Janssen
Constitutional Theology: Notes on the Book of Church Order of the Reformed Church In America

Gregg A. Mast, editor
Raising the Dead: Sermons of Howard G. Hageman

James Hart Brumm, editor
Equipping the Saints: The Synod of New York, 1800-2000

Joel R. Beeke, editor
Forerunner of the Great Awakening

Russell L. Gasero
Historical Directory of the Reformed Church in America, 1628-2000

Eugene Heideman
From Mission to Church: The Reformed Church in America in India

Harry Boonstra
Our School: Calvin College and the Christian Reformed Church

James I. Cook, editor
The Church Speaks, Vol. 2: Papers of the Commission on Theology of the Reformed Church in America, 1985-2000

John W. Coakley
Concord Makes Strength

Robert P. Swierenga
Dutch Chicago: A History of the Hollanders in the Windy City

Paul L. Armerding
Doctors for the Kingdom, The Work of the American Mission Hospitals in the Kingdom of Saudi Arabia

Donald J. Bruggink & Kim N. Baker
By Grace Alone, Stories of the Reformed Church in America

June Potter Durkee
Travels of an American Girl

Mary L. Kansfield
Letters to Hazel, Ministry Within the Women's Board of Foreign Missions of the Reformed Church in America